ʿĒṢ ḤAYYĪM

The Tree of Life
Part I

A Publication of the al-Qirqisani Center for the Promotion of Karaite Studies

By Aharon Ben-Eliyahu
Translated by Dr. Morris Charner

Library of Congress Card Number: pending

ISBN 0-9700775-9-9

ʿĒṢ ḤAYYĪM

PREFACE

In view of the technical language and nature of the work before us, the translator has endeavored to reproduce as accurately as possible the original Hebrew of Aharon Ben-Eliyahu by maintaining as exact and literal a rendering as is permissible within the limitations of accepted English usage. In so doing he has been guided rather by the method of Samuel ibn Tibbon who, in translating Maimonides' Guide, deliberately sacrificed elegance of style for the importance of accuracy, than by the example of Yehudah alHarisi, who was less interested in the correctness of his version than in its superior literary quality.

The Biblical references in this translation are quoted from the Hebrew Bible. In general, the rendering of Biblical verses into English follows the translation of the Jewish Publication Society, Philadelphia, 1917, save in those instances where Aharon Ben-Eliyahu's interpretation of a Scriptural passage is at variance with its commonly accepted meaning.

In concluding these brief prefatory remarks, I desire to express my sincere gratitude to Dr. Avraham S. Halkin who has generously given of his broad erudition and valuable time so that this effort might possess whatever merit it has. I am also under obligation to Professor Arthur W. Jeffery and Dr. Isaac

Mendelsohn for their kind assistance in the special problems connected with this work. Finally, it gives me real pleasure to acknowledge profound thanks to my wife, who has constantly been of aid in innumerable ways throughout the writing of this dissertation and its preparation for publication.

Morris Charner
New York
September, 1949

INTRODUCTION

I. AHARON BEN-ELIYAHU OF NICOMEDIA, HIS LIFE AND WORKS

The history of the mediæval Jew, in contradistinction to that of the ancient Israelite and the modern Israeli, is to a large extent a record of spiritual achievements and literary monuments. Yet in striking contrast to the significance of the realm of ideas that engrossed the attention of the Jewish spirit during this period there is a conspicuous lack of historical interest in the biographical details regarding the exponents of these same ideas. Hence, the unfortunate dearth of information that envelops in obscurity the lives and circumstances surrounding the Jewish celebrities of this era.[1] In keeping with this the few statements that can be made regarding the life of the eminent Karaite philosopher, *halakhist* and exegete, Aharon Ben-Eliyahu of Nicomedia, are based mainly on inferences from and speculation on scattered references rather than on direct information. He is known as Aharon the Younger - in order to distinguish him from the prominent Karaite theologian Aharon Ben-Yosef (the Elder),[2] who was born approximately half a century prior to the birth of our author. Aharon Ben-Eliyahu was born about the year 1300[3] possibly in Cairo,[4] a city that had been an important seat of Karaite learning for several centuries. Very little is known regarding his youth and formal education. It is abundantly clear from his three works, however, that he not only possessed a masterly command of the entire field of Karaite learning, but was also deeply versed in Rabbinic literature[5] as well as in the discussions revolving around the Arabic and Greek philosophy studied in his day. From this fact both Delitzsch[6] and Furst[7] infer that Aharon Ben-Eliyahu was reared in and engaged in intellectual pursuits amidst most favorable material circumstances.[8] From the modest and unassuming tone that he employs in his 'Es Hayyim against Maimonides, his chief adversary, one might assume that Aharon Ben-Eliyahu possessed a kindly character, and was a man of even temperament.[9] It may just as well be, however, that this modesty is due to his lack of positive conviction as to the views that he advocates, and that it is because of this consciousness of his fallibility that he shows himself so fair and impartial in his treatment of his opponent.[10] From his works we learn of three teachers who guided Aharon in his studies. H. Yehudah, a maternal uncle, who died prior to the completion of Aharon's philosophical treatise, in 1346, instructed him in Biblical exegesis.[11] His father-in-law H. Mosheh is also mentioned as his teacher, and from the context in which he is quoted it appears that he instructed Aharon in philosophical exegesis.[12] In the 'Es Hayyim Aharon speaks of his father-in-law as already deceased.[12a] Throughout, a certain H. Yosef,[13] is mentioned at the conclusion of a Leyden manuscript of Aharon's work on Karaite Law entitled Gan 'Eden.[14] This H. Yosef is there said to have died about five months before the death of Aharon Ben-Eliyahu in September 1369.[15] In an acrostic poem (No. 3 in the Evpatoria ed. of the Keter Torah), the first letters of whose verses spell out the name Aharon

Ben-Eliyahu, our author mentions as his student a certain Ya'aqov whom he compares with 'Anan and Yosef al-Basir and his disciples. From a similar acrostic (*ibid*. No.g) we learn that Aharon's father had traveled to a distant war-troubled land and the ship in which he was voyaging remained unheard of for what seemed to Aharon an insufferably long time. Upon the safe homecoming of his father, Aharon composed this song of praise to God.

When approximately thirty years old, Aharon settled in Nicomedia, one of the chief town's of Asia Minor, whence he derived the agnomen "Nicomedi".[16] It was here that during the years 1340-1346[17] he composed his *'Es Hayyim*[18] (The Tree of Life) a philosophical treatise, which earned for him among his coreligionists the reputation of being the Karaite counterpart of Maimonides; for like the renowned Rabbi Mosheh of Cairo, our author alone among the Karaites established a comprehensive system of religious philosophy.[19] Some eight years later - while in Constantinople, the Karaite center of the Byzantine empire - he wrote the *Gan 'Eden* (The Garden of Eden), a comprehensive work on Karaite *halakha* which became of paramount importance to his coreligionists. His third and final work of great significance, *Keter Torah* (The Crown of the Law) was completed in the year 1362.[20] Included in the introduction to this Pentateuchal commentary is an excursus on the differences between the Rabbanites and Karaites with regard to Scriptural exegesis.[20a] These three works on philosophy, *halakha*, and exegesis represent the epitome and zenith of Karaite scholarshlp[21] during the Post-classical period of Karaite endeavor, and for this reason Aharon Ben-Eliyahu was considered one of the most eminent of Karaite scholars. With the death of Aharon the Younger, as the result of a plague in 1369, there commenced a gradual decline of Karaite effort and achievement. Their numbers also declined; until a decade ago their total number did not exceed 12,000, and their every attempt towards a spiritual renaissance has terminated in failure.[23]

In presenting now a more detailed consideration of Aharon's works we shall take up first his contributions to Karaite *halakha*, exegesis, and poetry, and leave for a separate discussion his magnum opus in philosophy. The only complete edition of Aharon's book of Codes, entitled *Gan 'Eden*,[24] is that edited by Judah Sawaskan, based upon a study of four manuscripts,[25] published in 1866 in Evpatoria (also known as Köslov or Göslöw) a seaport town on the west coast of Crimea, which contains the principal Karaite synagogue. Prior to this edition, various sections[26] of the *Gan 'Eden* had been treated by several scholars.[27] This work is supplementary to the previously written philosophical treatise of our author, the *'Es Hayyim*, upon whose foundation it is based, and which it quotes frequently. Dealing comprehensively with Karaite ritual[28] as well as civil law[29] it became the accepted Code among the Karaites,[30] who consider it their counterpart of Maimonides' *Yad haZaqah*.

The ultimate purpose of the divine commandments, he holds, is to inculcate belief in the monotheistic principle and to demonstrate that God rules the destiny of the world.[31] Towards the attainment of these goals the divine precepts as well as the *hagadah* have been provided for our benefit even though we fail to perceive this relationship. Thus, the laws pertaining to specific days, months, seasons or years have for their special object the removal of every vestige of sphere worship or other pagan practice.[32] Similarly, the Sabbath is intended to strengthen the belief in Creation. Another reason for the Commandments is to remove God's chosen people from the false notions and evil ways of other nations. Hence, the dietary laws, precepts regarding purity and prohibitions with respect to marriage.

The non-canonical work of our author in the Evpatoria edition consists of forty-one sections, which are divided into two hundred and twenty-four chapters. In the larger portion of this work dealing with Karaite ritual law Aharon devotes considerable attention to the calendar and festivals (fifty-six chapters); to the various laws pertaining to marriage (forty chapters) and to matters of purity (thirty-nine chapters). The commandments dealing with the ritual slaughtering of animals comprise twenty-three chapters. The concluding portion of the *Gan 'Eden*, which deals with civil law, is prefaced by a censor's admonition that the laws herein contained relative to man and his fellowman do not apply in actuality and that in all these instances the law of the land shall prevail.[33] Here we find the laws dealing with torts, pledges, bailments, land, loans and interest, legal procedure, partnership, testimony, etc.,

Aharon makes extensive reference to the Talmud for the purpose of accepting or rejecting the notions therein stated. As his criterion towards this end, he employs three principles by which every Karaite law must be examined, viz., Scripture, reason, and accepted tradition.[34] The divine commandments are divided into intellectual laws (*miswoth sikhli-*

yyo'th) i.e., laws amenable to reason, and revealed precepts (*miswoth toriyyoth*) i.e., laws that are to be obeyed purely because of their divine origin. Each of these groups consists of positive and negative commandments, and all of them are intended for the intellectual perfection of man.[35] In an interesting excursus on the language to be employed in liturgical selections, Aharon concludes that it is most proper to employ only the Hebrew language, although Daniel employed the Aramaic tongue for prayer.[36] The work as a whole offered the best presentation of the Karaite system of law that had been formulated and hence was accepted as the standard Code of the Karaite community.[36a]

Aharon Ben-Eliyahu's contribution to philosophical exegesis is contained in his *Keter Torah* [Crown of the Teaching], a comprehensive commentary on the Pentateuch, patterned after the *Sefer hamMivhar* of Aharon the Elder,[37] which strives to emulate the fame of Ibn Ezra. This exegetical work, like the preceding system of Karaite *halakha*, rests upon the foundation of the *'Es Hayyim,* which it quotes extensively. A complete edition of this work based on a comparison of six manuscripts was published by Judah Sawaskan in Evpatoria, 1866.[38]

Like Ibn Ezra, Aharon introduces this work with an analysis of the various methods of Scriptural exegesis. In rhymed prose, Aharon continues to delineate in his introduction the basic differences between the Rabbanite and Karaite expositors of the Bible.[39] As in his *'Es Hayyim* and *Gan 'Eden* so here Aharon's eclectic method is evident. After subjecting his predecessors, both Karaite and Rabbanite, to a critical analysis, he presents his own view, though with far more positiveness than in his philosophical treatise, where it is frequently difficult to determine which side of a particular issue he espouses. Whereas in the latter work Maimonides served as the object of his attacks, here Aharon's chief opponent was his older namesake, the author of the *Sefer HaMivhar*. Aharon lays special stress on the literal sense of Scripture, which constitutes the raison d'etre of the Karaites, and gives meticulous regard to the grammatical and syntactical structure of the Biblical verse. Care is also taken to point out the delicate nuances that differentiate synonymous terms.[40] Throughout the work our author displays a masterly knowledge and command of the entire Bible as well as a thorough acquaintance with all of its most important expositors. There is little originality in any of the works of this writer, a fact that is abundantly evident in his last book. Almost every philosophical interpretation of a Biblical phrase in the *'Es Hayyim*, a large portion of which is dedicated to such exegetical exposition,[41] is restated in the *Keter Torah*. Similarly, the *halakhic* significance of the verses in the Pentateuch as explained in the *Gan 'Eden* can be found reiterated in similar terms in the *Keter Torah*. Aharon appears to have written this commentary in order to round out his work in the three major fields of Karaite learning, thus emulating the tripartite activity of Maimonides.

There remain now to be considered the few poems and liturgical compositions of Aharon Ben-Eliyahu.[42] His poems have been published among those in a collection that constitutes the first part of Sawaskan's edition of the *Keter Torah*. This collection comprises twenty-two poems of which Nos., 3, 5, 6, 18, 21, 22 are acrostics, the first letters of whose verses spell out the name Aharon Ben-(or Bar-) Eliyahu.[43]

Poem No. 9 has been mentioned above as describing the safe homecoming of Aharon's father.[44] Of the others, Nos., 12, 15, 19, and 20 appear to be the work of Aharon Ben-Eliyahu, and are so accepted by Davidson.[45] In the Karaite *Siddur* Vol. 3., on the Day of Atonement and the Ten Days of Mercy, p. 151b and 157a there are two liturgical acrostics of Aharon Ben-Eliyahu, the first a *Tokhahah* and the second a *Selihah*.

In his poetic writings Aharon is again the eclectic, selecting and cleverly matching together Biblical verses and phrases in the manner of his time, as is readily perceived in these liturgical selections. In the ninth poem of the Evpatoria group, however, we are made to feel the overpowering emotion that possessed Aharon while writing these verses.

II. THE PHILOSOPHY OF THE `ES HAYYIM

The first and greatest work of Aharon Ben-Eliyahu was the *'Es Hayyim*, a comprehensive philosophical treatise that set out to establish the fundamental principles of revelation upon a sound logical and philosophical foundation from the Karaite point of view. An exemplary edition of this work based upon two manuscripts was published in Leipzig in 1841 by Franz Delitzsch with the cooperation of M. Steinschneider.[46] Another edition of this work was printed in Evpatoria in 1847 together with the commentary of Simha Lutzki, entitled *Or Harayyim*.[47] In addition to this commentary just mentioned there are two unpublished commentaries: the *Derekh Seluldh* by Simha Ben-Solomon[48] and the `Es HaDa'ath by Mosheh Ben-Samuel Kalai.[49]

In treating Aharon's Tree of Life I shall confine myself for the most part within the scope of this dissertation which includes Chapters 1-78.

Characterized by an erudite admixture of Kalāmistic and peripatetic elements[50] this work consists of one hundred and fourteen chapters. Being philosophically inclined towards the doctrines of the "Men of Unity and Justice" the *'Es Hayyim* is patterned after their works. The first section comprises seventy-eight chapters dedicated to the vindication of God's unity; the second section consists of thirty-five chapters that reveal the omniscient justice of the Almighty.

The method of establishing one's theology upon the theory of the creation of the world is distinctive of the Kalām[51] and in keeping with this Aharon Ben-Eliyahu, after a historical introduction (Chap. 1) and a statement of his views on the sources of truth (Chap. 2), immediately proceeds to present the notions of the Philosophers and the Mutakallimūn on the nature of existing things (Chaps. 3, 4). After setting forth the theory of Creation, regardless of whether one accepts the Kalāmistic conception of nature as constituted of atoms and their accidents or the Aristotelian notion of a universe composed of matter and form, he shows that there logically follows the necessary existence of a Creator (Chaps. 1-11). This fact is further verified from Scripture (Chap. 12) and by the logical syllogism (Chap. 13). The existence of Separate Intelligences and their identification with the Angels of Scripture (Chap. 14) is followed by the demonstration of God's incorporeality (Chap. 15). The following forty-eight chapters are devoted to the rejection of anthropomorphism in connection with the divine essence. The first section of the *'Es Hayyim* concludes with the demonstration of the absolute unity of God (Chaps. 64-78). The section on divine Justice commences with an exposition of Aharon's views on Providence and the ultimate goal of existence (Chaps. 79-93). Revelation, prophecy and the purpose of the Law are treated in the subsequent chapters and the work concludes with a discussion of the immortality of the soul and of retribution in the hereafter.[51a] This rapid survey will serve to indicate the scope and disposition of the treatise under discussion.

Coming now to the essential elements of this work, our author informs us that the purpose of his endeavors is to demonstrate the direction of truth and to elucidate the heresy which results for those who follow the views of the Philosophers (i.e., those who subscribe to the Peripatetic school of thought in contradistinction to the notions of the Mutakallimūn which our author espouses and whom he designates as "Scholars of Investigation".)[52] Seeing that "even some of our own (Karaite) scholars are inclined towards views which the intellect cannot tolerate, my heart has moved me to approach this task in order to point out the way of truth to the extent that I am able to do so; for the word of the LORD was like a fire within me which I could no longer contain".[53] Judgments as to truth derive from four sources: speculative reason (*mūśkāl*), sense perception (*mūrgāsh*), what is considered axiomatic (*mefārsām*) and accepted tradition (*mequbbāl*). What is apprehended through speculative thought or logical inference as well as the knowledge ascertained by the perception of our senses can be classified under the first degree of truth, that which is entirely certain. Those notions determined by what is considered axiomatic, as, e.g., that to steal is evil, belong to the second degree of truth, the category which includes ideas that are for the most part true. In the last position is our knowledge derived from tradition. Aharon is careful, however, to add that in certain instances authentic tradition can enjoy the same validity as objective reflection.

It should be noted here that Aharon Ben-Eliyahu like his predecessor Maimonides, whose monumental work marks the culmination of mediæval Jewish philosophy and which our author frequently follows obsequiously, considers speculative reasoning not only as the primary source of truth, but as its determining and decisive element. The assured results of reason and the validity of logical inference as determined by demonstration and syllogistic proof constitute the paramount criterion in matters pertaining to God, the Universe and Man, which comprise the scope of religious philosophy. The imperious rule of reason through its prophet Aristotle, modified by the principles of the Kalām, dominates the intellectual expression of this Karaite Maimonides. To be sure, Scripture is held forth as a definitive truth, but it is so considered only to the extent that it confirms and corroborates the unquestioned results of observation and ratiocination.[55] Aharon is in complete accord with the fundamental doctrine of Maimonides expressed in the following words, "We do not reject the Eternity of the Universe, because certain passages in Scripture confirm the Creation; for such passages are not more numerous than those in which God is represented as a corporeal being nor is it impossible or difficult to find for them a suitable interpretation... We should perhaps have had an easier task in showing that the

Scriptural passages referred to are in harmony with the theory of the Eternity of the Universe if we accepted the latter, than we had in explaining the anthropomorphisms in the Bible when we rejected the idea that God is corporeal".[56] In accordance with the above Aharon establishes his conceptions of the nature of God and His attributes, His relation to the Universe and Man, the manner of the Creation, the existence of separate Intelligences which he identifies with the angels of Scripture, etc. These views are corroborated by what he considers as the metaphysics of the Bible, which is concealed in prophetic visions and allusions intended for the wise among men. Regarding this Hoshe'a (12.11) states, "I have also spoken unto the prophets, and I have multiplied visions; and by the ministry of the prophets have I used similitudes". In addition, he considers that the esoteric meaning contained in the account of the divine chariot known as the *Ma'aśēh Merkābāh* and in that of creation known as the *Ma'aśēh Be'rēshīth*[57] lends itself to extensive metaphysical interpretation. By expounding these metaphors and similes our philosopher propounds a system of allegorical values by means of which he alone among the Karaites reconciled Aristotelian philosophy and Kalāmistic doctrine with Jewish tradition in one complete system.

In proving the existence and nature of God, knowledge of which is the foundation and ultimate goal of religious experience, Aharon first sets forth the opposing views of the philosophers who maintain the theory of Eternity and those of the Mutakallimūn who believe in *creatio ex nihilo*. The opinions of these two schools of thought are determined by their respective notions on the nature of existence and the existent, that is, by their views on the principles of physics and metaphysics. Aharon Ben-Eliyahu's presentation of Aristotle's physics as well as his metaphysics is colored by the second hand sources of his knowledge concerning these Greek doctrines, which he learned of only through the somewhat distorted medium of Syriac, Arabic and Hebrew translations. Furthermore, the original works of Aristotle were at that period rarely consulted; even Maimonides who was a deep student of the Stagirite's ideas resorted to the commentaries of Alfarabi and Avicenna for his information regarding the Philosopher's teachings.[58] In spite of this Aharon succeeds in adducing dialectic proof for the refutation of the hypothesis of Eternity. This leads him to a detailed exposition of atomistic physics from which he demonstrates the theory of creation by proving that bodies cannot do without accidents originating in time and consequently bodies themselves must have their origin in time. Thus, it is established that the world was created and from this there logically follows the existence of a Creator who is proved to be a necessary existent. From the very nature of the proofs that are brought forward to demonstrate the reality of a necessarily existing Creator, Aharon deduces that He is perforce incorporeal. For were He corporeal, "then all the proofs that have led us to believe that bodies are created would indicate that He, too, is created. He would thus require a creator and the latter, in turn, another creator".[59] But infinite regress is inadmissible.

In order to remove every taint of corporeality and anthropomorphism from the supereminent Essence, Aharon devotes considerable space to the expounding of Scriptural terms and passages that appear to indicate the ascription of human characteristics to God. "When we find that a matter which has been demonstrated by the intellect is contradicted by Scripture then we must not compel the former to fit the literal sense of the Biblical verse. On the contrary, we must adapt Scripture to fit that which has been demonstrated by the intellect".[60] This is accomplished either by the addition of a word to the Scriptural verse in question, or by understanding it as a metaphorical expression, or by taking the word in doubt as a homonymous term. Thus, Aharon explains the anthropomorphisms in the Bible as figurative expressions that indicate the divine activities as they are related to man.

As in the matter of creation, so with regard to the doctrine of attributes Aharon opposes the views of Maimonides who rejects all but negative predicates. According to our author, there are five positive essential attributes: Omnipotent, Omniscient, Acting with Will, Living, and Existent. These attributes are identical with His essence and in no way infringe upon His unity and simplicity. Similarly, the names of God are identical with His Essence, even as Ya'aqov is identical with Israel. With regard to God's Will, certain of the Mutakallimūn argue that if this be eternal and unchangeable, as is His essence with which it is identified, then the universe created by this Will must also be eternal. Thus, they are forced to assume the existence of a divine will without a substratum. Aharon rejects this subject-less will with the assertion that God's Will like His Essence and Wisdom is inscrutable. Aharon ascribes sense perception to God not, of course, as we perceive things through physical organs, but that all perceptibles are known to Him. Thus, our author completes the first section of his treatise that deals with God's Unity.

Before concluding this review of Aharon Ben-Eliyahu's work mention should be made of the more interesting aspects of his literary style.[61] The task of converting the Hebrew language into a medium of expression for philosophical concepts was not an easy one. Thanks to the efforts of the Hebrew translators[62] and his own originality, Aharon nevertheless succeeded in developing a more lucid and flexible Hebrew style than most mediæval writers in the field of philosophy. His abundant knowledge of Rabbinic literature placed at his disposal all the literary achievements of the latter, which he employed to good advantage.[63]

The foremost characteristic of Aharon's style is his conciseness and brevity that in no way, however, mar the clarity of his expression. Only by comparing the mode of expression of our author with the well nigh undecipherable construction of Neo-Hebraisms and Neo-Arabisms contained in the translated works of men like Yeshu'ah Ben-Yehudah[64] can we appreciate the smoothness and flowing quality of Aharon's language, despite his condensed form of expression.

Aharon was not very successful in his attempt to coin new terms and expand verbal forms for the purpose of introducing a more exact philosophical terminology.[65] Although, in general, the presentation of our author is the characteristically formal, rigid, pregnant and unadorned prose of the School-men, nevertheless, here and there throughout the treatise, we are struck by a poetic turn of thought, or an artistic picture drawn in words.[66] The Karaite nature of this philosophical treatise can readily be determined by the numerous words and phrases that indicate their exclusively Karaite character, although these expressions are frequently of Arabic origin.

III. THE PERIPATETIC AND KALĀMISITIC INFLUENCES IN THE 'ES HAYYIM

"Aristotle", says Maimonides, "supplanted all his predecessors. The thorough understanding of Aristotle is the highest achievement to which man can attain, with the sole exception of the understanding of the prophets".[67] This opinion of the mediæval Jewish Philosopher, who exerted so great an influence upon Aharon Ben-Eliyahu,[68] would alone suffice to explain why our author is found to be substantially indebted to the philosophy of the Stagirite. Aristotelianism, however, during the fourteenth century represented not merely a body of doctrines, but a mental attitude that had become an all embracing and motivating stimulus to Jewish mediæval thought; it represented a system of rationalism that effected the abandonment of the anthropocentric view of the universe, the subordination of moral perfection to intellectual perfection as the *summum bonum* of human life, and led Gersonides to maintain the Aristotelian doctrine of the eternity of the universe. No wonder then that Aharon's method and terminology[69] are dominated by the Peripatetic influence whose founder is mentioned by name throughout the 'Es Hayyim[70] and is quoted frequently as "The Philosopher".[71] Even where Aharon rejects Aristotelian views[72] the dialectic proof employed is that of the Stagirite. Aharon's condemnation of philosophy as well as philosophers (i.e., Aristotelians)[73] in no way inhibits his acceptance of the philosophical method of ratiocination. Indeed, Aharon is in accord with the Aristotelians in regard to the unity and incorporeality of God. It is only those philosophic views which would repudiate the fundamental doctrines of the Torah that Aharon rejects.[74] It should be noted at this point, however, that although Maimonides, to whom our author is deeply indebted, rallied the forces of Aristotle against the Mutakallimūn, the Karaite Aharon Ben-Eliyahu opposed both these Philosophers to vindicate the opinions of the Kalām.

At the outset of his discussion on the nature of things[75] Aharon mentions incidentally the Aristotelian distinction between intellectual and sense perception.[76] He then proceeds to an extensive exposition of the familiar Aristotelian concepts of matter and form,[77] and the natural properties of the elements[78] whence are comprised the four categories of existence: mineral, plant, animal and man. In this same chapter are also considered the three first principles, namely, matter, form, and privation;[79] the influence of the celestial spheres upon terrestrial things and the dispute among philosophers as to whether the former are constituted of matter and form.[80] In the following chapter, Aharon applies the Aristotelian definition of body[81] to the Kalāmistic theory of atoms. The 'before' and 'after' relative to time[82] are considered in connection with the motion of the celestial spheres. Aharon is thoroughly acquainted with Aristotle's explanation of the motion of the first heaven, i.e., the outermost sphere of the universe in which the fixed stars are set, as being due to the fact that this sphere is the object of desire and the object of thought.[83] In one of his interesting comparisons with the words of the Philosopher[84] our author relates concrete nouns, abstract nouns and nouns of nonbeing with the Stagirite's three basic principles of matter, form and privation.[85]

In his exhaustive section on anthropomorphic expression in the Bible, we find frequent digressions in which the Peripatetic influence is felt, as in the explanation of the homonymity of the term "place".[86] In his treatment of the Hebrew *selem*, Aharon quotes almost verbatim the opinion of Aristotle to the effect that the affections of the soul such as passion, fear, love and hate produce a correlative affection of the body.[87] The Aristotelian definition of transparency[88] is quoted in the words of Maimonides.[89] We again come across an Aristotelian notion of time[90] in connection with the explanation of the various meanings of the term *āḥōr*. The Separate Intelligences of Aristotle,[91] which are identified with the angels of Scripture, are also met with in this chapter. The Aristotelian view that what is infinite is not contained by time, measured by time nor affected by time[92] is applied to the question of the possibility of two deities.[93] In demonstrating the view that God's attributes are identical with His essence, and in no way infringe upon His unity and simplicity, Aharon quotes the Peripatetic notion of identity.[94] Finally, in vindicating the Karaite doctrine that God is possessed of sense-perception, we find the Aristotelian view in intelligibles and objects of sense perception.[95]

Now, in all the aforementioned examples of Peripatetic influence, the sources are palpably and assertedly Aristotelian. What is for more interesting, however, as has been shown by H. A. Wolfson in his brilliant article on the Kalām arguments for creation,[96] is that even those notions which Aharon Ben-Eliyahu considered to be exclusively Kalāmisitic in origin and character are either based upon Aristotelian principles or revolve around propositions asserted by the Stagirite. Let us take, as an example, Aharon's first proof for creation.[97] This argument involves three propositions: 1) All bodies are composed of matter and form; 2) Forms are transient and no form borne upon matter is eternal; 3) That which cannot do without things originating in time must itself have its origin in time. The first proposition in its original Kalāmistic form is phrased in terms of atom and accident,[98] as it appears in Maimonides,[99] rather than in the matter and form of Aristotle.[100] This argument can be refuted, however, by the contention that an infinite succession of different things can be borne upon an eternal substrate. In answer to this, Aharon demonstrates the impossibility of an infinite series of causes and effects (accidental infinite) which is in reality an Aristotelian principle.[101] Similarly, take Aharon's second proof for creation: 1) All bodies are composed of matter and form; 2) Composition is the cause of a body's existence; 3) What is possible of existence must be created. The first proposition is obviously Aristotelian[102] and the second also derives from the Peripatetic school.[103] Likewise, Aharon's distinction between "characters" and "accidents" which he ascribes to the Mutakallimūn Investigators in contradistinction to the philosophers[104] bears a striking resemblance to the Stagirite's distinction between "definition" and "property".[105] From the preceding discussion, it becomes clear that the spirit of Aristotle hovers over the entire work of Aharon Ben-Eliyahu.

"It is true that the whole framework, scope and material of Arabic philosophy is to be traced to the civilization of the empires which the Arabs conquered, and that Greek philosophy predominates in their system".[106] Nevertheless, a constant struggle was maintained by the scholars of Islam to free themselves from this influence.[107] Thus, the Arab theologians adopted the atomistic doctrine and the denial of casual relationship from the pre-Aristotelian philosophers, Leucippus and Democritus, as the basis for their system of physics. Despite this, they evolved religio-philosophical notions that were fundamentally opposed to the views of their predecessors.[108] This system of thought known as Kalām[109] exerted considerable influence upon mediæval Jewish philosophers[110] from Saadia[111] (10th Cent.)[112] until Aharon Ben-Eliyahu (14th Cent.),[113] The principal doctrines of the Mutakallimūn, especially those of the Mu'tazila, which influenced our author[114] include, in addition to the aforementioned views on physics, the necessary existence of God based upon *creatio ex nihilo*, His absolute unity and simplicity (doctrine of divine attributes) and His incorporeality. The Kalāmists also developed views characteristically their own with regard to divine justice, the immortality of the soul, reward, and punishment and the nature of good and evil.

Aharon's views on the nature of sublunar existence, in keeping with the doctrines of the Kalām, are founded upon the theory of atoms.[115] The indivisible particle or atom is the basic substance, and accidents are its qualities or attributes. He denies the necessity of cause and effect, and repudiates the validity of natural law. God, unassisted by intermediates, is responsible for what occurs in the terrestrial world as among the supralunar spheres. The theory of atoms does not necessarily argue the creation of the universe; for Epicurus subscribes to the theory, and nevertheless maintains the theory of eternity.[116] Aharon rejects the views of the Ash'ariya who maintain that accidents must be successively recreated in order for them to continue to exist.

Like Saadia, al-Basir, Yeshu'ah Ben-Yehudah, and Bahya before him, he employs the Kalāmistic arguments for creation,[117] from which there logically follows the necessary existence of a Creator[118] and the fact of His incorporeality.[119] Coming to the matter of God's unity, we are confronted with the much discussed question of God's attributes. Here again our author adopts the Kalāmistic notion of God's unity in an absolute sense as excluding any and every kind of plurality. Against the view of Maimonides who insists that only negative attributes can be ascribed to God, Aharon maintains that we can predicate five positive essential attributes of the Divine Being, viz., Omnipotent, Omniscient, Acting with Will, Living and Existent.[120] In ascribing these attributes to God, however, they must not be considered as five distinct entities separate from the essence of God. On the contrary, they are identical with one another and at one with His essence, although we do not understand the nature of this identity as we are ignorant of His essence. Aharon rejects the Asharite view of a subjectless Will maintaining that God's Will is identical with his essence.[121] Finally, Aharon ascribes a kind of sense-perception to God, so that he perceives intelligibles as well as objects of the senses although this is not acquired by corporeal organs which are inconceivable with regard to God.[122]

IV. INFLUENCE OF MAIMONIDES' GUIDE UPON AHARON'S TREE OF LIFE

Both the external disposition and the essential spirit of Aharon's *'Es Hayyim* and the *Moreh Nebukhim* of Maimonides are fundamentally one and the same.[123] It is also abundantly evident from Aharon's treatment of the anthropomorphic expressions in the Bible[124] that he has made verbatim use of his predecessors' work.[125] Maimonides is quoted by name even more frequently than Aristotle,[126] and it appears that the Peripatetic notions of Aharon are derived from Maimonides' presentation of the same. As to the extent of Aharon's dependence upon the Guide and the commentary *Meshārēth Mōsheh* thereon by Kalonymos[127] we find two extreme views expressed by critics: one asserts that Aharon's religio-philosophical system contains nothing new whatsoever, being an eclectic work based for the most part on the views already expressed by the *Mōreh*;[128] the other, while admitting the similarity between the two works, insists that the *'Es Hayyim* is an original work that sheds light upon the doubtful parts of the *Mōreh*, thus completing and supplementing it.[129] The truth, as usual, is to be found in neither extreme, although the former view is more nearly correct. The eminent Rabbi Mosheh of Cairo is indeed the central figure in the picture, and his views constitute the point of departure for the development of our author's opinions.[130] Nevertheless, the *'Es Hayyim* possesses many features which render it a real contribution whose value is not alone to the Karaites, but to any student of Jewish philosophy, who will find in this treatise an intermediary position between the Kalāmistic notions of an al-Basir and the Aristotelianism of a Gershonides.

The basic principle that underlies the respective works of Maimonides and Aharon is their common acceptance of speculative reasoning as the definitive source of truth. In this regard, the former, as a strict follower of the Stagirite in well nigh everything save Creation and Providence, is more consistent than our author, whose avowed aim[131] is to rid his coreligionists of the destructive influences of Aristotelian rationalism. With Aharon[132] as well as his Rabbinic guide, Scripture is adduced not to substantiate, but to corroborate and confirm the assured results of observation and ratiocination. Maimonides' arrangement of his *Magnum Opus* was motivated by his desire to guide a limited circle of religiously perplexed students to whom the anthropomorphic language of the Bible presented a conception of God that was diametrically opposed to the results of their philosophical studies.[133] Hence, he commences his treatise with the spiritualization of the Scriptural anthropomorphisms and the negation of positive attributes, and only then does he proceed to discuss Creation and the existence of God. Aharon, on the other hand, follows a more logical order by presenting first the arguments for creation, followed by proofs for the incorporeality and unity of God. With regard to anthropomorphisms, Aharon and Maimonides are again in full agreement as to the hermeneutical principles of philosophical exegesis. After stating the four criteria for the literal understanding of Scripture, which he takes almost verbatim from his Karaite predecessor Aharon the Elder,[134] our author asserts that any Biblical statement which does not conform with these standards or in any way is opposed to what has been demonstrated by the intellect must be explained either as a metaphor, a homonym or as requiring an additional word.[135] Aharon is careful to indicate, lest anyone accuse him of plagiarism, that his Karaite predecessors had employed the same exegetical method in expounding the Bible as he is about to use.[136] He makes a special point of noting that Yehudah Hadassi's work, the *'Eshk'ol HaKofer* which contains a detailed exposition of this subject appeared some twenty-nine years prior to the *Sefer HaMaddā'* of Maimonides. The Karaite Kalev Afendopolo adduces the fact that Aharon expounds many terms not found in the *Mōreh* as proof that he did not derive his views on the matter of homonymity from Maimonides.[137] In the approximately forty-five chapters, which both Aharon and Maimonides devote to the explanation of anthropomorphisms in their respective works, the number of instances where Aharon derives his views directly or indirectly from Maimonides are far too numerous to mention. These have been indicated throughout the notes to the English translation. A singularly novel interpretation of the transgression of Adam and Eve is expounded by our author[138] in connection with the verse, "And they heard the voice of the LORD God walking in the garden" (Gen. 3.8). Based upon Maimonides' treatment of Adam's fall as an allegory representing the relation that exists between sensation, moral faculty and intellect,[139] Aharon explains that Adam and Eve were made to descend from the intellectual sphere to the realm of moral truths because they failed to heed the divine admonition that they should eat from both the Tree of Life and the Tree of Wisdom. Another interesting view is Aharon's interpretation of Psalm 103, 2022 where he explains the "angels" as identical with the separate Intelligences; the "hosts" as one with the spheres; and "his works" as representing the things of the terrestrial world.[140] This is in keeping with view of

Maimonides who identifies the separate Intelligences of Aristotle with the angels of Scripture.[141]

Both Aharon and Maimonides are agreed that true Philosophical knowledge was the original possession of the Jews,[142] but whereas the latter asserts that this knowledge is primarily Aristotelian in essence, our author contends that the Mut'azilites are the real heirs. It is here that we perceive the fundamental difference between Aharon Ben-Eliyahu and Maimonides. The latter is a staunch disciple of the Stagirite and has no use whatsoever for the Mu'tazila,[143] while Aharon is an avowed follower of the Kalāmistic school and repudiates Aristotelianism as a destructive influence against the Law of Mosheh.[144] Thus, Maimonides tentatively adopts the Aristotelian theory of eternity in order to prove with one stroke God's existence, unity and incorporeality. The Kalāmistic Aharon, defender of his faith against the inroads of the Peripatetics, will not permit such a heretical thought to enter his mind. He establishes Creation upon the firm foundation of atomistic physics and from this he derives the existence, incorporeality and absolute unity of the Creator. Maimonides' argument for creation, based upon the peculiarities of the heavenly motions which Aristotle cannot account for, is rejected by Aharon who explains that the reasons for these aberrations may be quite in accord with the hypothesis of mechanical causation although they are yet unknown.[145] Hence, one must turn to the Kalām for the correct proof of Creation. Our two philosophers are in full agreement as regards the incorporeality of God although their results are derived from the opposing concepts that characterize their respective views. In Maimonides' classic exposition of the nature of divine attributes,[146] he concludes that only negative attributes may be ascribed to God with the exception of those positive predicates which describe the effects of the divine energies and activities upon man and the rest of sublunar existence. Taking the last mentioned view as his point of departure, Aharon insists that the five positive attributes that may be ascribed to God are to be considered only as representing the divine acts as they are related to the terrestrial world. These essential attributes are identical with one another and with God's essence and in no way infringe upon His absolute unity and simplicity. Thus, in reality, Aharon agrees in principle with Maimonides, although he takes considerable pains to refute the notion of Maimonides that only negative attributes may be ascribed to God.[147] Finally, our philosophers disagree on the ascription of sense perception to God, which Aharon maintains as a necessary corollary of His attribute, Living.

V. THE POSITION OF AHARON BEN-ELIYAHU IN KARAITE PHILOSOPHY

In considering the development of Karaite religio-philosophical thought we may conveniently divide our subject into three periods corresponding to the youth, manhood and maturity of this system of ideas.[148] In so doing, we shall attain a proper perspective for Aharon Ben-Eliyahu's place in the evolution of the Karaite theological and speculative doctrine. What is true of Jewish philosophy in general, viz., that its spirit has been stirred and inspired by its exposure to and contact with external culture, is particularly applicable to the religious philosophy of the Jewish sect under discussion. As Philo was stirred by Hellenic culture, Solomon ibn Gabirol and Maimonides were inspired by NeoPlatonism and the Aristotelian doctrine respectively and Herman Cohen was influenced by Kantian idealism, so Karaite dogma developed through its contact with the Islamic Kalām.[149]

The early and formative stage of Karaite religious philosophy which we have designated as the period of its youth embraces the latter part of the eighth and the whole of the ninth centuries and is distinguished by the writings of the two theologians, Benyamin Nahawandi[150] (ca. 830) and Dani'el alQumisi (ca. 890). The work of the former, who may be considered the first Karaite religious philosopher and, incidentally, the first Karaite to employ the Hebrew language, was permeated with the fundamental conceptions of Mu'tazilite thought. In his effort to harmonize the physical and human characteristics of God that are contained in the expressions of Scripture, especially those associated with revelation and creations, Nahawandi propounded a transcendent conception of the Most High that pictured His relation to the universe as one of remote contact effected by a hierarchy of spiritual beings that was dominated by a primate angel. The latter alone were created by God, while all things terrestrial were brought into existence by the angels. Accordingly, this Karaite thinker makes all anthropomorphic and anthropological expressions concerning God that are found in Scripture referable to the Angle.[151] This notion was later thoroughly refuted by alBasir.[152] Aharon Ben-Eliyahu quotes Nahawandi as maintaining the eternity of matter although the latter admits the well known Kalāmistic principle that bodies cannot do without accidents originating in time, from which they deduce that these bodies themselves must have their origin in time.[153] This notion is also repudiated by alBasir. Nahawandi adopts the Mu'tazilite theory of attributes in accordance with which such predicates as Life, Power and Knowledge are identical with one another, and are at one with His essence. Thus, God's spirituality is vindicated and His absolute unity maintained.

The second philosopher of this early period Dani'el alQumisi (ca. 890), presents a reaction against the preceding views. With him, speculative reasoning cannot constitute a definitive source of knowledge, and he clings to a literalistic interpretation of both the legalistic and theological aspects of the Bible. This attitude is in opposition to the generally accepted Mu'tazilite view which considers it a "duty" to arrive at the knowledge of God by speculation and rational proof. Unlike his predecessor, alQumisi denies the existence of angels; when they are mentioned in Scripture they do not refer to rational articulate beings, but to the forces of nature,[154] such as lightning, clouds, winds, etc.[155]

That stage in the development of Karaite religio-philosophical thought, which we have designated here as the period of manhood, is the most brilliant age of Karaite literature. This period, embracing the tenth, eleventh and twelfth centuries is distinguished by the philosophical achievements of alQirqisani, alBasir, Yeshu'ah Ben-Yehudah and Yehudah Hadassi. The first mentioned scholar, alQirqisani (ca. 935);[156] composed the Kit'ab alAnwar (Book of Lights)[157] in which are defended the dictates of commonsense and reason in religious matters. He accepts without modification the Mu'tazilite view of the Kalām, and formulates the criteria by means of which one is to determine when to interpret Scripture literally and when to expound it according to its inner or figurative sense. The schism which divided the rationalistic

Mu'tazila and the orthodox Ash'ariya in the Islamic Kalām is reflected in the divergent notions of alQirqisani and other Karaite scholars of this period, as Sahl Ben-Masliah and Shelomo Ben-Yeruham who were hostile to secular knowledge and decried those who went too far in the direction of rationalistic thinking.

The foremost Karaite philosophical theologian and the source from which Aharon Ben-Eliyahu obtained most[158] if not all[159] his Kalāmistic opinions is Yosef alBasir (ca. 1025).[160] This most renowned Karaite scholar formulated five principles in connection with the unity of God:[161]

1. The necessary assumption of atoms and accidents

2. The necessary assumption of a creator

3. The necessary assumption of divine attributes

4. The necessary rejection of attributes falsely ascribed to God

5. The necessary assumption of His unity notwithstanding the plurality of His attributes

These principles in their application to Karaite dogma, as has been pointed out by Schreiner,[162] constitute the foundation as well as the framework of Aharon's philosophical system. Although alBasir's philosophical works have no claim to originality, they provide us with an earlier, more comprehensive and less prejudiced account of the Mu'tazilite doctrine than that presented by Maimonides.[163] As a matter of fact, the Muhtawi, alBasir's chief philosophical treatise, might easily be taken for the work of an Arabic Mu'tazilite, were it not for the few Biblical quotations that it contains. AlBasir unequivocally affirms that speculative reason is logically prior to revelation as a source of truth; knowledge of the existence, power and wisdom of the Creator must precede our belief in the prophet's mission.[164] The universe is constituted of atoms whose four primary accidents are combination, separation, motion and rest.[165] These accidents are brought into being by a creator whose attributes are inferred from the nature of His activities relative to the universe. For this reason no analogy or comparison whatever can be established between God and terrestrial existence;[166] the finite human intellect cannot pierce the inscrutable transcendence of His essence. This is the foundation upon which the Kalām builds its conception of God's absolute unity and simplicity.

The fact that Aharon Ben-Eliyahu obtained his knowledge of the Kalām from his Karaite predecessors is clear not only from his dependence upon alBasir but from his frequent reference to the latter's pupil Yeshu'ah Ben-Yehudah (ca. 1060).[167] The philosophic position of Yeshu'ah is exactly like that of his master in that it is completely dominated by the Mu'tazilite Kalām. His arguments for creation although differently formulated are essentially those of alBasir and the same applies to his notions of God's incorporeality and unity.

Like Aharon Ben-Eliyahu so Yehudah Hadassi is primarily indebted to Yosef alBasir for the views expressed in his 'Eshkol HaKofer.[168] What has been stated regarding the philosophic notions of Yeshu'ah Ben-Yehudah is equally applicable to Yehudah Hadassi.[169]

The period of maturity in the development of Karaite religious philosophy begins with the Sefer HaMivhar of Aharon Ben-Yosef (ca.1260-1320).[170] The views of Aharon the Elder are generally based upon the Kalām, but they show decided leanings towards an Aristotelian doctrine[171] that is tinged with NeoPlatonism. Thus, Aharon the Elder, although primarily following the doctrines of his Karaite predecessors alBasir and Yeshu'ah Ben-Yehudah, nevertheless conceives of the angels mentioned in Scripture as separate Intelligences that emanated from God. He is also inclined to assume the Platonic view of the preexistence of formless matter. In Aharon Ben-Eliyahu, however, we perceive what Schreiner describes as a "singular coalition of Kalāmistic and Aristotelian doctrines".[172] In our foregoing sketch of the Peripatetic and Kalāmistic influence to which Aharon is indebted (Part III) we have seen how these two forces have affected our author. Although he was chiefly concerned to guard the Mu'tazilite Kalām against the Stagirite's teachings, which had found their way into Judaism largely through the writings of Maimonides, nevertheless Aharon Ben-Eliyahu's 'Es Hayyim is profoundly dominated by the spirit of Aristotle.

ʿĒ Ṣ ḤAYYĪM

[THE TREE OF LIFE]

BY

AHARON BEN-ELIYAHU OF NICOMEDIA

O nobles, behold this book, incline your ears,
For it is unto the wise a light for their eyes.
The clarity of its words unto all peoples
Array with the sound of tabret and cymbal.

Its exposition is worthier than all that have
preceded,
Shall Gihon boast by the waters of Eglaim!
Its wisdom being well arranged
Open your eyes, man of understanding, gird
your loins.

Men of intelligence and understanding who believe

In the existence of God and comprehend His unity,

And that He is neither corporeal nor a power residing within a body

You know the glory of Him Who dwells in heaven.

His essential attributes through scientific reasoning, not by mere tradition

You have comprehended by means of authentic proofs.

They are: Omnipotent, Omniscient, Living and Existent

From His essence these are inseparable, nor do they reside in Him.

And with the band of His kindness He girds

Every created being with the goodness which He has laid up.

His Law through the words of the prophets

To comprehend the inner secret beyond the concealing clouds

He has bestowed with lovingkindness from the holy heavens

Upon the seed of Ya'aqov, keeper of the faith,

And also reward and punishment to make righteous

His ways that they may be proper.

Behold this book, perfect in beauty, and search

Through its pages you wise and men of understanding

Which contain the principles of our faith.

In knowledge it is more precious than pearls.

Then you will be found worthy of beholding the pleasantness of the LORD

In Eden the divine garden which awaits you.

The Tree of Life, that quickens the soul,

I have called it in honor of the Guardian of the faithful.

INTRODUCTION

Rejoice the soul of Your servant, for unto You,
O LORD, do I lift up my soul (Tehillim 86.4).

Said Aharon, the son of Eliyahu: Since man's
intelligence finds great delight in discovering truth,
this delight will be enhanced in proportion to the
quality of the object in his search for truth. We know
that the existence of this world, which we shall presently investigate and examine, has come into being *ex
nihilo* as regards both its quality and its quantity; that
it is not capable of maintaining itself, but requires a
force external to itself that has brought it into being *ex
nihilo* and has endowed it with existence, perfecting
its form and sustaining its being. Consequently, it is
incumbent upon us to know that Being, to believe in
His existence and His perfection, to negate from Him
any defect by authentic proofs and to affirm the truths
pertaining to Him; to adorn Him with every manner
of perfection since he is perfect in the highest degree
of perfection as is proved by authentic investigation.
That Being is God alone, and there is no Rock besides
Him, Who has brought about existence in orderly
arrangement, creating in the beginning the upper,
middle and lower worlds[173] and in His great wisdom
beginning with the largest and ending with the smallest and giving to each the portion which is its due.

1

Exalted and praised be He Who has placed man's spirit within him and knowledge and understanding in his heart. In truth God is the first Existent and man the last created being. Man is the tabernacle of God in the sublunar world. Around Him are darkness, clouds and thick darkness, and the place where He abides is in the intelligence of man, with which he alone is endowed of all living creatures beneath the heavens. Man beholds the vision of the Almighty and is obliged to know its what and its wherefore. Consummate matter was united with a soul that ascends on high elevating the lowly and bringing down the sublime, marvelous in counsel, great in wisdom. Then man became a living soul so that he could rise intellectually to remove the mask from his thoughts, in order to understand the inner secret of the clouds, to draw nigh unto the thick darkness amidst which God is to be found, for there God appeared to him; to behold the pleasantness of the LORD to shine in the light of life, that the knowledge of God might be upon the earth and the presence of God in the land of the living. Then he will believe and know, know that there is a God and that the LORD is God. This is the law of the elevated man. Yet man, despite his excellence, with his foolish soul, did not understand, so the LORD drove him out from the garden of 'Eden to till the soil whence he was taken; for he was similar to the animal. Then there arose the father and head of believers, Avraham, our father, may he rest in peace. He comprehended the existence of God by intellectual investigation[174] and proclaimed the name of the LORD, the eternal God. This faith was transmitted to his children after him, as it is said, "For I have known him, to the end that he may command his children and his household after him, that they may keep the way of the LORD" (Gen. 18.19). Then there came the father

2

and head of the prophets, Mosheh, our teacher, may he rest in peace, who strengthened this faith by giving of the authentic Law. He confined them (i.e., the sons of Avraham) within the limits of this faith through reward and punishment, which constitute the end of all men, and designated their recompense for good or evil by means of proof. For Israel is the purpose of the sublunar world and has been created for His Glory, as it is written, "Every one that is called by My name, and whom I have created for My glory" (Isa. 43.7), and the Israelites are those who have been called by His name, as Scripture states, "And all the peoples of the earth shall see that the name of the LORD is called upon you; and they shall be afraid of you" (Deut. 28.10). It is also said, "I have called upon your name, you are Mine, Israel, in whom I will be glorified" (Isa. 49.3). They are His treasured possession and His people and therefore He is destined to redeem them with an everlasting redemption in honor of His name. God explained this purpose when Israel departed from the path of righteousness by saying "And that which comes into your mind shall not be at all; in that you say: We will be as the nations as the families of the countries" (Ezek. 20.32). For Israel has been privileged with this excellence owing to the merits of Avraham, our father, may he rest in peace, the first of believers. Consequently, it is incumbent upon us to emulate his faith,[175] to investigate and know the soul, which comprehends the existence of God by means of the reflection of the intellect. Indeed, all this depends solely upon the comprehension of the intellect and with this knowledge man may consider himself praiseworthy, as the prophet has stated, "But let him that glories, glory in this, that he understands and knows Me" (Jer, 9.23). Mosheh, too, has said, "Know this day and lay it to your heart" (Deut. 4.39). And

David said to Solomon, his son, "Know you the God of your father" (I Chron. 28.9).

The goal of our knowledge of Him is that we should conceive Him as without beginning or end, a necessary existent *per se*, Who is removed from corporeality and from the accidents of corporeality; that He is One and necessary by virtue of the attributes of the soul by which His existence is ascertained. The latter constitute one Being that is simple without any composition whatsoever. And everything depends upon his power by the thread of His kindness that is stretched forth from the gate of His goodness between celestial and terrestrial beings; the fulfillment of Providence, the authenticity of prophecy and the secret of the giving of the Law. There is no doubt that our truth is glorified by these opinions for they are the end of wisdom, which is the advantage of man; for through it man approaches the divine. This concept is alluded to in the verse, "surely a wise and understanding people" (Deut. 4.6).

However, when Israel strayed from the belief in God, Scripture states regarding them, "And the wisdom of their wise men has perished",[176] which is their advantage, "and the prudence of their prudent men has been hid" (Isa. 29.14). That prophet himself awakened them to the direction that their thoughts should take[177] by saying, "Lift up your eyes on high and see; Who has created these?" (Isa. 40.26). For that generation was the generation of Yishayahu in which they believed in the existence of God, but their belief was not the result of investigation. But, when there came the generation of Yerumiahu, and they denied the existence of God, and did not believe in the existence of God, as it is written, "They have belied the

Lord, and said: It is not He" (Jer. 5.12), he awakened them to seek proofs, saying "Stand you in the ways and see, and ask for the old paths" (Jer. 6.16). Now, if this condition existed during the time of the kingdom when there were among Israel prophets and the great Sanhedrin, how much more so is it true of us who have gone into exile because of that transgression and have remained empty and void of all wisdom after afflictions have been increased upon us among the nations and the vision of prophecy has been sealed, as it is written "Her prophets find no vision from the Lord" (Lam. 2.9); it is also written "My people are destroyed for lack of knowledge" (Hos. 4.6). There has been fulfilled upon us the statement, "Now, for long seasons Israel is without the true God" (II Chron. 15.3). Yet, after all this He has promised us that we shall again know Him, as is alluded to in the verse, "And I will scatter you among the nations, and disperse you through the countries; and I will consume your filthiness out of you. And you shall be profaned in yourself in the sight of the nations; and you shall know that I am the Lord" (Ezek. 22.15, 16). After all these misfortunes He has promised us that we shall know him by saying, "And you shall know the Lord" (Hos. 2.22). And by the good hand of God upon us, He has aroused the spirit of the wise men of our exile as it is written, "And they that are wise among the people shall cause the many to understand" (Dan. 11.33). And the latter have brought light regarding His unity to the eyes of our intelligence, to each one according to the perfection of his intellect.

CHAPTER 1[178]

Since the ultimate goal of our investigation is a single fact, namely, the existence of God, although the methods of proof that demonstrate His existence are different among the wise men of Israel, I have seen fit to inform you of the circumstances which brought about these differences of opinion as regards the methods of proof.

When the people of Israel were exiled into foreign lands because of their iniquities and affliction prevailed over them, there were fulfilled upon them the prophecies of evil, as Scripture asserts "And the wisdom of their wise men shall perish and the understanding of their prudent men shall be hid" (Isa. 29.14); "My people are destroyed for lack of knowledge " (Hos. 4.6). In accordance with their sins were they smitten. Indeed, it is not to be wondered at how these things (i.e., philosophical investigations) were lost from among us. If disagreement fell into matters which were continually with us and we do not know them with certainty, how much less agreement is there bound to he in matters of the intellect known only to one man in a thousand! But when the LORD's kindness prevailed over us by granting us a short respite from our toil as He had promised through the man of purest matter, when He said, "And yet for all that, when they are in the land of their enemies" (Lev. 36.44), He aroused certain men of pure soul whose

6

minds He motivated to seek after truth and perfection. Those–the remnant whom the LORD called–were the eyes of the mind that sought truth. It is significant for you to know that after Avraham, our father, the first believer, had set his mind to learn of the existence of God and understood the methods of proof by which the existence of God can be ascertained, he taught us those methods of proof through which he had acquired knowledge of the existence of God, as it is written, "For I have known him to the end that he may command his children and his household after him that they may keep the way of the LORD" (Gen. 18.19). That sufficed for us until the time of the Torah. And when the Torah came, containing opinions of peerless beauty, the latter were joined to the opinions of our faith and were as one in our hands. You have known that the Gentiles hated and envied Israel for their superiority in that they were the chosen ones of the LORD, and that they possessed true beliefs. Because of their hateful envy they endeavored to refute the true opinions and to establish opposing beliefs in their stead. These were the ancient Greek philosophers who are called "hateful, enemies and arrogant", as it is written, "Do I not hate them, O LORD, that hate You?..... I hate them with utmost hatred" (Psalms 139.21); "They gush out, they speak arrogancy" (Psalms 94.4). Such verses and others similar to them are manifold. At the time of the second Temple when the authority of the Greeks ruled the people of Israel, the former, as a result of their contact with the Jews, their religion and its true teachings, upon the advent of Jesus the son of Mary, immediately adopted his false teachings in order not to accept the faith of Israel, thus demonstrating their envy and hatred. You know that everyone who believes the Bible must refute the teachings of these philosophers[179] and believe in those other principles by which the Bible can be verified. Because the Greeks intermingled with the Israelites the former[180] learned their methods of proof.[181] Regarding this, the prophet exclaims "They have given their pleasant things for food" (Lam. 1.11). Nevertheless they remained ignorant of the true nature of God; they neither knew nor understood, but walked in darkness for their eyes were shut and they could not see; their hearts could not understand. Then, following the principles of the Torah which they received in accordance with the methods of proof which they learned from Israel, the Christians were divided according to the opinions of the philosophers and rejected their former views. Then came the Arabs who also trod the path of the Greek Christians. The Arabs believed in a teaching that had been transmitted to them and they adopted from the Greeks those principles by which their own teaching, could be verified. These are the Mu'tazila and the Ash'ariya, although the sect of the Ash'ariya was divided by alien doctrines as will be explained further. In fine, both peoples held views by which their revealed teachings could be verified, and maintained those proofs that justified their respective faiths, which they had borrowed from Israel.

After all this, when the people of Israel had been exiled into lands not their own among those same nations and their minds' eyes were groping to find the truth, they were divided into two factions, viz., the Karaites[182] and the Rabbanites. The scholars of the Karaites and some of the Rabbanite sages followed the opinions of the Mu'tazila, seeing that their views coincided with the principles of the Bible and that they were originally the views of Israel, as we have explained. As regards the propositions of the philosophers, however, since they stand opposed to the fundamental doctrines of the Bible and refute the latter, they turned their faces away and rejected them. This they did, not in accordance with preconceived notions but after intellectual research. Nevertheless some Rabbanite scholars[183] were inclined to accept the views of the philosophers[184] though believing in the Bible, and took upon themselves the burden of removing every view contained in the opinions of the philosophers that is opposed to the fundamental doctrines of the Torah. This, however, is impossible; for if the Greeks, to whom philosophy was paramount, rejected the views of the philosophers and turned to other opinions which coincided with the tenets of their revealed teachings at the time when the doctrines of Christianity prevailed—how can we, who believe in the law of Mosheh, follow the views of the philosophers which refute the basic principles of the Bible? Now, it would be improper for anyone to misconstrue our statement, when we assert that the fundamental principles of the Bible appear to direct us to one particular view, taking it to imply that what in reality is primary has become secondary;[185] for truth assists others while requiring no assistance for itself. Our reply would be that we have not said this, nor has such a thought entered our minds.

It is merely the effect of habit that certain people maintain opinions similar to the views of the philosophers that we have mentioned and consequently are led to heresy. This is hardly because they are in possession of truth, but as it is stated in the Biblical rhetoric, "For the lips of a strange woman drop honey" (Prov. 5.3); "With the blandishments of her lips she entices him away" (Prov. 7.21); "But her

9

end is bitter as wormwood" (Prov. 5.4); "Her guests are in the depths of the netherworld" (Prov. 9.18).

I have seen that the scholars of these two factions are divided in their opinions, certain among them finding pride in strange views. Regarding them Scripture states, "And they please themselves with the doctrines of aliens" (Isa. 2.6).[186] These men murmured and even spoke boldly against our sages,[187] peace be upon them, who were possessed of true beliefs. Therefore, I have come to point out the direction of truth and to elucidate the heresy which results from those who follow the views of the philosophers.[188] Then wickedness will stop its mouth.

Two motives have induced me to write this book. First, to preserve the results of my studies; for you will know the superior strength of learning by this course which I shall follow. Secondly, some of our own scholars, although not all, are inclined towards views which intelligence cannot bear. Hence, my heart has moved me to approach this task in order to point out the way of truth to the extent that I am able to do so; for the word of the LORD was like a fire within me which I could no longer contain.[189] I shall, therefore, include the doctrines of faith and the doctrines of the Bible so that they may be as one in your hand. Nor shall I be deterred by anyone whose evil desire prevails over his intellect to misconstrue my intentions in the matter; for my intention is dedicated to God's faith, to elucidate matters to the utmost of my ability. May the God of my salvation be with me.

Owing to the extraordinary character of this task and the importunities of the exile which we suffer[190] some matters may be concealed from me. Therefore, let me not be judged guilty by the reader of

10

this book because it was hidden from me, for I trust in my Rock that this error might occur in a corollary, but not in reference to the fundamental principles of our faith. With these words I commence, placing my hope and trust in the LORD.

CHAPTER 2[191]

It is an accepted fact that the function of the intellect is to distinguish truth from falsehood; to befriend truth and to reject falsehood. It is also known that the truth or falsehood of anything is classified by logic into five categories, viz., that which is entirely true or entirely false, that which is mostly true or mostly false, or that which is equally true and false. The two categories, viz., that which is entirely false and that which is mostly false we need not investigate. There remain then three categories that constitute varying degrees of truth. The first degree is that which is entirely true. The second degree is that which is mostly true. And the third degree is that which is equally true and false. Our investigation will be concerned with these three which the intellect acquires from four sources. They are as follows: speculative thought, sense perception, and the faculty of judgment and authentic tradition. That which is ascertained by logic or through the senses is included in the first degree of truth, that category which is entirely true. That which is determined by our judgment of values is included in the second degree of truth, that category which is mostly true. That which is accepted by tradition may be classed in the third degree of truth, the category that is equally true and false.

There are axioms such as our notion that the whole is greater than any of its parts. There are also less certain logical inferences, but this is not the place to describe them. An example of sense perception is our knowledge that a certain object is white and another black. An illustration of the faculty of judgment is the conception that stealing is evil and that filial respect is good. Tradition is that which is received from a reliable individual or community stating that a certain fact is true. Now, there is no disagreement in the faculties of speculative thought and sense perception. Hence, they are classed in the first degree of truth. Matters of judgment on the other hand, are subject to differences of opinion; for that which is accepted by one nation may not be considered true by another, for the views of judgment are those constituted by a consensus of opinion regarding the proper establishment of a political order. Consequently, this faculty is classed in the second degree of truth. Finally, there is greater disagreement in reference to tradition than in matters of judgment, hence the former is of the third degree of truth.

The substance of our knowledge is actually derived from three sources, viz., speculative thought, sense perception and the faculty of judgment, while authentic tradition includes all three of these. Indeed, where tradition is very strong in connection with one of these three categories, it has the same validity as they do. That tradition, however, concerning which there are differences has been designated for the third degree of truth. Certain matters are known solely through tradition, viz., the laws of Mosheh, which cannot be confirmed by the intellect although we are informed by tradition that they are of advantage to the soul.

It is further known that the existence of God cannot be ascertained by sense perception since God is not a thing that can be perceived through the senses. Nor can He be known by the faculty of judgment, for His existence does not depend upon the consensus of opinion in relation to the proper establishment of a political order. How could His existence be founded upon judgment seeing that the latter's province treats of the good and the bad, whereas the existence of God must be sought in the categories of true or false which are the qualities of thought and perception.

We have arrived at the conclusion that the existence of God is determined by speculative thought. It has already been explained that tradition includes thought. Therefore, it is possible that the existence of God, which is proved by speculation, may be also considered a tradition. We have stated the value of a fact concluded by logical inference as being in the first degree of truth while tradition is in the third degree of truth. Man must be firm in his knowledge of God's existence in order to avoid any errors. Therefore, it is impossible to know the existence of God solely through intellect. Nor can His existence be known through prophetic utterances by tradition alone and even less so[192] than through intellect; for the word of God can be verified only after we know of His existence, since a derived principle cannot be prior to an essential principle.

CHAPTER 3¹⁹³

Scholars are of divided opinion in respect of the methods of proof concerning the knowledge of God, i.e., His necessarily independent existence, and regarding the fact that He is neither a body nor a force residing within a body, and that He is One. Some base their proofs on the assumption of *creation ex nihilo*, while others have established their knowledge of His existence upon belief in the eternity of the universe. Still others have founded their knowledge of Him upon their conception of the universe and rely to a certain extent upon the idea of creation without entering into a consideration of the eternity or the creation of the world. Now, before we present the proofs which have been established by these three opinions in reference to the existence of God and in so doing decide against the belief in the eternity of the world and sustain the arguments for its creation, we must first consider how the universe is conceived according to each of these theories.

Things that exist in the world about us we perceive as bodies with accidents inherent in them. We have been taught, however, by scientific investigation that there are matters that cannot be apprehended through sense perception and this conclusion has been verified. Only by means of the intellect can such matters be tested. For thought is distinguished from sensation in two respects: first, thought apprehends the species or class, while the faculties of sensation perceive only the individual; secondly, the intellect comprehends the internal properties of things whereas the senses behold only externalities.[194]

Now, in reference to the forms of existing objects the philosophers, in accordance with their respective beliefs in the creation or eternity of the universe, have affirmed the existence of principles that cannot be discerned through sense perception. Concerning the divergence of their opinions as regards the quality of existents it is important to distinguish whether the nature of things in reality points to the teachings of each of the two differing schools of thought,[195] although each school is divided into sects, or whether a preconceived belief in creation or eternity has forced them to adopt notions regarding the principles of existence in conformity with this belief. It must further be determined whether the view of the quality of existents resulting from one of these two beliefs is merely possible or actually necessary and whether an opposing view predicated upon the same belief is also possible or not. These considerations require minute and unprejudiced investigation. The difference in view is between the Aristotelians (philosophers) and the Mutakallimūn.

The philosophers assert that all things are composed of matter. and form.[196] This can be demonstrated by the changes with which matter is affected by means of accidents, for we observe in matter only the accidents. The form, however, cannot be perceived through the senses. Now, accidents fall into three categories, viz., certain accidents reside in all matter, no matter existing without them, other accidents vary in accordance with the particular object, and a third class of accidents are those found in an object at one time and not at another. Hence, they derived the existence of form, which can be demonstrated as follows. There are accidents which are found in certain bodies[197] and not in others, as those affecting animals and those contained in plants. Now, the properties of animals are not evident in plants and there must therefore be an agent, namely, form, as a result of which a particular body is affected with the characteristics of an animal. This agent is its essential form. If this is not true, why are certain accidents found in one body and not in another hen the substratum of matter in both is the same. The same argument applies to plants as compared with minerals. As long as that force exists, i.e., the essential form, the plant possesses its characteristic accidents. Were it not for the essential form one object could not be affected with a form differing from that of another object since the underlying matter is the same. Similarly, respecting the elements which are differentiated by their accidents, if they were not possessed of a natural principle, then heated water, for example, if it did not have a natural principle, i.e., form, which restores it to its original nature, it would never return to its original state. Hence, the philosophers have concluded that form assembles and combines separables.

Magnitude is an accident which includes all matter and every magnitude is divisible an infinite number of times. Now, matter is divisible by virtue of its being matter and its composition is a resultant of its form. For separation and combination are two opposites and how could one subject bear two opposites? It must, therefore, be that separation is predicated upon matter and combination upon form. It follows then that all bodies are composed of matter and form.

Matter does not exist without form. For if an object were divided until it could no longer actually be divided and there remained the smallest particle which retains its form, and which is termed the first movable, that particle is of necessity divisible potentially. The proof for this is that anything which moves has a "before" and an "after" and must, therefore, be divisible.[198] A second proof is as follows: if we say that a body can be composed of parts which are not potentially divisible, let us consider a series of three points set in a row. This is divided through the center and we must assert that the middle point is either divided or not. If we say that the series can be divided into two equal parts, then the middle point is divisible. On the other hand, if we assert that the middle point is not divisible, it follows that the three points cannot be equally divided which is absurd. Thus, it has been demonstrated that since the minutest particle is potentially divisible, it is composed of matter and form. For, since it is divisible, it follows that it is affected with combination and combination is a resultant of form. Hence, it has been fully established that all bodies are composed of matter and form. It cannot be maintained, however, that all things are composed of body and form since the parts of a body themselves are a combination of matter and form. And matter does not imply combination, only form does, and the term body implies three dimensions.[199] Similarly, the Philosopher (Aristotle) stated that natural objects are possessed of a first principle (form) which is the essential quality that affects the object with existence. This principle, however, can be discovered only by the intellect, and its existence ascertained by rational proof. Now, since this property is concealed from the organs of perception and there are investigators[200] who do not believe in its existence, as will be explained, we must examine the nature of things from the simple element to the most complex combination of elements, i.e., man, for his nature is most complex and the existence of his form, which maintains him, is more palpable. The proof that man is the highest combination is that all the natural elements found in the sublunar world are contained in him. For the things which exist in the sublunar world are: the four elements; minerals which are composed of the latter and are of the second degree since they contain the four elements; plants which are of the third degree since they contain the elements and minerals; animals which are of the fourth degree since they are constituted of the elements, minerals and plants; and finally articulate man who is of the fifth degree since he is made up of the elements, minerals, plants, animals and he possesses in addition the power of reason. There is no combination higher than he. Now, the nature of these bodies is comprehended only through the knowledge of the different properties that are manifested by each of them. Nevertheless, the activities of the rational soul in the body of man, the highest in the scale of existence, more clearly demonstrate and establish the nature of that body by virtue of which those properties are made evident so that from its activity the philosophers have been able to determine its character,[201] viz., that it is an entity which is separated from man at his death and that it exists independently, as will be elucidated in the proper place in Chapter 109. Moreover, since the philosophers understood that the above mentioned characteristics are not accidents residing within the body of man as a first principle, but are brought into existence by a certain entity (the soul) which is the source of these characteristics, they concluded that the same applies to all natural objects, viz., that their essential powers are not accidents superimposed upon these objects but are engendered by an entity (form) which is not an accident, as can be demonstrated from its analogy with the soul of man which is not an accident since it is an independent entity separate from the body, while an accident cannot exist independently dissociated from a body.

The logicians have proposed three distinctions between that which is essential and that which is accidental:

1. It is impossible to comprehend the nature of a subject possessed of an entity essential to it without a previous knowledge of the essential thing itself, just as one cannot understand the essence of man if he has no prior understanding of that faculty by which man is distinguished to the exclusion of all other sublunar beings, i.e., the rational faculty. On the other hand, that which is accidental does not define the nature of its subject so that knowledge concerning the latter must precede.

2. Essential form, a universal concept apprehended through the intellect, is by nature prior to the subject with which it is associated. This is not so as regards accidents. For the concept of living must in our knowledge precede the existence of man. Likewise, the category of quan-

tity is prior to the number four since the first is the essence of the latter. Not so is the characteristic of laughter in relation to man. For it is possible to understand the nature of man and subsequently consider laughter, which is an accidental quality and attribute of man. For this reason laughter may be predicated of man and man predicated of laughter.

3. No cause is to be sought for essence. For example, one would not ask why man is a living, articulate creature or why is four a quantity and white a color. As regards accidents, however, a reason can be sought for them, e.g., why is a particular garment white or why is it red? There is also a fourth distinction between form and accident: with the genesis of form a subject is transformed from its natural state, as, e.g., where bread becomes blood. Accidents, however, when they inhere in a subject do not alter its original nature; a white garment that is dyed black still remains a garment.

We know that man was created the last of all beings and that he is constituted of the greatest combination of elements. Between the first creature and the last in the scale of existence there are beings simple and composite in a relative sense. The most simple substances we designate as a combination of prime matter and prime form. These are the foundations (elements), the bases of all genesis in which form does not exist without matter nor matter without form. They constitute the elements of all things that come into being in the sublunar world for everything that exists is composed of them (i.e., of the four elements) and when decomposed returns to them.

The elements exist only potentially in all objects made up of them since they do not retain their actual forms in these bodies. For the form of an element disappears when that element is transformed into an integral part of a body. Nevertheless, it remains there potentially. This can be established by the fact that when this body disintegrates, its elements revert to their original state or form. This is true only by virtue of the potential existence of the forms of the elements in the bodies, which the latter comprise.

Proof for the existence of four elements is derived from the correlative accidents that are inherent in them. These accidents or qualities point to the existence of only four elements and all other qualities can be subsumed under the original four. Since these respective qualities are found in the four elements in their most extreme state as, for example, there is no heat more intense than that of fire, and similarly, for the others, consequently they are termed "elements". Another reason for their being named elements is that all things that come into being are constituted frown them and when decomposed revert back to them.

The transformation of one element into another does not constitute a process of composition or decomposition in which one element serves as the basis or foundation of the other as is the case in composite bodies. No element can be considered the first principle of a second in the sense that the latter has come into being and will eventually return to the former since the matter of all four elements is one and the same. Still, matter cannot be found separate from form, nor form from matter. Only in reference to the human species can form be conceived as a substance that exists even after having departed from its body. For the philosophers assert that there is a question of doubt as regards the intellect and knowledge, whether they are separable or not. In a similar vein Aristotle stated concerning the intellect that it is a predominant aspect of the soul and that it is possible for it to exist eternally apart from that which is destroyed. It is impossible that any intelligent person should be ignorant of the existence of that essence conceived as the human intellect. Furthermore, the philosophers have concluded that there exists in the animal also an essence (the animal soul) in addition to its matter by virtue of which the animal possesses the powers of sensation, consciousness and nutrition. These powers are not separable from the body and cease to exist with the dissolution of the body. The animal soul is the perfection of the natural body whence is derived its power of motion by means of which it moves itself. Plants are also understood to possess an essence in addition to their matter by virtue of which they are endowed with additional powers. Now, these three intelligible souls (the vegetative, animal and human souls) have an existence in addition to the matter in which they reside, for after they cease to exist in a body the matter remains void of them.

All the powers that are found in plants are also to be found in animals, and those found in animals are also possessed by man. This does not mean to imply that man has three distinct souls or that animals have two. Rather, man possesses one essence by virtue of which he enjoys the powers of the rational being, the animal being and the vegetative being. Similarly, animals have one essence by means of which they enjoy animal powers and vegetative powers. This can be demonstrated by the fact that when this essence is gone from man, he does not lose the power of reason while his other powers remain. All his powers cease. We can conclude, therefore, that one essence provides all the powers enumerated. When we consider the powers apart from one another, their separation is a mental dissolution, not something else. In addition to the matter of which minerals are composed, our reason also concedes that minerals possess forms. The function of this form is to combine and amalgamate the four elements to the end that they become a composite whole. Without this combining form the elements could not coalesce.

It is also known that the changes to which bodies are subject are of four kinds:[202]

a) Change of substance, i.e., genesis and destruction,

b) Change of quality, i.e., transformation,

c) Change of quantity, i.e., increase and decrease,

d) Change of place, i.e., motion.

It is apparent from the words of Aristotle–who asserts that amalgamation is neither genesis, transformation, nor increase–that he does not consider it either a substance or an accident. In truth, however, amalgamation is an accident or quality and denotes the fusing of the elements into a composite unit, as will be explained further. In accordance with how harmonious the blending of the combined elements is, the composite will receive higher or lower form, e.g., the form of man or the form of an inanimate object.

There are four elements: fire, water, air and earth. These are distinguished by their correlative qualities, viz., heat, cold, moistness and dryness. All qualitative change to which matter is subject derives from these elemental qualities and for this reason it has been agreed that there are four elements. These elements are composed of matter and form, although the form can be apprehended only through the intellect. The existence of form as a component of the element is established by the fact that any element which departs from its original nature is returned thereto by an essential principle inherent in that particular element. For example, water which has been heated will return to its natural coldness and air which has been forced down will rise again when the pressure forcing it down is removed: The above mentioned facts demonstrate the existence of an essential principle residing in the elements. We are able to perceive, however, only matter and the accidents of which it is the subject. Furthermore, it is false to affirm that these accidents are their essential forms since we have already pointed out the distinction that exists between the essential and the, accidental. Another distinguishing characteristic of the essential, e.g., life, is that it cannot pass over from one subject to another while the accidental, e.g., heat, does pass over from subject to subject.

Similarly, the Philosopher has asserted that composite things, as can be perceived, are composed of substance and accidents. A specific object is a body by virtue of its being an actuality. Its actuality is not derived from its matter, nor from its accidents, which came to be after matter, although the accidents are present actually in the object. Consequently, it is clear that it is an essence in actuality and that this essence is neither an element nor an elemental quality. The essence of a thing is its form, which is neither the matter of which the thing is composed, nor an element nor an accident. Form denotes the essential nature of a thing.

I have seen, however, a statement of Aristotle to the effect that the accidents of the elements are their forms. He asserts in one passage, "The forms of the elements are their qualities, viz., heat, cold, etc". His words are indeed puzzling. For these qualities are accidents. How then can the existence of an object reside in its accident? The Stagirite states further that the fundamentals of the ten categories are three, viz., matter, form and nonexistence.[203] In substance, for example, the heat of fire is its form, cold is the nonexistence of heat and hylic matter is the substratum of both. In quality, whiteness is a form corresponding to the heat of fire and blackness is its negation corresponding to the cold of fire.

In fire, according to the opinions of both Aristotle and his followers, the elements are composed of matter and form and each form is associated with two qualities. Fire, for instance, has the form of fire and with this form are associated two qualities, viz., heat and dryness. Likewise, air has the form of air and that form possesses two qualities, viz., moistness and heat. The same applies to the elements of water and earth, that is, each is associated with two qualities.

If any element were divided to a point beyond which it could no longer be divided, actually the final particle, known as the prime movable, would move in the same direction as would be taken by the element as a whole. It must consequently possess a principle or force, which moves it to return to its natural place. This principle is its essential form. Moreover, since it moves it follows that it is divisible, if not actually then potentially. Now, it is divisible only by virtue of its matter. It cannot, therefore, be also combinable by virtue of its matter since it is impossible for one factor to be the cause of two opposites. Surely then it is divisible by virtue of matter and is subject to combination by virtue of form. It is consequently established that all bodies are composed of matter and form.

All composite beings have their origin in the four elements, into which they resolve again when their existence terminates. No genesis is prior to them; the elements make up the first composite and the first genesis since matter is not found without form, nor form without matter. Each of the elements, however, can assume the form of another element thus demonstrating that there is one substance common to all of them.

This substance or matter is potentially disposed and prepared to receive any form. The elements and their respective properties, however, constitute the basis of all composition and they form beings according to the relative qualities and harmonious amalgamation of their constituent parts. In proportion to the mildness or intensity of the heat or the moistness contained in them the elements assumed the variegated forms of different species. It is not intended here to imply that when the elements are combined in proper proportion this combination will bring into being its own form. For it is impossible that an object should be the agent who brings into existence its own form[204] since it cannot be both the agent and the receiver of the form. On the contrary, the forms of transient being are brought to effect through a different agent which itself is form, for only what is similar to itself can a being impart to others.

The motion of the spheres together with light and darkness determine the constitution of composites.[205] For there is a direct relationship between this motion and the coming into being of a particular thing. Similarly, with the termination of the motion the thing likewise ceases to exist. Hence, there resulted the belief in astrology.[206]

The reader might ask at this point concerning the simple matter common to all four elements, as attested by the identity of their rectilinear motion, in which there is no combination: How did this matter come to assume four distinct forms? The Philosopher (Aristotle) offers the following reason: Matter exists within the concavity of the lunar sphere which is the center of the spheres and in relation to its proximity or remoteness to the former matter receives different forms, as elucidated by him.[207] A question arises here. Do the proximity and the remoteness of the matter depend upon its inherent quality or are its different positions governed by chance? If the former supposition were correct, how can one element assume the form of another? In either case it is not to be understood that when matter is prepared to receive a form that this disposition effects its form. This is not true, for that which brings form into being is itself a form which is continually active in endowing matter with form save in those instances where the matter is not yet prepared to receive its form. The motion of the celestial spheres accomplishes this disposition of matter. A second question presents itself here. Since the properties of the simple elements are correlated with their respective forms, how do these properties remain in composite bodies after the original form of the element has ceased to exist ?[208]

It is only with difficulty that we can comprehend the existence of form in the elements and in inanimate objects. One who is skilled in the science of alchemy, however, can transmute one metal into another, for the essential form of a thing depends upon the relative proportion of its constituent parts as determined by the influence of the spheres. Philosophy does not inform us explicitly that the forms of the four elements and of minerals are derived from the active intellect as are the forms of animate beings, although the Traditionalists have admitted this to be true. There is still a difference of opinion among the philosophers as regards the function of the active intellect. Some assert that it endows only rational beings with form while others maintain that it also provides the animal and vegetative souls, as will be explained later.[209] In reference to the four elements and the minerals, however, no philosopher has stated that their forms are derived from the active intellect.

It is known to me that the dispute among the Philosophers in reference to the active intellect, viz., some assert that it acts only on the form of man while others claim that its activity extends to the forms of animals and plants, is based upon a fundamental problem: Flow can we assume that the universal forms which we conceive are true essences if they are not found to exist outside of the rational intellect? It was this difficulty which constrained Plato to hypostatize individual forms which govern the individual species of living beings. In reality, however, the solution lies in the fact that knowledge which is found potentially in the rational capacity of man must necessarily exist outside of the human intellect. For every category of which one constituent part (the passive intellect) is, potential must possess a corresponding actuality (the active intellect). Similarly, since the intelligibles are in the beginning potential and are motivated by the active intellect, thereby becoming actual concepts, it follows that these concepts perforce exist in actuality. This is the gist of the solution as proposed by the Philosopher.

Let us return now to the original subject of our discussion, viz., no investigator has required the aid of the active intellect for endowing the forms of the elements and minerals. Now, if one were to claim that the matter of lower bodies is derived from the matter of the celestial sphere, and their form from its form, i.e., the form of the sphere which is inseparable from the sphere, and that the human intellect proceeds from the Separate Intelligence (active intellect), he would thus imply that the sphere is composed of matter and form. We can refute this proposition by stating that knowledge regarding an unknown cannot be determined from a thing which is more unknown; for the substance of the sphere, i.e., whether it is a composite of matter and form, is a subject of dispute among the philosophers. Furthermore, they point out that it is not axiomatic that bodies are composed of matter and form. It is impossible, therefore, to compare the celestial bodies with terrestrial objects since the changes which occur in the latter demonstrate that they are composed of matter and form, whereas in the former we perceive only change of position from which we can infer simply that the heavenly beings are bodies. But we are not cognizant of any essential change that takes place in them. By what analogy them can we conclude that the celestial sphere is a combination of matter and form? On the contrary, most scholars, in order to exclude the spheres from the category of the possible, have not stated positively that the sphere is composed of matter and form. In conclusion; speculative philosophy has discovered no agent that brings into being the forms of the elements and minerals.

The process of the understanding of existence as conceived by the human intellect commences with accidents that reside in bodies. Since these accidents are seen to come into being, are destroyed and reside in certain bodies to the exclusion of others, the Philosophers comprehended that they must have an agent. This immediate agent is the essential form of a body. They realized further that matter, which is potentially able to receive any form, assumes specific forms by virtue of its disposition. This disposition is governed by the motion of the spheres. It does not endow matter with form, however, but acts upon matter incidentally. But form must come into being through an agent. This agent is a Separate Form (active intellect). Philosophic speculation has brought them thus far.

CHAPTER 4[210]

The Mutakallimūn, on the other hand, perceive in material objects only body and its accidents, the latter being elements superadded to the body itself, although physical substance is described by attributes. All of these are elements superimposed upon substance. Some of these attributes are termed "characters", others are called "accidents",[211] while still others are in part characters and in part accidents. The distinction between character and accident is that the former cannot be separated from the substance which is "characterized", rather the substance is coexistent with that character, whereas accidents may disappear while the body remains. By reason of this difference the Mutakallimūn distinguish between characters and accidents. Every attribute which is predicated of a body and which at one time comes into being and subsequently disappears is termed a "superimposed accident" according to their theory. These accidents exist in the human intellect despite their nonexistence in actuality. Characters, however, are not separable elements that can have existence in the human intellect alone.

Accordingly, the Mutakallimūn affirm that there are two classes of attributes, viz., those that are in existence and those that are nonexistent.[212] The latter are entities which are conceivable. Other entities are not conceivable, namely, those that have no independent being in a state of nonexistence. These are known as "characters". Character is a quality that is inseparable from its substratum while, on the contrary, an accidental attribute may or may not reside in its body. It was concluded therefore, that the cause of the presence and disappearance of accidents is the essence of the accident. For they claim that since body may exist either combined or disjoined[213] there must be a cause which effects tile union of bodies that were previously separate. This cause they call "union".

The Mutakallimūn have divided the possible causes for the union of bodies into the following necessary divisions: the essence of body, its existence, its nonexistence, the existence of a property, the absence of a separate property, and the maker of body.[214] They rejected the hypothesis that the essence of body is the cause of its union since its essence remains unaltered even when disjoined. Neither is the existence of the body the true cause. For the existence which it possessed when combined is identical with that which it possessed when it was disjoined. Nor can we accept the nonexistence of body as being the cause of its union after it has come into being because the postulate of combination is applicable only where body exists; of a nonexistent body it cannot be postulated. How, then, can that to which a postulate is inapplicable be its cause? Similarly, the absence of a property may not be considered a cause. For what is nonexistent cannot serve as the cause of an existent and is in no manner related to it. They also reject the maker of body as the cause of its union since the maker is engaged with what is made only at the time of its being made. Body, however, remains combined even after the time of its making. The only possible cause for its being combined then can be the existence of a certain property, i.e., "union". Likewise, everything else which is in the category of the contingent—i.e., that may, or may not exist—must be produced by some cause. These facts perforce led them to believe that every body possessed of magnitude is divisible. Furthermore, since it is divisible it must have union. We understand, hence, that union may or may not be present in its substratum and, consequently, is not a character. In any case, union is of such a nature [i.e., an accident superadded to body and separable from it]. It follows, therefore, that substance can exist without union. This is possible only on the assumption that there exists a non-dimensional entity; for only then could it be void of union. This necessarily led them to believe in the existence of the atom which is indivisible and which comes forth from nonexistence. For the Mutakallimūn postulate nonexistence only of the souls of entities that exist by themselves, not in combination since composition is possible only after coming into being has taken place.

The atom's quality of spatiality they term a "character". For no reason can be sought for this quality of the atom. It does not occupy place at one time and not at another so as to be subject to explanation since every atom that exists occupies space. The nature of union, on the other hand, is not of this kind. Union may come into being and disappear while body continues, but we do not find that the attribute of spatiality comes into being and disappears while body continues. Consequently, they call the latter quality a "character". The same type of quality is found in other attributes as, e.g., the attribute of sensation in animals.[215] There is no animal that is not sentient. Consequently, sensation is a character of animals. No reason can be sought for the sensation of animals to the end that it would be established that they are sensitive as a result of sensation. For animals do not cease to be sentient, thus enabling them to be sentient at one time and not at another. Granting that there is no physical defect in the animal, no external impediment and the existence of a stimulant, it will always receive the stimulus.

The character of the atom is its occupancy of space, and since it occupies space one atom can combine with another and a body is formed of them. No individual atom has magnitude. But when one joins another they assume magnitude, i.e., length. Two additional atoms by the side of the first two produce breadth. Four additional atoms above the first give us depth. This then is the true notion of body, viz., that which possesses length, breadth and depth.[216] What is termed "body" therefore must be constituted of at least eight atoms.

According to their theory the composition of atoms is a juxtaposition, not a fusion. One atom cannot merge with another since that implies the penetration of atoms into each other and their divisibility. But the Mutakallimūn have laid down the principle that the atom exists independently and is indivisible. This necessarily follows from the fact that one atom occupying a specific place would prevent another from simultaneously being in the same place.

The philosophers (i.e., Aristotelians) do not believe that a line is made up of points, a plane of lines and a body of planes. These figures are divisible, according to the philosophers, only theoretically, but not by actual separation and division.[217] On the other hand, the Mutakallimūn affirm that body is actually composed of planes; planes are made up of lines; and lines of points. These are the atom which our Sages (i.e., the Karaites) term Particle.[218] In a similar vein one Sage has stated that we are unable to see the atom, but the Almighty can perceive it for He sees, but not through eyes.[219] The Mutakallimūn assert further that atoms exist independently and are not subject to division, either potential or actual, by ourselves or by any being other than ourselves; for in their view it is inconceivable that the atom be divided.[220]

It is my own belief that they (the Mutakallimūn) have asserted the existence of the atom not through sense perception but by force of rational speculation. According to them, human reason has fully established the truth of the existence of the atom. They believe further that heaven and earth and all that is contained in them are constituted of identical atoms, which are distinguished only by their accidents. The atom is disposed to receive any accident. When it receives certain accidents and not others, this is due to the intention of an Intender and Designer.

In accordance with the aforementioned principles, there perforce follow certain propositions which they are constrained to accept:

1. No accident can serve as the substratum of another accident. Since accidents have no independent existence they cannot conceivably form the substratum for other accidents.

2.   An accident cannot pass from one object to another for motion can be predicated only of body.

3.   Accidents do not result from the combination of atoms, for the Mutakallimūn deny all causal relationship,[221] but each atom is provided with certain accidents except the accident of quantity, for it has no magnitude.

4.   Accidents do not continue in existence for two time-units.

Concerning this last proposition, however, these investigators are of divided opinion. Some contend that every accident is destroyed immediately after it has come to be and another is created in its place.[222] Others, however, hold that there are certain accidents which last for a longer period. They assert that atoms are of two kinds, viz., there is one kind of atom which endures for two [or more] time units and a second kind which disappears immediately, e.g., sounds. This will be elucidated further by the arguments for their theory, that the atom, time and accident are units that are indivisible. These conclusions were reached by the proofs of scientific speculation.

As a general statement I wish to say that the Mutakallimūn do not admit that the existence of accidents in bodies is due to a cause which in turn is due to a second cause, and so on. For this chain of causes would have to continue *ad infinitum*, which is impossible. That one accident should be the cause of another is equally inadmissible for this would imply that one accident forms the substratum of another.

This is also impossible for the reason that accidents do not exist independently and consequently cannot form the substratum of other accidents. According to the Mutakallimūn every element which is superadded to the substance is considered an accident. They do not subscribe to the theory of the Aristotelians in accordance with which accidents are caused by essential forms. And with reference to these forms one cannot ask, why are they so? For one cannot ask concerning a human being, Why is he a human being? Actually, forms are endowed through an agent by means of the disposition of matter [to receive a certain form]. This disposition is dependent upon the influences of the spheres.

The Mutakallimūn, on the other hand, have concluded by logical analogy, that all elements which are superimposed upon substance are accidents by virtue of the fact that they are borne by substrates and cannot exist independently, i.e., without a substratum or substance. Hence, it can be asked of all attributes why they are so and these questions would continue without end. Consequently, the Mutakallimūn have put an end to this by asserting that every accident is directly connected with its own subject and is not determined by any other accident. It is created by God, without any intermediary cause: They say further that substance is predisposed to receive any accident that God intends to grant it. For all atoms are of one kind and are identical in essence, each atom existing independently with no addition to its essence save the character of spatiality.

I deny that the belief in the atomic theory necessarily depends upon belief in creation since Epicurus[223] who did not believe in creation nevertheless

38

maintained that body is composed of indivisible atoms and that these atoms are eternal. In reality, belief in the atomic theory is necessitated by the reasons that we stated above. Epicurus believed that the joining and the composition of atoms are purely a matter of chance. But the Mutakallimūn attributed these facts to the First Agent without any intermediary causes. This sect is divided into factions.[224]

In fine, according to the opinion of the Mutakallimūn the existence of the atom can be apprehended only by the intellect. By the method of division and separation a particle is reached which can no longer be divided and which has come into being *ex nihilo*. It is characterized only by the attribute of position and no other accident is necessarily superadded to it. For the accident of union is one that comes into existence. And since it disappears there must be a substance without union. It is this that comes into being *ex nihilo*. Now, the Mutakallimūn do not believe that a composite body is created *ex nihilo* since such a body requires attributes superadded to itself which might be the causes of its existence. Hence, they declared that it is in the category of the impossible that a composite body be created *ex nihilo*. Only the atom is originated *ex nihilo*. The fact that the atom is either at rest or in motion and is never deprived of both rest and motion leads to the demonstration of its creation.[225] For rest and motion are attributes which alternately originate in time, and since the atom cannot do without accidents originating in time, the atom itself likewise has its origin in time.[226]

Rest denotes remaining in one place during two time-units and motion consists of moving from one place to another without pausing in one place for two time-units. At the moment that the atom comes into existence *ex nihilo* and finds its place when it is first originated, it cannot be described as either at rest or in motion. For a body at rest is one which remains in one place during two time-units, but the moment of the atom's origin does not last for two time-units. And a body in motion is one that has previously been at rest, but in our instance the atom had not been at rest previously. Hence, they termed this moment "coming-to-be". As a result of "coming-to-be" the atom is found in one particular place. The above is the opinion of H. Yefet haLevi, who maintains that what is termed "coming-to-be" is neither a state of rest nor a state of motion. His son, H. Levi, however, is of the opinion that "coming-to-be" may properly be considered as implying a state of rest whether the atom remains at rest [for two time-units] or whether it is at rest for merely a part of this period. He asserts that rest during its coming into being means its endurance in this state. For rest denotes either coming into being or remaining. The scholar, H. Yosef, of blessed memory, is also in accord with the last mentioned view.

At this point it is necessary to investigate the differences of opinion of the Philosophers and of the Mutakallimūn respectively in connection with the continuity of accidents after they have come into being. According to the opinion of the former, certain accidents are associated with matter while others are identified with form. As has been explained previously, all this depends upon the disposition of matter, in terms of the relative proportion of its constituent elements.227 Now, so long as the disposition of matter remains subject to the forces of the spheres, forms will continue to exist as a result of the active intellect.

According to the Kalām, however, which denies the existence of intermediary causal relationships and claims that things are created directly by the First Agent, a difficulty presents itself, viz., by what cause do accidents subsequently cease to exist after having endured for a certain length of time? To assume that accidents continue to exist by themselves without the aid of God and that after a time God, by His will, brings about their nonexistence, is rejected by the Kalām as inadmissible. The principle here is that the Agent cannot produce nonexistence. It is also considered as impossible, in conformance with their theory, to deprive a thing of its existence after it has once come into being. The Mutakallimūn accept as fact the creation of things *ex nihilo*, but deny the possibility of bringing about their nonexistence; for nonexistence does not require any agent at all. Consequently, these investigators have split into two sects. The Ash'ariya says that an accident, after being produced, requires an agent throughout every unit of time that it continues in existence. This necessitates the belief that an accident is incapable of enduring for two time-units; however, the Creator successively renews its existence after each atom of time and if He leaves off acting then the accident ceases to exist. The Mu'tazila, on the other hand, assert that after the Creator has produced an accident, it endures by itself for a certain period without requiring any agent to renew its existence. Similarly, our Sages, of blessed memory, have stated that the agent does not continue to act upon that which remains in existence.[228] Accordingly, the Mu'tazila believe that accidents are of two kinds: some accidents do not last for two time-units, but cease to exist during the second atom of time following their creation, e.g., sounds, other accidents do last for a period of time, e.g., blackness and whiteness, without

41

requiring any agent whatever.[229] In the last instance, what cause deprives these accidents of their existence seeing that nonexistence is not brought about by any agent? They reply that every positive accident has a correlative negative accident that exists without any substratum and when God desires to bring an end to any property of a substance, He creates its opposite property in that substance and thereby the first ceases to exist. For example, the universe, which was created by God, exists by itself. The negative accident correlative to the existence of the universe would be that of destruction. Now, if it pleased the Almighty to destroy the world, He would create the accident of destruction, free of any substance, and the world would cease of exist. To take another case, He would remove whiteness by means of its opposite property, namely, blackness. Their speculation has led them thus far. From the aforegoing they infer that the absence of a property is itself an actual property. However, with reference to an accident which does not remain in existence during two consecutive time-units they were not compelled to believe that its nonexistence is effected by means of an actual negative accident, but the absence of endurance constitutes its nonexistence. The Mu'tazila contend, for example, that ignorance is not the negative of knowledge; rather ignorance is merely the absence of knowledge. Similarly, the absence of a "character" is not a real property but a nonentity. Nevertheless, separation is the negative of combination, and rest is an actual accident, the negative of motion, and they are existing properties.

The Ash'ariya do not believe that an accident can exist without any substratum, and which would supersede an existing property; for every accident requires a substratum and furthermore no agent can produce nonexistence. Hence, they are compelled to deny the proposition that an agent does not act upon that which he has already brought into existence, but they claim that as long as an object remains in existence it is the result of the action of a producer and as soon as the latter leaves off acting the product likewise ceases to exist. This led them to the belief that no atom can last for two time-units without the aid of an agent.

The Mu'tazila argue that if all atoms were similar in the sense that they do not last during two consecutive units of time, it would be impossible for some to remain in existence and for others not to remain. Yet we actually see accidents which do not remain because of a reason, yet remain because of themselves by necessity without the activity of any agent at all.

According to the opinion which holds that no accident can last for two time units but is successively renewed after each unit of time—in accordance with this view, when a garment has been placed into a red dye it is not the red pigment which has dyed it, but God created the red color in the garment. Nevertheless, God generally acts in such a way that the color is not created in the garment unless it is brought into contact with the red dye. The same applies to the motion of a pen that is apparently moved by a hand. The pen is not set in motion as a result of the moving hand, but God creates the accident of motion in the pen and He has so regulated the nature of things that motion is created in the pen only following a movement of the head. They have also established another principle; namely, an accident cannot pass beyond the substance in which it is since this would imply that an accident is subject to motion whereas motion can be predicated only of atoms. Now, the accident of motion in the hand is also created anew after each unit of time; and the effect, which is seemingly produced by means of man's ability, is, in actuality, produced by God. There is no power of agency in man's ability, only in God, for the accident of ability is constantly reproduced and does not remain in man. The sole cause is God.

The Mu'tazila on the other hand admit, in conformance with their views, that man's ability does remain in existence after God creates it and that it possesses a power of agency. Indeed, some of the Ash'ariya concede a certain amount of power to man's created ability when they say that the occurrence of an act is effected by the occurrence of ability. This [special power] is termed "permission" in the language of our sages.[231] In the refutation of their views on Providence this subject will be fully elucidated.[232] It was merely intended at this point to explain how certain accidents are combined with certain bodies to the exclusion of others, not the continued existence or disappearance of accidents.

The results of their investigations led the Mutakallimūn to the conclusion that bodies are composed of atoms, which are similar in reference to essentiality. And since we find that specific accidents unite with specific bodies their research compelled them to believe that this is caused by a determining cause that endows certain bodies with particular accidents. This theory leads to the demonstration of the creation of the universe, as will be explained.[233] Now, if this were adequate, it would be considered an authentic proof. But, as you know, the Philosopher has explained the union of specific accidents with bodies by proceeding from one cause to another until the influence of the spheres. Indeed, some investigators have conceded this view.[234] However, they discovered in reference to the spheres themselves and their stars that certain among them are endowed with particular forms to the exclusion of others; that their motions have different velocities, that they are unlike each other as regards relative position, proximity, distance and eccentricity, as a result of which it is necessary to assume either the existence of a vacuum between every two spheres or the presence of some substance, different from that of the spheres, which would fill this space and which would not encompass the world. Now, there must be a cause that is responsible for all these different phenomena. Since no other cause was found it was attributed to the determination of a Designer. This teaches that the world was created.[235] But this reasoning can be refuted. For it can be maintained that the deficiency of our intellects is responsible for our ignorance, nevertheless there actually is a cause, although hidden from us, which determines all the aforementioned phenomena. Hence, the matter remains in doubt.

After the comprehensive presentation that has preceded, I find it necessary to restate the fundamental propositions of both theories, as I understand them. According to the Aristotelians all bodies are composed of matter and form and possess at least three attributes, viz., quantity, quality and position. The Mutakallimūn, on the other hand, assert that body is constituted of indivisible atoms which are free of any addition to their essence save the accident of position. These two conflicting theories can exist because our senses perceive only body and its accidents. The Aristotelians state further that the essential form is the cause that determines the accidents of a body. Indeed, all objects are composed of matter and form since every object is possessed of accidents from which there follows a necessarily existing form which itself is derived from the Active Intellect. The above has been proved in connection with the divisibility of particles. It has also been shown that the souls of plants, animals and humans are in reality their essential forms. Hence, they concluded by analogy that all bodies are composed of matter and form. The Muta-kallimūn deny any intermediary cause for the accidents which are found in an object, but claim that they are brought into existence by the First Agent without any intervening cause. Hence, they were led to believe that bodies are composed of indivisible atoms.

H. Yehudah *HaAvel*, however, rejected the theory that bodies are composed of atoms and contended that all things are made up of the four elements, which were created *ex nihilo*.[236] He argued against those who believe in the existence of the atom and its indivisibility, stating that atom is limited [by space] and whatsoever is limited is *ipso facto* divisible. He contended further that just as the atom is void of any of the four elemental qualities (cold, heat, moistness, and dryness) so body should be without any of these properties. Nevertheless we perceive that this is not the case. It is thus demonstrated that even among our own scholars there is a division of opinion; some believe that things are composed of the four elements while others maintain that they are constituted of atoms. According to the latter theory the vegetative, animal and rational souls are termed "accidents".

46

According to either view, neither the belief in matter and form nor the theory of atoms is based upon sense perception, nor can either be considered axiomatic. Instead each theory is the logical conclusion of a conception of the nature of things to which the advocates of either opinion subscribe; each faction maintaining that what it believes is a true concept while the others believe it to be a product of the imagination rather than of the intellect.

Now, I see no reason to believe that the proponents of either theory have fashioned their conception of the nature of things in accordance with a preconceived notion of the creation of the world or its eternity. On the contrary, it appears to me that the advocates of both opinions base their respective views upon the existing system of things, as each school comprehends it. In fact, both in accordance with the Aristotelian and the Kalāmistic views of the nature of the existent, the creation of the world is a necessary corollary of the principle established by the Mutakallimūn which asserts that if an object cannot do without an attribute originating in time, the object itself has its origin in time.[237] For according to either view— whether it be that of the Aristotelians, who claim that body is a composite of matter and form; that matter cannot be found without form; that form has its origin in matter and that accidents subsequently come into being in matter—or the theory of the Mutakallimūn which contends that body consists of accidents; that body cannot be found without accidents and that accidents have their origin in matter—one common principle demonstrates the creation of matter in either instance. ,for just as we conclude that matter is created from the premise that matter cannot do without accidents which originate for it and matter is never found without accidents, so we can derive the conclusion that matter is created because of the forms which originate in time since matter cannot be found without form, as has already been established.

It was to this purpose that our efforts were directed in this presentation, namely, to demonstrate that the principle, in accordance with which proof for the creation of the world is established, applies not only to the Kalāmistic conception of the nature of things, but this same principle is equally applicable to the Aristotelian view of the constitution of the existent. The difference of opinion between the Philosophers and the Mutakallimūn concerns only the acceptance of this principle itself. Maimonides, likewise, has stated:[238] "some of the Mutakallimūn have endeavored to establish their proposition [concerning the accidental infinite]–i.e., to demonstrate its impossibility by means of a method which I shall explain in this work". Others say that this impossibility is a self-evident axiom and requires no further proof. But if it were unquestionably false to assume as possible the successive existence of an infinite number of things, although that part of the series which exists at present is finite, the inadmissibility of the eternity of the world would be equally self-evident and would not require any other proposition for its proof. This, however, is not the place for investigating this subject. Al Nahawandi is in accord with the theory of the eternity of matter, although he does not concede the eternity of things originating in time.[239] But his words require examination as will be elucidated in our solution of this problem.

The ideas of H. Yeshu'ah, however, as expressed in his commentary on Genesis are well founded. He states there that our proof for creation rests upon two propositions: first, if an object cannot do without an attribute originating in time, the object itself has its origin in time—this proposition is axiomatic; the second proposition treats of the nature of those characteristics without which matter is never found and as a result of which change occurs in bodies.[240] It is concerning the essence of these characteristics that there is a difference of opinion among scholars, since knowledge regarding them is acquired only by means of the intellect. Some say that these attributes are accidents superadded to body and without which body is never found. Combination and separation, for example, are attributes originating in time without which body cannot do. Hence, body itself has its origin in time. Others, however, contend that combination and separation are not two real existent opposites, rather one exists while the other is nonexistent. Consequently, H. Yeshu'ah asserts by way of generalization that since we know change to be impossible without the addition of some element to matter, although we do not comprehend the specific nature of this element, the essence of change indicates that this element has originated in time. And since matter or body cannot do without that element, matter itself must have its origin in time. This element the Aristotelians term "form". Hence, they assert that body is composed of matter and form, although his (i.e., H. Yeshu'ah's) conception of form is divergent from that of the Aristotelians.

CHAPTER 5[241]

In reference to those philosophers who have constructed their proof for the existence of God upon the basis of belief in the eternity of the universe and who have thus established that God is a necessary existent; that He is neither corporeal nor a force residing within a body and that He is one, we must understand the nature of this proof. It rests upon the true principle, which asserts that matter does not move itself. Furthermore, the prime moving agent itself cannot be in motion for it would then require another force to set the former in motion and this would continue *ad infinitum*. In truth, however, the existence of an infinite series of causes is impossible.[242] It must come to an end with a moving agent, which is motionless itself and is eternal since motion is perpetual. The eternity of the moving object is deducible only from the perpetuity of motion. The proofs that the philosophers offer in support of the eternity of this motion will be treated in a subsequent chapter.

The moving agent itself must reside either within the sphere or without it and each of these possibilities can be further subdivided into two alternatives. Thus, we have in all four alternatives:

1. The motive element is either within the sphere,

a) as a force spread throughout the substance of the sphere as is the case with the heat in fire,

b) or an undistributed and indivisible force like the soul of man;

2. Or it exists outside the sphere

a) as a corporeal object,

b) or an incorporeal object.

Now, it is impossible that the moving agent be a corporeal thing without the sphere since a corporeal body that imparts motion to another material object can only effect this by simultaneously being set in motion itself. The reason for this is that all physical motion is produced either by pushing or pulling. Now, if the moving agent is itself in motion it would require another force to effect this state and if the latter force is a body, it would need to have still another agent to impart motion to it, and so on *ad infinitum*. But the existence of an infinite series of causes is impossible, and we must eventually stop at one motive force that does not move itself, and is consequently incorporeal. This conclusion is true.

The basic proposition, however, upon which the preceding proof is established, viz., a corporeal thing that sets another material object in motion can accomplish this only by being set in motion itself, [depends upon the nature of this corporeal thing, i.e.,] whether it be a simple material object or a material object possessing a particular quality. In the first instance the proposition is true. In the second, it would not be correct for there exists a material body possessed of a certain property which enables it to impart motion to another corporeal object and nevertheless remain motionless itself; viz., a magnet is able to effect motion in iron by virtue of its peculiar characteristic, but does not itself move at the same time.[243] The moving agent of the sphere might accordingly be a corporeal object similar to this. For the proponent of this proof has established the incorporeality [of the prime motor force] upon the principles of motion in accordance with which we would eventually arrive at a motionless mover since an infinite number of causes is impossible and this mover would be God. But, as we have already explained, it is possible for the series to end with a corporeal body possessed of a certain property which effects motion without itself being moved. Therefore, this proof, viz., that there must finally be a motionless mover, is not sufficient to establish the incorporeality of the mover since the advocate of this reasoning has not founded his proof upon the impossibility of its potential motion, either essential or accidental; he has merely taken into consideration the actual motion that it causes. If, however, he had based his proof upon the eternity of motion which requires a perpetual moving force that is a necessary existent *per se* and therefore cannot possibly be a corporeal object possessing a peculiar property, then his reasoning would be correct. Moreover, if he had stated that every material body is possessed of magnitude and its force is finite, and it would consequently be impossible for a finite force to effect infinite motion, this proof would also be true.

The second alternative, viz., that the moving agent of the sphere is a force distributed throughout the whole body, is likewise impossible. For this force by virtue of its substratum is finite and could consequently not produce an infinite motion.

The third alternative is similarly impossible, viz., that the motion of the sphere is due to an indivisible soul residing within the sphere in the same manner as the soul resides in the body of man. For a force of this kind would not be sufficient to cause infinite motion; because the moving agent of the sphere would have an accidental motion while the motion of the sphere is essential. When the body (i.e., the sphere) in which the prime mover resides is in motion, the latter moves accidentally. But an accident cannot continue in existence infinitely. We consequently arrive at the proposition that a thing that moves accidentally must come to rest. Now, if the motion of the moving agent must come to an end, it follows that the motive element does not constantly maintain a state of motion in the sphere; because if the latter did not cease moving, then the accidental motion would not come to an end. We must therefore conclude that the eternal motion of the sphere is due to some force that does not form part of things composed of two elements, viz., a moving agent and an object moved. If this force ceases to act, the motive element of that compound discontinues its activity, which in turn brings the motion of the sphere to an end. This is in accordance with the necessity for accidental motion to come to rest. Our case, however, treats of eternal motion.

I am aware that certain philosophers desire to reject the proposition that asserts that all things that move accidentally must come to rest. They adduce the fact that those spheres that are found within the outermost sphere move accidentally and nevertheless their accidental motion does not come to an end. A great difficulty presents itself in connection with this proof. For its proponent[244] is unwilling to accept the hypothesis that the prime mover is the soul of the sphere on the grounds that the latter would thus be subject to accidental motion. In spite of this he is not troubled in accepting the theory that the sphere is possessed of a soul as long as the sphere is motivated by an external force. We must, however, respect the truth. For he intended to deny the existence of accidental motion in the soul of the sphere only if it is the prime mover; in order that the latter shall not be subject to any contingency [of motion or rest]. But, if the soul of the sphere is a thing that is moved, he does not mind [if this soul participates in motion accidentally]. For eternity of motion can be effected only where the mover is not subject to any motion whether it be essential or accidental. The parts of the sphere, however, can participate in accidental motion that is eternal because of the prime mover. And this is not more astonishing than the phenomenon of the sphere itself, which is not a necessary existent, since it is composed of matter and form, but exists by reason of its efficient cause. Motion itself is thus an accident that is maintained in existence by the prime mover.

You will learn our own opinion in connection with the verification of this proposition, [viz., all things that move accidentally must come to rest] when we decide in favor of the theory of creation in preference to that of the eternity of the world.[245]

There remains finally the alternative in accordance with which the mover of the sphere is a force separate from it. It is eternal because of the eternity of motion, and it is neither corporeal nor a power residing within a body, as has been established. There is only one mover of the sphere because incorporeal beings cannot be counted except as cause and effect, and an infinite series of causes is impossible. Thus, the philosophers have constructed their proof for the knowledge of God on the basis of the belief in the eternity of the world.

We must now investigate the nature of the world to determine whether it is eternal or created. If it is found impossible to believe that it is eternal, it must have been created. Now, if it was indeed created, it is proper to point out first the errors in the proofs which demonstrate the eternity of the world and then to elucidate the nature of the opinions of the philosophers, who hold that the world is eternal, with reference to their proof for the existence of God in order to determine whether truth is with them or not. Subsequently we shall establish proof of the creation of the world. Now, if it is proved that the world was created, it must perforce have had a creator. This Maker is God. For it is axiomatic that anything that has come into being from nonexistence could not possibly have brought itself into being but must have come to be through an agency other than itself.

CHAPTER 6[246]

Before we proceed to establish the proof for the creation of the world, we shall first demonstrate the fallacies inherent in the theory of its eternity by disproving the arguments that have been adduced to indicate that the universe is eternal. The arguments that the philosophers have brought forward to demonstrate the eternity of the world are apparently based upon the nature of things at present in existence. In accordance with their belief, the nonexistence of our system of nature is inconceivable.

FIRST METHOD The philosophers assert that all change is preceded by motion. Now, if this motion were brought into being, it would need another motion [to effect the change] and the latter motion would require still another motion. But it is impossible to continue *ad infinitum*. One must perforce stop at a certain motion that is not subject to either genesis or destruction. This is the motion of the heavens.

The above proof can be refuted since its reasoning follows that which is apparent to the eye, viz., that all genesis is preceded by motion. Indeed this is so with objects that are brought into being by the Prime Mover through intermediary causes; for things that are corporeal intermediaries move other objects and are themselves set in motion until we arrive at the motion of the sphere. Furthermore, all change is subject to motion. If, however, the philosophers comprehended that change emanated from the Prime Mover, then it would require a motive force, not motion. If they do not believe this to be so, they must maintain that sphere is capable of effecting change, whereas God is not! This is utterly inadmissible especially when it is believed that God actually is the Prime Agent. Moreover, a thing that comes into being requires motion or a motivating force only when that thing possesses an already existing substratum, which will receive the genesis or destruction. It is this substratum that requires a motivating force or motion. But if things came into being, as we believe they did, from absolute nonexistence, they would require neither motion nor a motivating force. Proof of our words is that Form, which originates in matter and comes into being from nonexistence, does not require either a motive force or motion. For when the philosophers attribute motion to essential change, motion is not predicated of change itself but of the existing matter which requires preparation [to receive its form]; not of the non-existing form. Indeed, they do not apply the term motion to essential change. Thus, we have a thing that comes into being which does not require motion.

SECOND METHOD Circular motion is without beginning or end. The Aristotelians therefore assume as axiomatic that since we cannot conceive the rotating sphere as having a beginning it must consequently be eternal. For circular motion cannot come into existence, nor can it be destroyed. This can be refuted as follows: While it is true that we cannot imagine the beginning of the motion of the rotating sphere, nevertheless it is not within the category of the impossible that it should come to be after a state of nonexistence

57

in the form of a continuous circular motion. Further-more, a finite rotating body moves a finite distance and it is impossible that it should move an infinite number of times consecutively as will be demon-strated below.[247] Finally, since it has already been proved that all motion is composed of potentiality and actuality, and that there is no motion which was not preceded by its nonexistence, it follows that all motion has originated in time whether it be continuous or intermittent.

THIRD METHOD The actual coming into ex-istence of a thing is preceded in time by the possibility of its coming into being. This possibility requires a substratum that is antecedent to the thing which is actually, produced. Now, there is no "before" or "after" except in time, and time can only be perceived by the motion of the sphere.[248] Hence, the sphere must have been in existence. This demonstrates the eternity of the universe on two grounds: first, from the necessary existence of possibility in a substratum; secondly, from the existence of time.

Now, hear our refutation: It is true that the actual production of a thing is preceded by its possi-bility and that this possibility requires a substratum. But these propositions are only applicable to things as they exist at present, when everything produced is of the nature of attributes, not of substrata. For the essential characteristic of genesis concerns the form which is borne upon matter. Thus, the substratum of existing things is always prior to their attributes, and consequently the actual genesis of the latter is pre-ceded by the possibility of its substratum. If, however, nature came to be as we believe it did, viz., that the substratum itself was created, then upon what possible thing could it have been supported seeing that there was no substratum in existence upon which the possibility could be borne?

Now, regarding the alternatives adduced by the Aristotelians, viz., the existence of a thing is either necessary or impossible or possible: If it is necessary, it must always have been in existence; if impossible, it could never have been in existence; if possible, it might or might not be in existence. But the possibility of its existence rests solely with the agent when it comes into being from absolute nonexistence; ,for there is no substratum before its production upon which its possibility could be borne.

It has further been asserted that the possibility of creation preceded factual creation that precedence exists in time and that time is found only in motion.[249] This necessarily implies motion in the sphere before creation. It is not correct, however, to reason thus. For time is neither of the essence of motion, nor is time, as counted in seconds, hours and days, the measure of motion. On the contrary, it is a concept separate and distinct from motion. For it is possible to ask: Does the sphere move in time or not? It is inadmissible to assert that it does not move in time; but it can be maintained that it does move in time.[250] Hence, it follows that motion is not identical with time. For an authentic test of the aforementioned, one should consider the following three factors: a curtain, a cubit by means of which the curtain can be measured, and number by which cubits are counted. Now, the cubit is comparable to the measure of the sphere's motion and number is a quality of this measurement. It can be seen then that there is something distinct from motion of which motion is the measure. Indeed, if motion were to disappear, it would not effect the disappearance of this something. In reality we do not comprehend nor can we conceive the essence of this entity. We do know, nevertheless, that it is a concept distinct from motion and number. The Philosophers themselves are perplexed about it to such an extent that Galen has declared it to be a divine entity that we cannot conceive.[251]

FOURTH METHOD The substance of the heavens, since it contains no opposite elements within itself, is neither generated nor destroyed the proof of this is that genesis and destruction are possible only in an object that possesses opposite elements where one opposite is superseded by another. Now, the substance of the sphere contains no opposite elements because its motion does not include opposite directions; for whatsoever contains opposite elements within itself can move in opposite directions. And since the body of the heavens does not move in opposite directions, it contains no opposite elements within itself. Consequently, it is neither generated nor destroyed.

Now, the significance of this assertion, viz., that it is neither generated nor destroyed can be understood in two ways. It can denote that [the sphere] does not change forms or it may mean that it neither comes into existence from nonexistence nor disappears into nonexistence. If it is intended to mean that the sphere does not remove one form and assume another because it contains no opposite elements, then it is true. For genesis and destruction are found only where there are opposites. If, on the other hand, it means to establish that the sphere could not have come into being from nothingness since it possesses no opposite components, this proof can be confuted by the example of the sublunar matter common to the four elements. For here we have something that is a recipient of opposites, yet the Philosophers admit that it is not subject to genesis or destruction. They mean that it was not originated from something nor can it be reduced to that when it ceases to exist, and it certainly could not have been produced from nothingness, nor could it disappear into nonexistence. In accordance with our belief, however, that the sphere did come into being from absolute nonexistence the argument from opposite elements cannot disprove our conviction. Furthermore, careful consideration will destroy the basis of this proof. It maintains that whatsoever possesses opposites within itself revolves in opposite directions so that we can derive logically the proposition that whatsoever has no opposite directions in its motion contains no opposite elements within itself.

The substance of this syllogism is not suited to syllogistic form. The oppositeness [of the elements] should be absolute from every possible aspect within the category of quality.²⁵² Nevertheless, we find that the opposite properties of the elemental qualities are not absolute, as in the case of the opposite properties of fire and water. Nor is the direction of their motions opposite in the extreme. Similarly, we find that absolute oppositeness does not include all the qualities, e.g., fire and earth; for one quality is common to both; nevertheless the directions of their motions are diametrically opposite.

FIFTH METHOD The Substance common to the four elements is eternal. Proof of this is as follows: The Substance of the elements is of the first degree;

the qualities, of the second degree; and the elements, of the third degree. The existence of Substance and its qualities attains perfection in the elements as Substance and form do not enjoy independent existences. Indeed, all things are produced of it (Substance) and again reduced to it when they cease to exist. Now, if we remove all forms including the form of the elements, then Substance would remain void of all Form. If, then, Substance had come to be, it would have had to have an additional form distinct from that of the elements, as coming to be is nothing else than receiving Form. But we mean by "Substance" a formless substance. It can therefore not have had a beginning. The basis of this proof rests upon the proposition that asserts that a thing cannot be produced from nothing, only from something. Consequently, that which has come into being—which exists within the substance of a thing that has come into being from some other thing—is merely an addition to that which is already in existence and which changed one quality for another. This [changing quality] is Form.

According to our belief, however, Substance was created from absolute nonexistence. There is no changing of qualities and the existence of a form besides that of the elements is unnecessary to verify its coming into existence since [Substance] itself came into being from nonexistence together with the forms of the elements.

SIXTH METHOD Seeing that everything produced originates from something, not from anything at all but from a specific origin, the Philosophers deduce that a thing could certainly not come to be from nothing. But this point is an argument against themselves. For nothingness has the same relationship to all things. Moreover since the combination of form and matter is the cause for the existence of certain things, and form, which originates from nothingness, establishes the essence and existence of these things, then why should it be considered impossible that matter has been produced *ex nihilo*? If nothing at all had originated *ex nihilo*, they would be correct. But, since we find that certain things do come into being from nothingness the same can apply to everything.

CHAPTER 7[253]

The aforementioned arguments pointing to the eternity of the universe, which we have refuted, have all been derived from the nature of existing things. The philosophers employ in addition other proofs to demonstrate the eternity of the universe based upon the nature of God. For it appears that if we subscribe to the theory of creation then in accordance with this belief there will result certain defects in the essence of God, whereas we conceive of that Essence as perfect beyond comparison. They have presented the following proofs:

FIRST ARGUMENT An agent that performs an act after a period of inactivity must have been a potential agent before becoming an actual one. Now, if he has passed from a state of potentiality into that of actuality, the agent (i.e., God) must be subject to change.

Our refutation is that the transition from potentiality to actuality can be applied in three references:

a) to the substance acted upon that has passed from potentiality to actuality;

b) to the means (instrument) through which the latter substance has become a reality;

c) to the agent that was first a potential agent and later became an actual one.

Let us consider first the subject acted upon and the agent. The absence of action in them can be attributed to two causes; the agent fails to act either because of a want or an obstacle. Similarly, the thing is not acted upon because of a want or an obstacle. Now, it is true that the thing acted upon as well as the instrument through which it became an actuality are subject to change if they pass from a state of potentiality into that of actuality. Indeed, if the inaction of an agent resulted from a want or an obstacle then change would take place also in him. It is possible, however, for an agent to be perfect in every respect and nevertheless be inactive for reasons associated with the subject to be acted upon. In this instance, the transition from potentiality to actuality could not be considered a change [in the agent] since activity constantly emanated from him. An example of the above taken from nature would be the light of the sun which had shone potentially and afterwards shone in reality, while no change took place in the essence of the sun; the absence of light being caused by some obstacle associated with the recipient of the light. Hence, God, who is inherently perfect, does not undergo any change when He acts after a period of inactivity and [this action] does not constitute a transition from potentiality to actuality nor does any change occur in His essence. But some might insist,[254] it is true that when we attribute the prevention of action upon a substance to a want or obstacle connected with it no change can be ascribed to the essence of the perfect Agent. However, where the substance is absolutely nonexistent what kind of obstacle can be associated

65

with it to remove the possibility of change from the Agent? I reply thus: Our investigation and speculation do not concern themselves with the reason for the inaction of the Agent, but with the fact that this inaction does not constitute a change in the Agent whether the inaction is due to the substance acted upon itself or because of something external to the substance acted upon. But one might object, even if we admit the correctness of what has just been explained, viz., that the cause of the inaction of the perfect Agent upon a substance already in existence should be attributed to a want or obstacle in the latter, we should nevertheless seek the cause of the inaction of the perfect Agent upon non-existing substance. For existing matter has been created from absolute non-existence and prior to its coming into being God existed alone without want or obstacle, a perfect Agent from whom omnipotent action emanated continuously in the same manner. Furthermore, the value of that which was brought into being from nonexistence is identical at all times as regards the perfect Agent. Why then did He act at one time and not at another, seeing that before creation nothing was in existence in reference to which we could conceive the presence of a want or the removal of an obstacle? I answer that this depends solely upon the divine will; the duration of matter's nonexistence before coming to be as well as its creation after nonbeing are determined by God's will.

A serious difficulty presents itself here: Since God's will changed by desiring after a state of nondesire does this not imply change in the will itself and hence change in the divine Essence? Our reply is that will does not change by itself, but because of favorable or unfavorable circumstances. The former produce desire while the latter prevent desire. A new desire is created only by a circumstance outside of the will itself and because of that circumstance (goal) a desire is produced. Now, if that desire is not produced by a goal distinct from the will itself, then no change occurs within that will. And since the will of the incorporeal Being is not influenced by any circumstance outside itself hence His will is immutable. It follows from the above that we can reply to those who inquire concerning the present universe, which came into being after an infinite duration of nonexistence, that thus God willed. Indeed we have included the nonexistence as well as the coming into being of the world within one Will; it was His will that our system of nature should remain nonexistent for an infinite period of time and that subsequently it should become an actuality. As there is no change in His knowledge due to changes occurring in known things, so changes of desire do not produce any change in His will; for known things originate from His knowledge and desires from His desire. According to this reasoning we can also obviate the difficulty of why God acted at the time He did and not at any other time seeing that the Agent is perfect and the non-existing matter of identical value at all times as regards the Agent; for our final reply is: thus He willed and thus His knowledge determined.

CHAPTER 8[255]

After having explained all the proofs derived from the nature of existing things which demonstrate the eternity of the universe, having, rejected some and pointed out the possibility of others, the following remains to be added. It is not correct to deduce anything regarding the nature of a thing's origin from the properties which it possesses when fully developed. Moreover, it can be established from the system of nature which unfolds before us, when we consider the properties of a thing when it comes into being and its qualities in the final stage of its development, that a person unacquainted with the nature of a thing's origin will adduce proof from its present attributes to discount the story of its origin; he might even consider such an origin within the realm of the impossible.

Take, e.g., a man who has seen a bird, but does not know how it came into being nor from what it has developed.[256] Someone tells him the manner of its production. A tiny yolk about the size of a mustard seed is born within the body, it has veins and draws its sustenance therefrom. Thus, it grows until it matures into an egg possessed of a yolk, albumen and an enveloping membrane. Afterwards the veins become dried up. The membrane is moist, but when it leaves the body it becomes hard as you see it. Subsequently, when the fowl incubates the egg for a certain period of time at a certain degree of warmth, there emerge to towards the shell two veins from that part of the albumen which is present in the yolk. By means of these veins the embryo is nourished until it assumes the form of a bird within the egg and being thus enclosed it nevertheless breathes and becomes covered with plumage. If a person were to point out to the aforementioned man that this bird had originated from that egg, he would commence to refute the statements of this account from the properties of a fully developed bird; he would present proofs that this living being which is unable to exist without breathing air for a short time could not remain alive enclosed within a shell; and being thus shut in, whence came life to it? How could there develop from this yolk possessing a watery form the several forms of bone, flesh and plumage? What fashioner formed it within the closed shell? He would begin to contradict the entire account [of its development] from its properties as presently constituted.

All the proofs derived from the nature of existing things which attempt to determine the origin of a thing from its fully developed state may be likened to the above illustration. Regarding this the Bible states, "Where were you when I laid the foundations of the earth?" (Job 38.4).

In reference to the proof for the eternity of the universe based on our notion of God, viz., if we believe in Creation there would ensue defects in the essence of God, we reply in the following manner: There is no comparison between His essence and ourselves, nor are His deeds comparable to our own; as His essence is distinguished from ours so are His acts distinguished from our acts, and no likeness whatever exists between them. How then can we compare His acts to our own with the result that a defect would arise in

His essence, seeing that all our acts are performed through contact with or without an intermediary while the acts of the Most Sublime are without contact; how can these acts have the same value or be related to one another! Indeed, the term "activity" is applied to both (man and God) merely homonymously.

CHAPTER 9[257]

Following our decision in favor of the eternity of the universe it behooves us to investigate this theory for the sake of completeness in order to determine upon what grounds it demonstrates the existence of God and how it has established the entire system of nature as an intelligible order, faithful to fact and without contradictions. You are already aware that the exponents of the belief in the eternity of the world derived the existence of God from the motion of the celestial spheres, viz., everything that is moved requires a mover, and since it is impossible to proceed *ad infinitum* it is necessary to stop at a Prime Mover. This is God. It is also known that all motion of translation which takes place in the substance of the thing moved is divisible into three categories: natural, voluntary or compelled motion. The last category cannot be applied to the motion of the heavens since this implies that motion has originated in time while those who believe in Eternity do not think thus. Furthermore, compelled motion is effected by pushing or pulling which constitutes corporeal movement. Accordingly when one body sets another in motion, the former must move likewise. But we wish to arrive at an unmoved mover, and in accordance with their theory this would require that he be incorporeal. Hence, if the mover is incorporeal motion is not compelled. Neither is this motion natural, for every object in nature is possessed of an inherent principle which moves the object until it satisfies that principle and when it has satisfied that principle, its motion ceases. The motion of the sphere, however, does not come to rest and this demonstrates that its motion is not natural. Moreover, natural motion can only be properly applied to rectilinear motion, for the latter has opposite direction whereas circular motion has no opposite direction. Consequently, circular motion could not be due to a natural principle. If then, the object that is moved is not affected by an external force nor by a natural property, its motion must be voluntary, and volition can be attributed only to a being endowed with a soul. We know that such a being moves either by perception, by imagination or by conception and that where the motion is produced by imagination or perception, the mover is a body. After the thing being moved has obtained the object of its desire its motion comes to and end. It is known, however, that the mover of the sphere is incorporeal; for there is no end to the motion of the sphere and it does not change its place by its circular motion since it moves toward the same point from which it has moved away. Its motion must therefore have its origin in a conception which resides in the intellect of the sphere. The intellect conceives the concept and because of the conceiver's desire for the concept the heavenly sphere moves. Thus, we find three elements superadded to the substance of the sphere, viz., its sphericity, its soul and its intellect. It follows that the sphere is composed of matter and form.

You are aware of the proposition which asserts that every composite is of possible existence. You also know the conclusion of Averroës with regard to the words of Aristotle who states in one of his treatises that all bodies are composed of matter and form and are therefore possible existents since their existence depends upon that of their two component parts. [Aristotle] includes among the above the body of the heavens. Averroes states in this reference that if this is true, then [the sphere] is a possible existent because of its composition. Avicenna is in agreement with Aristotle's assertion although he is inclined to accept a differing view regarding necessary existents. Avicenna holds that necessity of existence is of two kinds, viz., necessity by virtue of the object itself or necessity by virtue of its cause. His words, however, are clearly contradictory if subjected to examination. In short, Averroes insists that if a thing is composite, it is possible and this being the case it must at one time or another have come into actuality.

Thus, the theory of the eternity of the universe maintained by Aristotle, according to the system from which he derived the existence of God is refuted; for according to that system which necessitates a conception of the spheres as animate beings Aristotle admits that they are composed of matter and form, and if they are composite their existence is possible, as Averroes holds. Besides, if the sphere is a possible existent it is subject to nonexistence and if subject to nonexistence, it requires an agent to bring it into being from a state of nonexistence; for everything that ceases to exist must have been brought into being. Now, if it required an agent, then as it received its actuality without contact through the agent so did it receive its power of motion without contact since that essence (the agent) is neither corporeal nor a force residing within a body and it sets in motion without being itself moved. Hence, by his admission that the sphere is composed of matter and form following the proposition that all bodies are composed of matter and form, the necessity of believing that the heavenly spheres are animate beings, in accordance with the theory of Eternity, is refuted.

Now, let it not appear difficult to you that we believe that the Mover is not himself moved despite the fact that the object which is moved is not a being endowed with a will. For Averroes likewise, by desiring to demonstrate the necessity of the sphere's existence and to avoid being caught in the net of possibility, has reached the conclusion that the sphere is not composed of matter and form. Consequently, he believes that the sphere is not animate, demonstrating that there exists a method of determining the existence of the Prime Mover different from the method of Aristotle.

It has been stated previously that the mover of the heavenly bodies is a Form superadded to the bodies and hence it is apparent that these bodies are necessarily possessed of a soul. If, on the other hand, they are inanimate beings, then their motion is not voluntary. Despite all this Averroes believed that their Mover does not himself move while setting them in motion.

I have presented [Averroes'] opinions to support my own views, as follows: How can he believe, in view of the fact that celestial motion is not voluntary, that its mover remains unmoved? This may be likened to one who flees from a lion and is confronted by a bear. For every motion of translation falls into one of three categories: voluntary, natural or compelled motion. The first two categories imply the existence of an inherent principle within the substance of the object moved, by means of which it is set in motion.

Hence, it is a compound. But Averroes desires absolute simplicity. There remains then only the category of compelled motion and this indicates that celestial motion was determined by a Creator who designated motion to it in accordance with his will. Averroes in his desire to maintain the theory of Eternity vindicates the belief that the sphere is eternal and removes from it all composition. Nevertheless, he will never attain his end for all his arguments merely serve to strengthen his assumption. In later chapters of this treatise discussions will be presented that will elucidate all these matters.[258] It follows also from the foregoing views that if one believes the heavenly sphere to be a body, then its power must be finite. And if one holds that it is a being endowed with a soul, then the latter participates in motion accidentally and must eventually come to rest.

An even stronger refutation is that of the stars within the outermost sphere which move by participation in the motion of another thing. This is similar to accidental motion. Now, since the motion of the sphere is perpetual it follows that the external mover has designated that this moving object shall move continuously although the sphere *per se* is subject to cessation. The statement of Aristotle to the effect that the sphere receives its motion from a non-hylic Form is in agreement with the preceding. It is apparent then that the sphere itself is a potential existent. In any event therefore it is impossible for an intelligent person to conceive that a potential existent and a necessary existent should be equivalent as regards existence and that one dial not precede the other.

CHAPTER 10²⁵⁹

Since we have dismissed the arguments of those who believe in Eternity and have indicated the weakness of their assertions and proofs, let us now commence to make clear the demonstrations that prove the theory of Creation. They are as follows:

FIRST PROOF You must know that every body is composed of matter and form. Proof of this is our knowledge that combination and separation are two opposites of which matter is presumably the recipient. Since it is impossible for that thing which receives combination to be itself the cause of separation we must rather say that combination is the resultant of one factor and separation the resultant of another. Consequently, bodies are possessed of two factors, namely matter, and form, separation arising from matter and combination from form.

The forms succeed each other upon matter as evidenced by the changes visible in the latter. This leads us to the conclusion that forms are transient; no form inherent in matter is eternal. By analogy [this reasoning applies] even to the bodies of the spheres: it is also known that matter is never found without form, and form has originated in time. Therefore, that which necessarily applies to form must likewise be applicable to matter, namely, that matter also originates in time. In the words of our sages: Whatever cannot do without something created must itself have been created.[260] This proof leads to [the belief in] the creation of the universe.

It is necessary to indicate the occasion for doubt that our opponent raises with regard to this demonstration, and to answer it in order to remove every objection. You realize that matter is constantly removing one form and assuming another, and that matter is not found without form. These forms supervene upon matter in rotation and succeed each other in an infinite series.[261] Thus, it follows that the existence of matter is infinite. But we do not believe this to be true. Every existent form was preceded by nonexistence; there exists no material form which was not preceded by nonexistence. Now, despite their successive appearances and disappearances all forms are contained within the measurement of number. Every measure is a concept of quantity, and number is of the genus of quantity. Hence, number is measurable, anything measurable is confined and limited, and its existence is finite. [262] Now, since every form inhering in matter is of limited duration it follows that all the forms successively found in matter are included in the measure of number and everything that is subject to measurement is finite in its existence. And in view of the fact that matter is not prior to that which is necessarily finite it too must have had a beginning.

If one objects that finiteness is a necessary quality of number only as regards objects in actual existence it can be answered that finiteness is a necessary quality of number and number includes those things which have once existed and have since disappeared. To prove this take, e.g., a thousand forms that have appeared and disappeared in succession upon a substance. They are all included in number. Now, since number includes them and all number is measurable, it follows that the existence of an infinite series of things is inadmissible. You are aware that the subdivisions of quantity are two: contiguous and disjointed, and number is in the class of the disjointed. Since it is in that class it undoubtedly includes both those things which have been in existence and have disappeared, as well as those presently in existence. It cannot be argued that this is a theoretical measurement that has no real existence for all that has passed was (at one time) in existence and is also subject to measurement. For if this were not so we would have one infinite exceeding another by the number of successive geneses that were lacking in the latter over a period of a thousand years and were added to the former.

In accordance with the reasoning of the foregoing which treats of forms that supersede each other upon matter we can derive a proof for the beginning of celestial motion. The heaven is measurable since it is a body.[263] Consequently, the accident that adheres to it is likewise measurable. Hence, heavenly motion is measurable because of the nature of heaven. Thus, motion is limited and, if it is limited and measurable because the body is subject to measurement, then the concepts of motion, i.e., hour, day, and year are limited. For every thing which can be measured is necessarily limited, and since it is limited its series is finite. Now, since motion itself has originated in time as it is necessarily finite, there is refuted the proof for the eternity of motion which Aristotle derived from the continuity of motion.

SECOND PROOF It is known that all bodies are composed of matter and form, and composition is the cause of a body's existence; were it not for composition no body could exist since the parts of a composite have no independent existence outside of the composite; for their existence depends upon their cause which is composition. Furthermore, every possible existent has had a beginning. Therefore, the entire universe has originated in time since it is composed of matter and form.[264] Whoever doubts that the heavenly bodies are a combination of matter and form does so because he is constrained by his belief that they are eternal. For if he admits that the sphere is composite he will perforce be seized in the net of possibility. And if it be established that [the sphere] is a possible existent, it is proper to assume that its possible existence became an actuality at some certain time. Hence, it must have a beginning.

Avicenna is in agreement with this proposition, viz., that the heavens are composed of matter and form. Averrœs, however, disagrees with this and decides in favor of Eternity, which Aristotle has established. In one proposition [Aristotle] states that every body is composed of matter and form and he includes the body of heaven. It appears then that the latter is a possible existent. But he asserts elsewhere that the body of heaven is not subject to genesis or corruption. Thus, it can be seen that his statements contradict each other. Averrœs decides in favor of one of these two propositions, maintaining that the body of heaven is not composed of matter and form lest the element of possibility be found in it. This view he will never be able to demonstrate by proof; for, although he escapes by not believing that possibility is inherent in the sphere, what will he do with [Aristotle's] admission that the sphere has received motion from a non-hylic form, which implies that [the sphere] itself is possible?

Although [Averroes] appears to flee from the latter proposition, and seems to disagree with it, does he not mention among his own statements that the Prime Mover is the Form of that which is in actual existence, i.e., the body of heaven; and the existence of this [Form] does not depend upon it (i.e., the celestial body), but the establishment of the moving sphere is dependent upon the [Form]. Can it enter the mind of any intelligent person that these words differ in any respect from that which is taught by the proposition which asserts that the body of heaven has received motion from a non-hylic form? For, just as possibility is made necessary in the body of heaven by the statement of Aristotle [that the sphere] has received motion from a non-hylic form, so possibility is necessarily contained in the body of heaven by the statement of Averroes that its origination does not depend upon the body, rather the origination of the body is dependent upon it; in other words, the Form is not originated by the body of heaven, but the body of heaven is originated by the body of heaven, but the body of heaven is originated by the Form. There is no difference between these two statements, only a change of words with the same meaning. Besides, what will [Averroes] do with the possibility [of existence that follows from] divisibility? For every tridimensional body is necessarily divisible, whether actually, potentially, or possibly. (The divisibility that applies to the substance of the heavens is of the possible class.) And if he has removed the quality of composition from the substance of heaven because there is no change in it, since change proves that the sublunar world is composed of matter and form, we reply: It is true that since we find one body the recipient of two opposite elements, viz., combination and separation, we conclude that bodies are composed of matter and form. And this very proof applies to the substance of heaven for it possesses the element of spatiality, it has three dimensions and it is subject to possible division. Moreover it has been established[265] that no body exists without a form. Thus, every body is a compound and its composition is the cause of its existence. It is a possible existent *per se*, and, because it is a possible existent, it is not a necessary existent *per se*, but requires an agent that combines form with matter. This is God, praised be He, who has brought them (i.e., matter and form) into existence from nonexistence, since neither has an independent existence, and has united them.

THIRD PROOF It is known that existence is an accident peculiar to every existing object. Existence is not identical with the substance of an existing object for the quiddity of a thing can be examined even though it is not in existence. Hence, existence is a quality distinct from the essence of an existing thing. Now, if existence is an accident superadded to body it becomes evident that every accident borne upon body is finite since [its substratum] the body is finite. This can be demonstrated by the example of water, which is by nature cold, but when it is heated until it reaches a maximum heat its natural coldness disappears. This proves that there is a limit to its existence. Similarly, if this water is left by itself it will return to its natural coldness and the heat will disappear. This demonstrates that every accident found in a body is limited. Now, if existence is an accident superadded to body the accident will be limited by virtue of the fact that the body is limited and if existence is subject to limitation, then no body can be found whose existence is unlimited and infinite. Hence, it must have a beginning.

FOURTH PROOF Since existence inherent in body is perforce finite, what comparison and what relationship can there be between an existence which is necessarily finite and one that is not necessarily finite, namely, the existence of God? And how can these two existences be regarded as equivalent? This is utterly impossible.

CHAPTER 11[266]

Since it has been established by means of the preceding proofs which we have adduced that the world is created, it follows that it must have a creator. It is inadmissible that it came into existence without a creator who brought the universe into being from nothingness; for it is impossible that a thing should come to be of itself. It must therefore have an agent and creator who has brought it into existence from nonexistence. This is God, who is eternal and an essentially necessary existent. It is impossible that He, too, has been created for then the matter would proceed *ad infinitum*, which is inadmissible.[267]

There are also proofs derived from our conception of the world which demonstrate the existence of God. They are as follows:

FIRST PROOF From change which occurs in matter we understand that bodies are composed of matter and form. For matter *per se* does not undergo any change, but preserves its limitations, i.e., its three dimensions, its spatiality and its tactility; despite any change that affects it, it retains its limitations. Hence, change, which takes place in matter, is caused by an element superadded to matter. This is form. Now, every change is preceded by the absence of change, and were it not for its previous absence change would not come to be. Furthermore, this coming to be, in passing from potentiality to actuality, must have had a producer who brought it out from nonexistence to actuality. For it is impossible that a non-existing thing should effect its own existence since there is no relationship between a nonexistent and existence. Besides it is inadmissible that matter should be the agent because matter is the recipient of change and it is inconceivable that it (i.e., matter) should be both recipient and agent. Moreover, a material object acts only by contact. How, then, could it affect a nonexistent, seeing that contact cannot be applied to a non-existing thing? Hence, [change] requires an agent that is neither matter nor form. This is God, who has brought it forth from nonexistence into existence.

According to the principle of this proof, motion is composed of the potential and the actual; for whatever point is attained by motion its following point is nonexistent. And if this were true then [motion] requires a mover that effects motion. Hence, since it is impossible to continue *ad infinitum*, we must stop at one being. This is God, praised and exalted be He.

SECOND PROOF We know that all matter is essentially identical since every material object is included in the same limitations. Now, if this were true then it would be proper that all matter be characterized by a common form. But, since we see material objects of variegated forms, we know that the inherence of [diversified] forms in material objects is not due to matter but to the intention of an intender and designer who has designated for each material object the form he desired. For if this were not so, it would be fitting that material things should all possess one quality in common. But, since they are diversified, this proves that there exists an intender and designer. This proof includes the matter of the four elements, which are of the same degree. With regard to the spheres, too, this demonstration can be established. For each sphere is designated by its proper form, motion and its stars although the matter of all the spheres is identical since they all move in a circular direction, as we determined a common matter for the four elements since the latter all move in a rectilinear motion. The foregoing shows that there is a being who designs and determines the nature of every sphere. Some spheres move speedily, others slowly; some possess many stars, while others possess one; some are higher and others lower. Some stars are large, others small; some bright, while others are not bright. The stars are fixed in the spheres, and move by derived motion. For motion does not take place in the substance of the star, but in the substance of the sphere. The sphere is of one form, the star of another. Yet the matter of both is the same. There are those, however, who contend that spheres and stars have separate kinds of matter since the former moves essentially while the latter moves accidentally. This would indeed demonstrate the wondrous ability of the determining Being Who fixed one matter into a dissimilar matter.

All that we have presented points to the existence of a designing and determining agent. This is God, Who designed and determined all existence in accordance with His will.

THIRD PROOF The things of the world which we behold can be classified into three divisions, viz., either they are all created, or they are all eternal, or some are eternal while others are created. The first division, namely, that they are all created is inadmissible for every created thing requires a creator and if the latter in turn is also created the matter would proceed *ad infinitum*, which is impossible. Furthermore, every created thing is destroyable, therefore, all existing things will be destroyed and none will remain in the universe. The second division, viz., that all things are eternal is similarly inadmissible for we do see things coming into being. There remains then the third division, namely, that some are created and others eternal. Among the created things, we should include the entire universe as we conceive it through speculative reason, and that which is eternal is God Who has brought the world into being from nothingness. Our sages, who delved into speculative thought, after having established the theory of creation by proof, contended regarding the matter of that wherein lay the reality of creation. Some assert that in creating the world [God] produced only existence. Since existence is an accident of existing things it necessarily requires a substratum to receive existence and this substratum must be prior to that which it bears. The soul of the thing (its quintessence), which forms the substratum of existence, is in a state of nonbeing. Hence, they divided objects into existents and nonexistents. Thus, the souls of things are nonexistents, and these souls are not the result of any maker; [God] contributed to them only existence. Their opponents on the other hand contend that through this chain of reasoning it is impossible to maintain the concept of the soul of a thing in a state of nonbeing. For when we deny that there exists a second to God, and negation constitutes an assertion, it necessarily follows that there is a second to Him in a state of nonbeing. But this is not true. Consequently, the scholar Yeshu'ah states in his *Berē'shīth Rabbah*, "Therefore, we must remain skeptical about accepting [the concept] of existence in a state of nonbeing". They believe that the soul of a thing itself is a created object, i.e., God creates a thing in its essence.

It is necessary to understand that those who believe in the reality of nonexistents are constrained to do so by the force of speculative reason. They find certain things that are necessarily just as they are; they are immutable, for to change them is impossible; e.g., that substance should change to accident or vice versa, or that two opposites be present in the same subject simultaneously. Now, since they are necessarily just as they are, they are not caused by an agent and consequently they are compelled to believe in the reality of things in nonexistence.

Those, however, who assert that the souls of things are themselves created originally and are [subsequently] actualized must concede that substance can change to accident and vice versa, and that two opposites can be present simultaneously in one subject. For in accordance with their view, one would not contradict the other save by the act and intention of a determining agent. If he does not will it, they do not contradict each other. It is also evident that destruction is not caused by one opposite being superseded by another, but is due to the will of an agent. And their belief that nonexistence is not in want of an agent necessarily leads them to believe that the agent continues to act upon existents and when he ceases to act destruction ensues.

However, the words of the latter are far from the truth, as demonstrated by perception. For we see that certain things remain while others perforce do not remain. Now, this necessity is not the work of an agent. Hence, the agent does not act continually upon what remains in existence. Furthermore, we see that one accident destroys another and if the agent does act continually upon existents it would not be possible to destroy it nor would one thing be superseded only by its opposite, but it would be proper that a thing be superseded by other than its opposite. This reasoning forced them to believe in the existence of an accident without a substratum. In accordance with the foregoing the philosophers are justified in stating that substance has no opposite and is consequently not subject to destruction. For this reason we must not believe when we see a thing coming into existence which has no opposite that it is necessarily destructible. Rather its destruction is possible and when some force determines its destruction, there is created for it the accident of destruction without substratum. Thus, they make privation a reality. Their speculation has reached thus far. On the other hand, if there is no force determining its destruction, its existence will continue forever.

In conclusion, with regard to the existence of accidents and their differences, the view of the Mu'tazila is more in conformance with logical reasoning and consequently our sages follow this opinion: you must know that all the scholars, as I have seen in the "Book of Unity", believe in the reality of nonexistents. Indeed I am astonished at the words of H. Yeshu'ah[268] who stated, "Therefore, we must remain skeptical about accepting [the concept] of existence in a state of nonbeing". For any view that is believed by every school of [Karaite] thought is asserted not by chance, but because reason demands it.

CHAPTER 12[269]

It is fitting for us to express our gratitude unto Him, praised be He, Who has benefited us with the following views. When He desired to perfect us through His practical decrees that can be verified only after the verification of intellectual notions; in other words, when He desired to establish the truth of prophecy by the belief in Providence, which is a metaphysical problem, seeing that Providence can be established only by establishing the creation of the world, the enlightening Torah revealed to our master Mosheh commences [with the following words] "In the beginning God created" (Gen. 1.1). From this one can understand that the belief in the existence of God is established by means of the belief in the creation of the world. Our father Avraham, the first believer, serves to support [this contention]. He was reared among atheists, the Sabean peoples, who believed in the eternity of the universe and that heaven is God. Nevertheless, Avraham departed from their midst and declared the unity of God. He believed in the creation of the world and from creation he derived the existence of God,[270] as is stated, "Blessed be God, the Most High, possessor of heaven and earth" (Gen. 14.22). Although the term "possessor" does not denote creation *ex nihilo* it does indicate that they are as slaves before a master and that He directs them. Since the evident heresy in their (i.e., the Sabean's) arguments was to make the sphere identical with God he

89

offered an evident argument to refute their assertions, by his contention that they (heaven and earth) are as slaves before a master and have a Prime Cause. For this reason he employs the term "possessor".

In truth, Avraham preceded the statement of Mosheh, viz., "In the beginning God created" (Gen. 1.1), which is a prophetic statement. It is impossible that Avraham received it from him. Moreover, no prophet preceded Avraham who taught this view so that the latter could receive it from him,[271] for if this were so it would be known by its narration in Scripture. It is also impossible that Avraham professed this through prophecy without intellectual comprehension; for he would not have been shown special favor in such a case. Besides, he taught the creation of the world before he prophesied and furthermore, what arguments could he have presented to his opponent if not intellectual proofs? Only after he had recognized the existence of God was he endowed with prophecy, but the existence of God he derived from the creation of the world. And if he derived his knowledge from tradition this would not prove a sufficient argument against his opponents for his words would not be more truthful than their assertions on the merits of argument alone. It is also inadmissible that Avraham received [his knowledge] from a teacher who taught him the creation of the world by intellectual proof. For then the favor with which Avraham was graced should more properly have been bestowed upon him from whom Avraham received [this knowledge]. It should be noted, on the other hand, that it is impossible that the truth was unknown to all the people of the world prior to the time of Avraham, as is attested [by Scripture]. However, not one of these openly disagreed with the people of his generation, but in the open he included himself in their faith, until Avraham arrived. He disagreed with them and placed his life in grave danger out of love for God. This, incidentally, is the meaning of, "The seed of Avraham, My friend" (Isa. 41.8). And he is the faithful friend who will suffer injury for the sake of the one he loves, as it is stated, "That brought you out of Ur of the Chaldees" (Gen. 15.7). And wheresoever he would go he used to arouse the minds of the people to the unity of God, as it states, "And the souls that they had gotten in Haran" (Gen. 12.5); "And he called there on the name of the LORD, the Everlasting God". (Gen. 21.33). Consequently, he was favored with the blessings that God destined for him and his seed after him, blessings that no other man merited after him.

From this entire exposition it becomes evident that Avraham taught the existence of God by proof which he derived from the creation of the world after intellectual investigation. And this teaches that there exists a proof for the creation of the universe by intellectual means. Therefore, it is proper for us, the community of those who profess the unity of God, that we agree with him and follow his views by teaching the creation of the world in order to arrive at a knowledge of the existence of God, in accordance with the prediction with which Avraham was favored, "For I have known him to the end that he may command his children and his household after him, that they may keep the way of the LORD..". (Gen. 18.19). Many people wonder about the desire of Avraham to have progeny. Do they not know that this is due to his love for God—for thus it is stated, "The seed of Avraham My friend" (Isa. 41.8)—in order to transmit to them His unity by means of intellect and tradition to the end that knowledge of God will be spread abroad all the days of the world through the existence of his seed. This is the significance of the verse, "For I have known him to the end that he may command his children and his household after him". (Gen. 18.19). It is known that when the Israelites were ignorant of the existence of God and the prophets awakened them to the existence of God you will find that they aroused them only by means of the example of the creation of the world as is evident from the words of Isaiah when he states, "Lift up your eyes on high, And see who has created (*bārā'*) these?" (Isa. 40.26). The term *berī'āh* denotes the production of something *ex nihilo*–although it is also found in connection with the production of something from something else, as, "And God created (*way-yibrā'*) man" (Gen. 1.27). There is a great scholar who teaches that here, also, it denotes the production of something *ex nihilo* and it alludes to the superadded form [of man] which comes to be out of nothingness.

The statement of the prophet, "Who has created these?" (Isa. 40.26) comes in the form of a question. Evidently, there is no doubt that they were created. Rather this is calculated to call attention to the Creator and, consequently, he answers, "He that brings out their host by number", (*ibid.*), lest it enter any one's mind that it be other than He. But his intention cannot be accomplished by this method of presentation. On the contrary, it is necessary to explain that his real intention was to indicate that they are created and from this there would perforce follow the existence of God. This prophet argued against those views that admitted the eternity of the universe and asserted the impossibility of its having a creator. For you see that the entire chapter revolves around this point. When he states, "Who has measured the waters in the hollow of his hand?", (Isa. 40.12), the prophet argues and asserts: You must comprehend that they are created and require a being that has created them. He also awakened them to the speculative outlook by means of intellectual proof and said, "Since they require an arranger and director in view of their design and determination, this demonstrates that they are created and require a creator, as he states, 'He that brings out their host by number' (Isa. 40.26)". The real meaning refers to the motion of the spheres. Some of them move speedily while others move slowly; some move from east to west and others from west to east. There are also additional differences related to the question of motion. Since motion is revealed only by means of the host of heaven, he links his discussion to the host of heaven.

Let us now return to our [original] subject, namely, if the creation of the world were not known through the intellect, it would not be proper to offer in rebuttal an intellectual proof such as his statement., "He that brings out their host by number" (*ibid.*). Furthermore, if the creation of the world were not known through the intellect, but by means of an oral tradition that teaches the creation of the world, this same [tradition] would teach the existence of God and it would not be correct to offer some of his statements as proof for the others. Hence, it is demonstrated from the foregoing statements that there is a proof for the creation of the world through intellectual investigation: praised be God Who has enlightened the eyes of our hearts through our prophets with counsels from afar, and with true faith.

Furthermore, in accordance with the syllogistic modes of the science of logic, it is inadmissible that the creation of the world should be known from prophecy. Syllogisms can be divided into what are termed conjunctive and disjunctive syllogisms.[272] The conjunctive syllogism is one that includes two propositions that have between them one common term. For every syllogistic proposition is composed of two terms: a subject and a predicate. Hence, that term which is common to both propositions is called "the middle term". Thus, there are three parts or terms in the two propositions, and the conclusion that follows from these two propositions is due to the middle term. The conclusion is also composed of two terms: a subject and a predicate. The subject of the conclusion is the minor term and the predicate of the conclusion is the major term. That which leads to the conclusion is called "the middle term"., For example: Every man is a living being, and Every living being is sensitive.[273] Every man is a living being constitutes the minor premise, and Every living being is sensitive, the major premise. Therefore, Every man is sensitive, is the conclusion because the term "a living being" is common to man and to sensitive. "Man" in this instance is called the minor term; "sensitive", the major term and "living being", the middle term. These three terms from which propositions are composed and conclusions drawn can be reduced to four forms, as follows:

    a)   the middle term is the subject of both extremes (terms),

    b)   the middle term is the predicate of both extremes (terms),

    c)   the middle term is the predicate of the minor term and subject of the major term,

d) the middle term is the subject of the minor term and the predicate of the major term.

I shall draw these four forms by means of four diagrams.

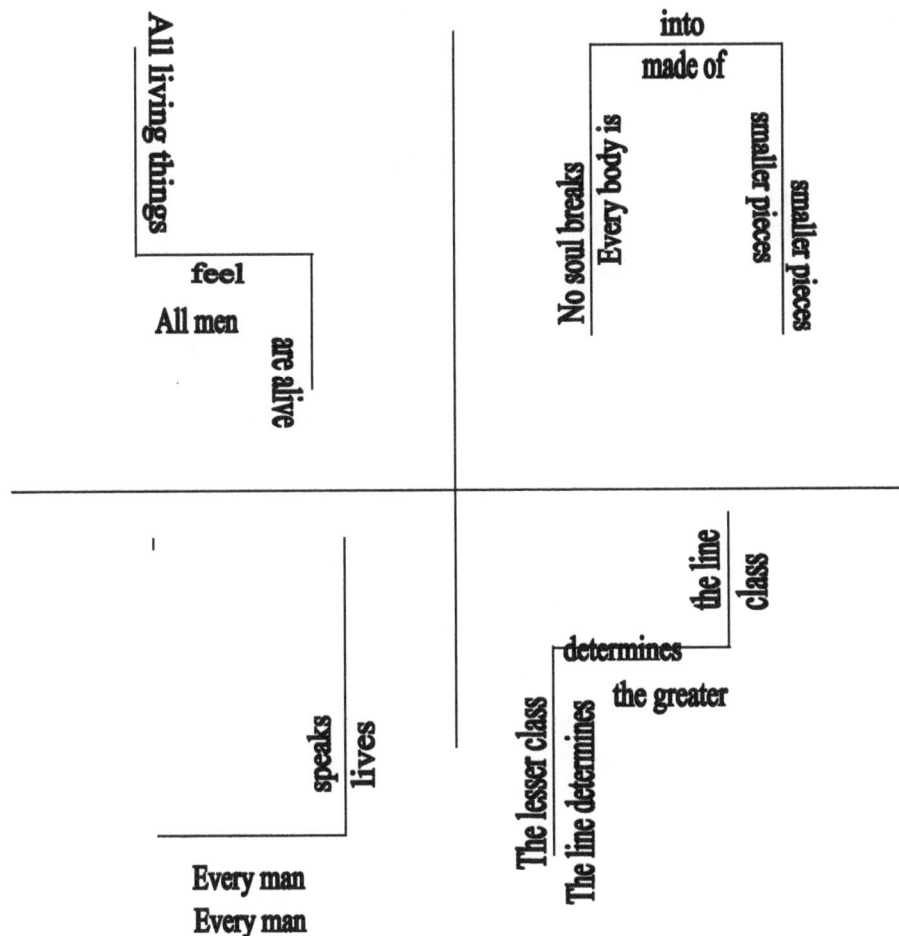

Now, three of these forms will yield a conclusion and there can be derived from them a true syllogism as has been explained in the science of logic. The fourth form, however, in which the middle term is the subject of the minor term and predicate of the major term is absurd and cannot be conceived. For the major term is naturally the predicate of the minor term; but if the predicate of the major term is the subject of the minor term, it follows that the minor term is the predicate of its predicate and the subject of its subject, also the middle term will be the predicate of its predicate and the subject of its subject, and thus it will be its own subject.

In conclusion, that which we are investigating, namely, the creation of the world, the existence of God and the prophetic statement, if you will examine them in all the three types of forms, you will find them true and there will come forth from them a true syllogism. According to the fourth form, however, if we consider as the minor term the creation of the world, and as the middle term the prophetic statement, and as the major term the existence of God, in other words, the creation of the world is verified by the prophetic statement and the prophetic statement is verified by the belief in the existence of God therefore the existence of God is known through the creation of the world, it follows that the thing is known through itself. Nor is there any foundation here from which a true conclusion can be derived. This is utterly impossible.

CHAPTER 13[274]

Considered from an intellectual point of view, the performance of miracles seems to demand [the acceptance of] the creation of the world; for one who believes in Eternity will not admit change in nature. If, however, there do occur changes in the nature of the world, it demonstrates that the world has been created and brought into being by the intention of a determining agent. You see then that when God desired to perfect us in the knowledge of the creation of the world, in order for us to stand up against the opinions of those who believe in the eternity of the universe and that the sphere itself is God, He did so only by the performance of the miracles that were wrought in Egypt which demonstrate the creation of the world. Indeed the [Egyptians] were smitten in accordance with their transgressions. Similarly, the Ten Commandments begin with, "I am the LORD your God, Who brought you out from the land of Egypt". (Exod. 20.2), and He does not say: Who created heaven and earth. For the exodus from Egypt is like the creation of the world.

In reality this is not a demonstrative syllogism (i.e., a conclusive proof) for the creation of the world. It must be understood that in the science of logic there are five types of syllogisms: the demonstrative, hypothetical, categorical, the analogical, which is also termed the inductive syllogism, and [finally] the compound syllogism. A demonstrative syllogism is one in which the major term is found within (i.e., is the predicate of) the minor term by means of the middle term. An inductive syllogism is one in which the major term is found in (i.e., is the predicate of) the middle term by means of the minor term. To believe that the world was created because of the performance of miracles is of the latter kind. For example, suppose you see a house that is produced and we say that it is produced because it has form. We have thus predicated production of that which is formed because of the production of the house. In this instance "production" is the major term, "form" the middle term and "house", is the minor term. The logicians, however, raise four objections to invalidate [this type of syllogism, asserting] that production cannot be predicated of form on the basis of the house that was produced, because it is possible that the production of the house rests upon another reason, not because of form. Thus, they have weakened this proof so that it cannot be [considered] an authentic syllogism. Nevertheless, for the advancement of the understanding of the common people it is proper to derive a proof from this [type of syllogism].

Besides, we have the statement of H. Yosef to the effect that the knowledge of an actual existent is secondary to that of its real essence although the latter is known clearly only through actual occurrences.[275] To this one may object that it is absurd that the secondary should be known clearly and the primary [merely] by proof. The sage, H. Menahem, nevertheless claims that the knowledge of an actual existent is, in truth, secondary to the knowledge of its real essence. [The former], however, is not known absolutely, but merely by vision. Indeed, when we know clearly that a certain order of existence has been disturbed then just as its actual existence is [known] clearly, so is its primary or real essence known clearly. He asserts further that those who entertain any doubt regarding the actuality of a certain phenomenon do so because they do not admit of its possibility on grounds of reason; for they assert that it is impossible for change to occur in the world's system of nature. Consequently, when they do see an unusual phenomenon they strongly insist that this has been accomplished by natural means or that a man performs this by means of a technique that he knows. Thus, the scholar has distinguished the method of speculation that is attained by intellectual proof from perceptual knowledge. This would be an educational method of gradually proceeding from the conception of the performance of miracles to the level of intellectual comprehension.

Similarly, the Psalmist declares, "I will give thanks unto the LORD with my whole heart, in the counsel of the upright and in the congregation (Psalm 111.1).[275a] He states, "With my whole heart", but the noun *lēb* (heart) mentioned here is used metaphorically for the intellect; for it is a homonymous term and since the heart is the principal seat of the intellect, the latter is termed "heart". The meaning of, "With my whole heart" is, "My mind entertains no doubts in regard to His existence that would render my mind divided concerning His existence, but I believe and acknowledge His existence with my whole heart (mind)". He states, "In the counsel of the upright and in the congregation" (*ibid.*), the meaning is: In the counsel of the congregation. And when he says, "In the counsel of the upright" this denotes the intellectual proofs that are known by the counsel of the upright to verify His existence. But when he states, "And in the congregation", it refers to the method by which the common people believe in the existence of God. Afterwards, he begins to explain through what means there may be derived the intellectual proofs for the existence of God which constitute the "counsel of the upright", and through what means there may be derived the methods of learning of His existence which constitute the "counsel of the congregation". He states further, "The works of the LORD, are great, sought out of all them that have delight therein", (*ibid.*, 2). By saying, "The works of the LORD" he includes the two kinds [of works] by means of which the two notions can be derived. Then he distinguishes each of the two types of works. That is, [first, he mentions] the works from which there can be derived the philosophical proofs which constitute the counsel of the upright. He states, "His work is glory and majesty, and His righteousness endures for ever". He includes in this passage the three divisions of existing things. By the term "glory", he implies the existence of angels. By the term "majesty", he refers to the nature of the spheres. And by the phrase, "And His righteousness endures for ever", he intends the world of genesis and destruction. When he elaborates the mosaic pattern (idea) of existence[275b] it has the same meaning in those words of Psalm 10, "O LORD my God, You are very great; You are clothed with glory and majesty. Who covers Yourself with light as with a garment, Who stretches out the heavens like a curtain", (Ps. 104.12). He alludes to the meaning of these words in the conclusion of the preceding Psalm by saying, "Bless the LORD, you angels of His, You mighty in strength that fulfill His words" (Ps. 103.20). This is the meaning of the term "glory". He says further, "bless the LORD, all you His hosts" (Ps. 103.21). This is the meaning of the term "majesty". Then he states, "Bless the LORD, all you His works" (*ibid.* 22). This is the meaning of the phrase, "Who covers Yourself with light as with a garment". Indeed these two Psalms are as one, but their author separated them to conceal a matter that he intended to clarify although our master Mosheh did not clarify it. For Mosheh did not indicate the existence of angels in the account of creation, while David did intend to make mention of the existence of angels. Consequently, he separated the Psalms to conceal this matter. Since the phrase, "And His righteousness endures for ever" (Ps. 111.3) alludes to the world of genesis and destruction, it is proper to define it precisely. The term "righteousness" indicates a double blessing. For God, having brought the sublunar world into existence, although it is subject to genesis and destruction, nevertheless, perpetuates its existence and maintains it through genesis and destruction.

From an analysis of the three divisions of existing things, proofs are derived for the knowledge of God. It is a known fact that in existence there are only God and His works, and through His works we know Him. By examining His works we can determine what attribute must be affirmed of Him and what attribute denied of Him. This is the counsel of the upright.

With regard to the counsel of the congregation, however, he states, "He has made a memorial for His wonderful works; The LORD is gracious and full of compassion (Ps. 111.4). This refers to the knowledge of God, which can be derived from the performance of miracles such as the wonders that were wrought in the land of Egypt.

CHAPTER 14[276]

We have called attention to the existence of the three divisions of existence and we know that the existence of two of theses divisions, namely, the middle world and the lower world, is verified by sense perception. Through scientific investigation we are aware further that they have been created since we comprehend that they are possible existents. The upper world on the other hand cannot be perceived. Its existence is confirmed by the intellect alone. Nor do we believe in its existence because prophetic utterances have indicated it in many passages as will be explained.[277] Consequently, we must indicate the methods of investigation adopted by the differing theories that have verified its existence intellectually.

The opinions of the philosophers, who have verified the existence of separate Intelligences through intellectual means by way of proof, are derived from the eternity of motion. For it is impossible that a finite body should move in a perpetual, infinite motion. The continuous motion of heaven has indicated to them the existence of separate Intelligences—and it is only through the latter, and because of them, that this perpetual motion can result. Thus, their speculation has deduced four causes for the continuous motion [of the sphere][278] as follows: its sphericity, its soul, its intellect and its desire. This has been demonstrated by proof. For it is impossible to have an infinite series of movers, but one must stop at a certain mover that produces motion without being itself moved. Now, since the mover of the heavenly body does not itself move, it is perforce evident that it effects motion in the manner that a conceived and desired object causes motion; for that which is cherished and desired generates motion without being itself moved.[279]

The essence of this desire of the celestial bodies is necessarily an idea conceived intellectually. For the conception of the desire must be one of three kinds: either a perceptual (or imaginative) idea, or a conceptual idea or an instinctive idea. That which is desired as a result of perception or instinct is corporeal. But demonstration shows that this desired object is incorporeal, since [in the former instance] that which moves towards the desired object will stop after attaining [its desire]. Thus, it remains that this desire is an intellectual concept and that which is conceived in the intellect is an Intelligence.

Maimonides points out that the causes of motion as explained by the Philosopher[280] are arguments that have not been proved. Nevertheless, they are the most acceptable since they are least open to doubt and more systematic [than other theories].[281] You are also aware that I have presented the decision of Averroes, in regard to Aristotle's theory, against the view that the celestial body is composed of matter and form. He (Averroes) offers [proof] that his (Aristotle's) words contradict each other. For at one time he states that it (the sphere) possesses no element of possibility at all and that there must not be found in it any composition. But this contradicts his assertion that every body is composed of matter and form. He also states elsewhere that the body of heaven [is composed] of matter and form because the principle upon which he establishes the perpetual motion [of the spheres] is that they are animated, intellectual beings capable of conceiving ideas. We have also explained that Averrœs decided against the opinion of Avicenna who agrees that it (the sphere) is composed of matter and form and contends that necessary existents are of two kinds: that which is necessary *per se* and that which is necessary by virtue of its cause. And although the body of heaven is composed of matter and form it is a possible existent *per se*, but a necessary existent by virtue of its cause. Averrœs is not in accord with all this. On the contrary, he objects to agreeing that a possible existent *per se* can become something eternal. He also points out that if there exists an eternal hylic (i.e., material) form we could not derive the existence of a non-hylic (i.e., nonmaterial) mover. Thus, he concludes that we must consider the body of heaven as being simple, without composition and that the term "body" is applied to it homonymously. He also decides that it is substratum alone, pure and clean, [consisting of] neither body nor matter. If this were not so, he continues, we could not arrive at an authentic proof for the existence of the Prime Mover being utterly devoid of matter. It is evident that this opinion is divergent from that of Avicenna, who believes that there is a method of explaining the existence of the Prime Mover different from the method of Aristotle. Nevertheless, from what has been explained, viz., that the mover of the celestial bodies is a form superadded to the body, it is seen that the latter are animate beings. I have presented the aforegoing in order to explain that the causes of motion, as explained in accordance with Aristotle's theory, and from which is derived the existence of separate Intelligences, do not meet with the acceptance of other philosophers.

By recognizing these causes the existence of separate Inteiligences is derived as follows: If there were one Intelligence towards which all the spheres moved and this were God [it would be proper that all spheres be characterized by one kind of motion].[281a] However, all the spheres do not have one and the same motion, but they differ in their motions; some [moving] from east to west and others from west to east. (In recent times, nevertheless, a system of astronomy has been discovered, according to which all the spheres move from east to west for each individual sphere is provided with two axes in addition to that of the outermost sphere.) Some move speedily while others move slowly. Their order is unsystematic; for a fast [sphere] is found higher than a slow one and a slow [sphere] higher than a fast one. He (Aristotle) asserts that the fact of all these differences–although all the spheres are characterized by circular motion–makes it necessary for us to believe, in accordance with our investigation of nature, that the idea which a certain sphere conceives and which causes it to complete its speedy motion in one day is not the same idea which another sphere conceives and which causes it to complete its motion once in thirty years. Consequently, he reached the decision that there exist separate Intelligences. It is impossible that their number be infinite for, since plurality depends upon causes and effects, it is inadmissible to proceed *ad infinitum*. He agrees that the separate Intelligences are equivalent in number to the spheres. Each sphere longs for that Intelligence which is its desideratum and its principle and which imparts to it its individual motion. This Intelligence then is the mover of this sphere. Thus, he arrived at the decision that the number of separate Intelligences is equal to the number of spheres. Eventually the Astronomer,[282] after careful investigation, asserted that the number of spheres is nine: the seven planets–Sun, Venus, Mercury, Moon, Saturn, Jupiter, Mars, the sphere of the constellations (i.e., of the fixed stars) and the outermost sphere. Averrœs, however, does not believe in the existence of a sphere without a star. Other [astronomers] contend that there are ten spheres[283] since they consider the sphere of fixed stars as distinct from the sphere of the constellations. In fine, the matter is agreed upon that there are nine spheres. Hence, there are nine Intelligences and the tenth is the dispenser of forms for the sublunar world, i.e., the world of genesis and destruction. For form is acted upon without contact and action without contact is the activity of a separate [Intelligence] as the dispenser of forms is a Form. Thus far systematic investigation in their opinion has led them in deducing the existence of separate Intelligences.

Maimonides considers it inadmissible that the motive agent of the highest sphere should be God.[284] For He would thus be associated with the other [Intelligences] in setting the spheres in motion. But it is necessary that God be outside of the category of those beings that produce motion in the spheres. (Aristotle, however, has replied to those who contend that the Prime Cause is not the motive agent of the first sphere that moves in a diurnal motion.) Although there are many Ideals it is impossible to number separate Intelligences save by virtue at their being causes and effects. Now, it is inadmissible to proceed *ad infinitum*, but one must stop at a certain mover. This, is God.

On the other hand, according to the view that does not agree that the motion of the sphere is due to a form superadded to a body it is not believed that they (the spheres) move because of a desire. How then does it (this view) derive the existence of separate Intelligences? One can reply that just as it does not suffice for those who believe that the sphere is animate and moves because of a desire far the ideal which it has conceived, that all the spheres should have one common ideal—and this would be God—but because of their variegated motions they affirm that each sphere possesses an ideal distinct from that of any other sphere and thus derive the existence of separate Intelligences, similarly if one believes that the spheres move involuntarily, even though it would be proper to believe that one mover—that is, God—moves all of them, nevertheless the correct view which the intellect favors is that because of the various motions of these many moving objects it is fitting that each sphere possess a separate mover. The latter constitute the separate Intelligences. For it is impossible that there be a throne without attendants. Indeed the words of the prophets, as they are customarily explained, indicate this. For one verse states, "The heaven is My throne", (Isa. 66.1), and another verse states, "The LORD has established His throne in the heavens" (Ps. 103.19). It is evident then that the throne is distinct from the heavens. It (the throne) is motion. [Isaiah] indicates the existence of Intelligences from the motion of the throne by asserting, "I saw the LORD sitting upon a throne high and lifted up" (Isa. 6.1), and he states further, "Above Him stood the seraphim". (*ibid.*). He teaches the existence of seraphim by virtue of the throne and distinguishes between God and the Angels in that He is seated while they stand. The scholar Aharon [Ben-they stand. The scholar Aharon [Ben-Yosef] has deduced the existence of angels from the foregoing words.[285]

Scripture supports the conclusions of scientific investigations regarding the existence of angels[286] by means of which there can be known the existence of God. Thus, the Psalmist arranges his verses and states: "Bless the LORD, you angels of His, you mighty in strength Bless the LORD, all you His hosts Bless the LORD, all you His works" (Ps. 103.20-22). It is stated further, "Praise the LORD from the heavens, praise Him in the heights. Praise you Him, all His angels; Praise you Him all His hosts", (Ps. 148.12). Now, it is necessary to examine these words, for their meaning and intention is surely not that he requested of them to bless the LORD in an imperative manner. How should a material, lowly and transient creature command the hosts of heaven that are of clean and pure matter existing perpetually, that are more elevated than he in rank and degree? Much less [could he command] the separate Intelligences that are free from matter and of a higher degree even than the host of heaven. Even as an exhortation this would be impossible; for how should one who is short-lived and intellectually deficient exhort those to bless God who bless Him incessantly and without change? The real meaning is: Through an analysis of their existence (i.e., of the spheres and Intelligences) he who examines them will conceive God [and will realize] that every existent requires that He bring it into existence and maintain it; that He is the Highest of all high; that all existence is sustained by His power through His generous grace and the open gate of His goodness. This is the blessing and the praise that will be offered to God through the examination of existing things.

Furthermore, it is impossible that the meaning is that he requested of them that they bless the LORD, even though they are animate beings that conceive and bless the LORD. For he has included in this blessing and praise also inanimate objects and it is not his intention at all that these should offer praise since this is impossible. But the meaning refers to the person who examines them and conceives their essence since through their essence it can be realized that they require an Agent that has brought them into existence and preserves them wholly without defect, blessed and praised be His name for ever! The same applies when he relates the blessing to the angels. The intention refers to the one who studies and conceives them; for through them he will attain knowledge of God and conceive Him—that He has brought them into existence and maintains them and that He is distinct from them. This is the object of the praise and acclaim. For it is inadmissible that one term [in the same stanza] should have different connotations. That is, in reference to the angels it would denote that he requested of them that they bless the LORD, whereas in regard to the inanimate objects it refers to the person who investigates them.

H. Yeshu'ah, in accepting the existence of angels from intellectual investigation, does so because he believes in the order of the creation of the world as mentioned in the Book of Genesis. This *Panhaq* that the existence of inanimate objects preceded the creation of animals and human beings. But, since the works of the LORD are in conformity with wisdom, and every existent which He brings into existence must have a purpose, this purpose being to benefit His creatures, then if there were no living being there could be no delight or benefit. Now, to say that He created inanimate objects for the benefit of living beings that were to be created subsequently is unacceptable. For what purpose could be served by creating the former first and the latter afterwards. For this reason he has been led by necessity to believe in the existence of living beings at the time of the creation of heaven and earth. These are the angels that David mentioned as prior to the existence of heaven and earth when he stated, "Bless the LORD, you angels of His". (Ps. 103.20). H. Yeshu'ah cites an allusion to the existence of angels in the words of Mosheh from the term *berē'shīth* (in the beginning) which is in the construct state and requires a governing word. It thus signifies, "In the beginning of living beings", It appears from his view that one must necessarily believe that angels are corporeal beings since they find delight in corporeal objects.[287] This is the essence of his view.

The most acceptable reason, from a consideration of existing things, for believing in the existence of angels is the following. We see things coming into being in the sublunar world by means of celestial motions. Investigation has taught us that these motions effect only the preparation [of matter]. We see also that those things that come into being are composed of matter and form and that it is matter that receives preparation through the mediacy of the motions of the spheres. The genesis of form, on the other hand, has another agent and one might be correct in claiming that it comes into being from the Prime Cause though direct genesis without any intermediate agency. But, since we see and comprehend that preparation does not take place as a direct act of the Prime Cause without mediacy, but preparation is from the Prime Cause through the mediacy of motion, the same should apply to the genesis of form, viz., that it comes into being from the Prime Cause through intermediate agents. These are the angels Who execute their acts without contact since it (i.e., form) comes into being without contact. For any act that is without contact is the action of a separate [Intelligence]. Hence, we believe that they are separate from matter. And since the celestial motions are intermediate agents for the things that come into being it is likewise true that the motions themselves [came into being] through intermediates. These are the separate Intelligences. They are incorporeal for we conceive no bodies save those of the elements and the spheres. And since the spheres are in motion because of these angels the latter could not produce this motion if they were corporeal beings. For every corporeal movement that is circular is composed of pulling and pushing and this would require another heaven for the angels in order that there be a place for the angel as it moves the sphere by pushing and pulling. But this is false.

It is necessary that the first intermediate be an intelligence which will command that the will of God be done. Any thing other than this is inadmissible since commanding is impossible for other than an intellectual being.

Prophecy also teaches that the acts of God are executed through the mediacy of His angels as is alluded to in the vision of the Chariot.[288] Also the verse, "For He will give His angels charge over you" (Ps. 91.11), [indicates the same]. Indeed it is not necessary to expatiate regarding this for [such verses] are exceedingly many. Let there suffice the remarks of David who states, "Bless the LORD, you angels of His, you mighty in strength... Bless the LORD, all you His hosts... Bless the LORD, all you His works", (Ps.

103.20-22) in which he indicates the three divisions of existence. The two [higher divisions] he describes as "agents" (doers), and the third [division] he describes by the term "works" (things done). Each one of the three divisions of existence demonstrates the might of God, blessed be He; that it is He alone Who has brought existence into being from absolute nothingness. Thus, the poet in the Psalm, "Praise you the LORD from the heavens" (Ps. 148), after having arranged all the three divisions of existence concludes with, "Let them praise the name of the LORD, for His name alone is exalted; His glory is above the earth and heaven" (Ps. 148.13). Now, since a thing done (a work) indicates a doer, and we find two classes of doers, namely, the angels and the hosts, we must consequently demonstrate by proof that God is incorporeal lest our reason err with regard to the hosts, His ministers that do His pleasure, [by believing] that they are God. And afterwards we must demonstrate His unity by proof lest we believe that God is more than one, and lest our reason err with regard to the angels, who are mighty in strength, that fulfill His word [by believing] that they are God. For the activity of the two aforementioned doers is [confined to] what is already in existence through the power of God, while the activity of, God [takes effect] upon absolute nothingness as the investigation of nature has demonstrated.

CHAPTER 15[289]

Since proofs have demonstrated to us the existence of God we must ascertain by intellectual investigation whether He is corporeal or incorporeal. Following are the methods of proof:

FIRST METHOD The proofs that demonstrate His existence also demonstrate to us that He is eternal, as follows. All existing things necessarily fall into three categories, viz., either all these things are transient or they are permanent or some are transient and others permanent. The first case, viz., that all things are transient is inadmissible for then it would not be proper that there be even one existent in the universe. Nor is it correct that all things are permanent since we see things coming to be and being destroyed. Hence, there remains the third case, namely, that some things are transient and others permanent, since it is impossible to proceed *ad infinitum*. This is God, blessed be He! He has brought all existence into being. Were it not for this Existent the universe could not remain in existence. Therefore, we must remove from Him anything that might tend to nullify His eternality. His being corporeal or a force residing within a body would nullify His being an independent, necessary Existent as will be clarified in these proofs.

SECOND METHOD If God were corporeal then all the proofs that have led us to profess that bodies are created would indicate that if His essence constitutes a body, He too, is created. He would thus require a creator and this creator, in turn, another creator. But it is impossible to proceed *ad infinitum* and we must stop at one creator. This creator is perforce incorporeal lest He be seized in the snare of creation.[290]

THIRD METHOD It is known that the activity of a body is always through contact and it is impossible that a body act merely by virtue of its being a body. ,for if this were true it would be proper that this activity should emanate from it (the body) continually since the cause [of the action], namely, its corporeality is ever present. It follows then that [a body] acts by virtue of some element superadded to itself, either because of its nature or because it is possessed of a soul. Now, in either of these two instances its activity is [effected] through contact. Nor can this assertion of ours be refuted by [the action of] a magnet which moves iron without contact. For this too is produced by the meeting of the magnet with air, by virtue of its peculiar properties, and of the air with the iron. Proof of this is the fact that [a magnet] does not attract from any distance at all, but only from a limited distance. Hence, bodies always [act] through contact, whether by means of an intermediate agency or not.[291]

Now, it is known that the universe has come into being from absolute nonexistence. And it is impossible that its Creator should have produced it through contact since there is no contractual relationship between existents and nonexistence. This demonstrates that the Creator of the universe is incorporeal.

FOURTH METHOD It is known that a body is not a unity *per se* both in view of its composition, since it is composed of matter and form, and in view of its divisibility, since it possesses dimensions, viz., length, breadth and height. Hence, it follows that its existence is dependent upon its composition and its union. Therefore, its existence is due to some cause and, consequently, it is essentially possible. But it is known that there is no possibility at all associated with the necessary Existent.

FIFTH METHOD It is known that every body requires space and since it requires space it is measurable. Every measurable object is finite and the power of a finite object is likewise finite; for it is inadmissible that an infinite power should be found to inhere in a finite body. This is absurd (*reductio ad absurdum*). Since speculation has made it necessary for us to believe that God is an infinite Being this demonstrates that He is neither corporeal, nor a force residing within a body, lest finiteness perforce be ascribed to Him.

SIXTH METHOD You are quite aware that a body must be at a certain place and is of necessity measurable. You must consequently seek a cause that has determined its being in one place rather than another and that has designated it with certain measurements rather than with others.[292] But it has already been made clear that the Prime Being was not caused.[293]

SEVENTH METHOD It is a known fact that it is impossible for a producer to be identical with his product.[294] For if this were not so it would be necessary that he produce himself. Consequently, since God has created bodies how is it possible that God be a body?

One might object and assert that the substance of His body [which is free] from all defect is different from the substance of other bodies as the substance of heaven differs from that of the elements. Consequently, He acts upon them [the bodies] with the result that the Producer is not similar to His product. It may be replied that our intention is not [here concerned] with the essential nature of substance. Nor does the term "body" indicate the essential character of substance and whether it be identical or not we need not regard the latter. Our intention is confined to the connotation of the term body. You know, from what has been explained in the "Book of Investigation", that a line consists of length without breadth or depth; that area consists of length and breadth without depth; and that body consists of length, breadth and depth. It is agreed then that the term body includes these dimensions. All substances whether similar or dissimilar that possess these three dimensions, namely length, breadth and depth are described by the term "body" by consensus of opinion. Now, if we assert that God is a body and has created bodies then the Producer would be identical with His product and would be producing Himself since He possesses dimensions and produces dimensions. This is utterly impossible.

The main proofs in our negation of [God's] corporeality are the three set forth in detail, namely, the first, third and seventh. The others necessarily follow from the first. Nevertheless, in order that this matter be made more explicit we have examined them minutely by number so that the proofs will be clear.

Regarding the order in which I have stated them he who speculates will investigate and comprehend.

CHAPTER 16295

Know that the negation of similitude in respect of God has been demonstrated by intellectual proofs. And if we find in Holy Writ prophetic utterances that indicate the opposite of what the intellect has demonstrated the matter should be considered. We assert that when we find a matter that has been demonstrated by the intellect and we find a Scriptural passage that contradicts it, i.e., contradicts our intellectual concept, then we must not compel the latter to fit the plain meaning of the Scriptural verse for it will remain unexplained. On the contrary, we must compel Scripture to fit that which has been demonstrated by the intellect. It is an evident fact that Scripture now and then speaks not in accordance with true measurement even with regard to, matters that are perceptible to the senses, concerning which Scripture speaks by way of exaggeration. For example, "The cities are great and fortified up to heaven". (Deut. 1.28 and 9.1); "Whose height was like the height of the cedars" (Amos 2.9). These are instances of hyperbole where an existent, whether man or other than man, is described by a quality that is greater than that which it possesses. There are other instances where something is characterized by a kind of quality which it does not possess at all, neither in lesser nor greater degree. However, [this quality] is a metaphorical figure that suggests a likeness to itself that is evident even to the ordinary person. These, too, are instances of hyperbole. It is impossible that it was intended that an ordinary person should consider the existent as possessing this quality that was attributed to it. An example of this type is, "And how I bore you on eagles' wings", (Ex. 19.4). There are many instances similar to this.

Such being the case, since we know that Scripture now and then does not speak in accordance with true measurement in respect of things that we have perceived with our senses, similarly, with regard to a matter that we have perceived by intellectual means when we find that Scripture contradicts it, it behooves us to adapt Scripture to conform to what has been demonstrated by intellect.

There are four instances which exclude a [Scriptural] statement from being [literally] true.[296]

FIRST INSTANCE When we perceive a thing through our senses and [Scripture] contradicts it we know that the latter is not true.

SECOND INSTANCE If we weigh the connation of a [Biblical] statement on the scales of the intellect and these testify that it is not true, we know that it is a figurative expression;

THIRD INSTANCE When we do not perceive it (i.e., a Scriptural statement) either by the senses or by the intellect yet many proofs bear evidence that it is not true, then we know that it is a figurative expression;

FOURTH INSTANCE If we compare it (i.e., one Scriptural statement) with another and the latter is dissimilar since it contradicts the first, we know that it is a figurative expression.

Now, the negation of corporeality in respect of God has been demonstrated by the intellect. Hence, if we find statements in Scripture that indicate that there exists any similitude to God we must react to these statements as requiring an additional word or as metaphorical expressions or as homonymous terms. Thus, we shall remove all doubts as will be explained in detail in the chapters of this treatise.[297] Similarly our Sages have urged us to adapt the Holy Writ by these three methods, viz., the addition of a word, the use of metaphor and the use of homonyms. Consequently, since we find that the intellect negates similitude with regard to God and Scriptural statements stand in opposition to the intellect, as it states, "And the LORD descended"; "The eyes of the LORD", "The hand of the LORD", and other passages similar to these, the intellect must prevail by excluding the literal meaning of these statements. This is all the more true since we find other Scriptural statements that indicate that which is approved by the intellect concerning the negation of similitude. For it states, "To whom then will you liken God" (Isa. 40.18); "To whom will you liken Me, and make Me equal" (Isa: 46.5); "There is none like unto You, O LORD" (Jer. 10.6), which [indicates] the negation of any likeness to His essence and even to His attributes. Hence, the latter verses that negate similitude contradict the former statements that favor similitude and nullify them because they are aided by the demonstration of the intellect. This is all the more true ,since if the former statements which in their plain meaning stand opposed to the intellect are subjected to an additional word, a metaphor or a homonym, it will be possible to reconcile these statements with the teachings of the intellect so that the former will not oppose the latter. This will be clarified in the following chapters in connection with metaphorical expressions and homonymous terms to the end that there will remain not one painful thorn against what the intellect has demonstrated.

CHAPTER 17[298]

A great necessity has led the Hebrews to employ metaphorical figures that are corporeal concepts in relation to God. This is because the intellectual soul dwells in a material abode, and there emanate from the former certain faculties. It is impossible that these faculties become visible save through material organs. Hence, [the soul] has adapted its language to those faculties and the language is permeated with corporeal content.

When it was desired further to make known that there are powers deriving from Him without the intermediacy of material means and the soul possessed no terms that were simple and untainted by corporeality with which to make known the powers of the Almighty it was led by necessity to make these powers known by means of expressions which it had adapted to its own needs and which are permeated with corporeal meaning. Such are: descended, ascended, sat, stood, did, worked, spoke, etc. But this did not suffice for the soul for when it desired to establish beyond doubt that activities do emanate from God it also attributed to Him those material organs that it associates with itself. For by means of these organs activities are effected. Such are: hand, foot, palm, fingers, arm, lip, mouth, tongue, nose, eye and ear.[299] Thus, when we desire to know that God is approaching or departing He is described metaphorically as: going, sitting, coming, descending or ascending. Since all these activities are [effected] by the organs of locomotion, i.e., the feet, these organs are ascribed to Him in a figurative sense as when it states, "And the earth is: My footstool" (Isa. 66.1); "The place of the soles of My feet" (Ezek. 43.7).

When it was desired to assert that actions emanate from Him there were applied to Him metaphorically acting and doing. All the latter actions are effected by means of the tactile organs, namely, hands, palm, fingers, and arm. These organs are ascribed to Him figuratively when it states, "The work of Your own hands" (Ps. 138.8); "And You has laid Your hand upon me" (Ps. 139.5); "Your right hand, O LORD" (Ex. 15.6); "By the greatness of Your arm" (Ex. 15.16). When we desired to make known that God perceives things there were applied to Him sight, hearing, and smell. All the latter perceptions are [attained] by means of the organs of perception, viz., the eyes, nose and ears: these organs are attributed to Him metaphorically when it states, "The eyes of the LORD" (Deut. 11.12); "His eyelids try the children of men" (Ps. 11.4); "Incline Your ear" (Ps. 17.6); "They shall put incense before Your nostril" (Deut. 33.10). Again when we desired to make known that matters are communicated from Him to the prophets, speech was ascribed to Him figuratively. But, since speech cannot take place save by means of the organs of speech, viz., lips, mouth, tongue and voice, the latter organs were applied to Him. For it states, "The mouth of the LORD" (Ex. 17.1); "and His tongue is as a devouring fire" (Isa. 30.27); "The voice of the LORD shakes the wilderness" (Ps. 29.8); "And open His lips against you" (Job 11.5). With regard to the matter of speech this question requires further discussion as will be clarified in several chapters of this treatise.[300]

In the following chapters there will appear, relative to the above, obvious instances of metaphoric use which will serve as evidence in confirmation of the general principle of metaphoric use when those words are applied to God.

You must also know that these metaphorical expressions denoting certain organs and the activities relative to such organs were employed solely because [the prophets] desired to attribute to God absolute perfection and to remove from Him any defect from the viewpoint of the ordinary mind. Thus, when they beheld certain powers emanating from ourselves and for each power within us there is a distinct organ, they also ascribed organs to Him in a metaphorical sense. For it appears to the ordinary man that this is the height of perfection. Hence, the necessity [engendered] by emanating powers has led them to the attribution of organs. It follows that when any power is found within ourselves which the imagination cannot conceive as emanating from God, then the organ related to that particular power will not be attributed to God; e.g., the nutritive and generative organs. From the foregoing we have proof that [the prophets] conceived Him in a corporeal sense only as regards certain activities since He is elevated above any defect of a corporeal being.

Finally, you must realize that there are terms that in certain passages are employed as metaphors and elsewhere are to be understood as absolute homonyms even though they refer to organs. This must be considered with great diligence lest we stumble in regard to the intention of the prophets' words. The advantage of the absolute homonym over the metaphor is like the advantage of light over darkness.

CHAPTER 18

Do not imagine that Karaite scholars have not preceded me in the explanation of these terms. On the contrary, the scholar H. Yosef, may his soul rest in peace, has already elucidated in a general sense the method of resolving doubts [engendered] by these terms as has been explained previously. And the scholar H. Yehudah *HaAvel*, may his soul rest in peace, has presented an elaborate exposition in his treatise, *"Eshkol HaKofer"* regarding every word of these terms to the best of his knowledge.[301] He explains that his mention of the elucidation of these terms [derives] from the exposition of the enlightened scholars, May God be gracious unto them, and from the exposition of Yehudah Ben-Koreh, may God be gracious unto him. Subsequent to this exposition Maimonides, of blessed memory, elucidated metaphorical expressions and homonymous terms in his *Sēfer HaMaddā'* (the first Book of the *Mishneh Tōrāh*). The interval between these two works is approximately twenty-nine years; for H. Yehudah the Mourner completed his work in the year 4,909 while the work of Maimonides appeared in 4,938.

I, too, have followed in their footsteps by expounding these terms in order to vindicate the truth of our language as it appears in the narrations of prophetic utterances in accordance with their true intention as it seems to my mind. Our effort will be directed only to clarify what appears in the words of Mosheh whose conceptions are not dominated by the imaginative faculty; and that which is stated in the utterances of those who speak through the Holy Spirit (i.e., the Hagiographa); and [finally, to explain] those prophetic statements which are of a narrative character, not those of prophetic visions which are engendered by the imaginative faculty.

You reader, who examine this treatise of mine, if in the exposition of these terms there occur to your mind something other than what I have declared, it is granted to you, but only after a minute analysis pursuant to the truth. Observe great care lest in your exposition you ascribe corporeal acts to the essence of God.

CHAPTER 19[302]

In this Chapter, we shall discuss the adaptations of nouns and determine to what extent metaphors may be properly employed and finally what kind of adapted terms may be fittingly ascribed to God.

In the science of logic nouns fall into three classes: a) these that denote a body whether sensitive or insensitive, e.g., man, field, stone, tree, fish, ox, lamb; b) those that do not denote a body, but an existent, e.g., wisdom, strength, life; c) those that denote nonexistence[302a] or the absence of a particular quality, e.g., blindness, death, poverty, affliction. Of these three divisions the third is most inferior and hence you will not find any noun of this class ascribed to God Who is elevated above all imperfection. There remain then the first two divisions. This may be likened to the statement of the Philosopher, viz., The principles [of all existing transient things] are three, namely, Matter, Form and Privation.[303] In accordance with this method of reasoning the Mutakallimūn asserted that nouns include all three and regarding the last division they declared that it is considered an entity although it is not known. Thus, there remain two divisions, namely, Matter and Form.

You must know that there are specific nouns for matter that indicate the essence of matter, viz., material, matter, substance, and body. There are also accidents that apply to matter *per se*; these are its properties, viz., length, breadth, depth, place, motion, touch, small and large. There are other accidents that are associated with matter by virtue of its union with form. The latter are five types of corporeal accidents which are perceived by the five senses: cold and heat which are perceived by the senses of touch and taste; appearance, perceived by the sense of sight; voice, perceptible to the sense of hearing; and odor which is perceived by the sense of smell. Of all these three categories you will find that because of their inferiority no nouns are ascribed to God save the terms "Place" and "great" of the second category, and, of the third category, the terms "appearance" and "voice" as well as the perceptibles of vision, i.e., everything that is perceived by the sense of sight, e.g., image, likeness, form, representation and description; and the perceptibles of sound, i.e., everything that is perceived by the sense of hearing, e.g., the sounds which a body emits through friction, blowing or shaking. Included in the matter is the sound of articulate speech. Now, whatever connotation of these four terms, namely, place, greatness, voice and appearance is ascribed to God in Scripture will be explained by us in their respective chapters so as to remove all doubts.

Again, you must know that there are specific nouns for Form, which is also termed "soul", and it has its own categories. The first category is the form of the elements; the second is the form of inanimate matter; the third is the soul of vegetation; the fourth, the soul of animal life; and the fifth category is that of the rational soul. The last is the highest and most significant of all. Now, you will not find attributed to God the form of the elements and its appurtenances, nor the form of inanimate matter and its appurtenances save the term Rock, nor the vegetative soul and its appurtenances, nor the animal soul and its appurtenances, which are present in those animate creatures not endowed with speech. For there are properties possessed by the lower animals that are not present in rational beings. Hence, you will not find them ascribed to God. And if we do find such words as roaring and. leaping forth, they are employed as similes for those that possess their properties. Thus, the meaning of, "And the LORD roars from Zion" (Amos 1.2.) is: He roars like a lion. The significance of, "He does leap forth out of His holy habitation" (Zach. 2.17) is: He leaps forth like a lion. The term wing [is employed] as an absolute homonym, as will be explained. Hence, you will not find the form of the animal soul nor its appurtenances ascribed to God by virtue of its being a vegetative soul, but by virtue of the fact that it is the substance of the rational soul.

All the names of the intellectual soul, viz., soul, life, breath, spirit, are ascribed to God. For the intellectual soul is an entity separate from body and is possessed of faculties that do not require aid from the body, e.g., knowledge, understanding, and thought. Proof of this is that notions are distinct from the accidents of the soul; for when the latter are active in the soul they also produce some effect upon the body as pallor in the coward and the redness of shame.[304] Notions on the other hand are not so, for when they are active in the soul they do not produce any effect at all upon the body and hence they may properly be applied to God since they are free of corporeality. It (the intellectual soul) also possesses certain properties by virtue of its union with matter through the vegetative soul. They are the five senses, viz., touch, sight, hearing, smell, taste, the imaginative faculty, the incentive faculty and in addition to these the rational part.

We find three senses attributed to God, namely, sight, hearing and smell, and the faculties of the soul, namely, the incentive, and the rational. These properties are figuratively ascribed to God as are the organs in which these properties are found, viz., eyes, ears and nose for the senses; and heart, feet, hands, palms, fingers and arms which are the organs of the incentive faculty.[305] For each organ there is a specific function among the properties of the incentive faculty as the desire for a certain thing or its avoidance and approaching a thing or keeping away from it, since all these are dependent upon the qualities of the soul relative to the incentive faculty such as anger, grace, fear, fortitude, cruelty, compassion, love, hate, etc. Among these [emotional states] are those which may properly be applied to God. Others, however, are not proper in that they would constitute an imperfection in Him, e.g., lips, mouth, tongue, the organs of the rational faculty. Now, any designation other than those of the intellectual soul and its properties which are unaided by the body will come within the category of metaphors. But a designation that can serve as a homonymous term adapted to the intellectual soul and its faculties, which are unaided by the body, is praiseworthy and free from error. And whosoever strives towards this elevated end will approach the Divine One.

Now, we shall commence to explain in an orderly fashion the various terms [employed in the Holy Writ].

CHAPTER 20[306]

The term *māqōm* (place) is a homonym. It signifies in the first instance "what a body occupies"; the boundary of this occupied space is termed "place". It also designates a boundary which is unoccupied as, "But at the place" (Deut. 16.6). Scholars are divided in their opinions regarding "place".[307] Some assert that it is the space contiguous to the surface of a body that surrounds it on all sides while others contend that it is the vacuum which encompasses [the body] circumferentially.[308] Again, the relationship of space is figuratively applied to that which is incorporeal as, "The place of justice, wickedness is there; and the place of righteousness, wickedness is there" (Eccles. 3.16), i.e., in the place of justice they perpetrate evil. Now, the place of righteousness and justice is the present world, which is the locality for deeds. According to this figurative meaning, it is stated, "Blessed be the glory of God from His place" (Ezek. 3.12). God forbid that this should denote a glory that was created and which occupies space. For then one who worships would worship a created being and whosoever believes in this would believe in two deities. Rather the phrase "The glory of the LORD" refers to the dispensation of the mighty Providence of God. In this precious vision He aroused the prophet, through the departure of His Providence that had continually been in the Sanctuary, to return to the interrelated system of the entire universe so that he could see [the truth] from the point of view of the world itself. When he reached the peak. and comprehended therefrom, by means of investigation, the existence of divine Providence it is as though the origin, whence his intellect endowed him with knowledge of divine Providence with true and firm belief, were the place of God. And it is as though he (the prophet) said that praise and laudation are God's when he states: Blessed is He from that place which indicates His providence. This is the allusion contained in the words, "I will go and return to My place" (Hos. 5.15). The same signification is also to be understood in the statement, "Behold, there is a place by Me, and you shall stand upon the rock" (Ex. 33.22), i.e., the high rank of investigation from which you can conceive Me. For this reason it states, "And you shah stand upon the rock". This standing refers to a standing of cognition and the term "rock" signifies the origin of existing things,[309] not that He is a corporeal being occupying space, God forbid!

CHAPTER 21

The word *gādōl* (large) denotes addition and is a homonym for every kind of increase whether quantitative or qualitative. With regard to quantity it is of two types, namely, joined quantity and disjoined quantity. [It is employed] in connection with a joined quantity in the verse, "He plants a baytree and the rain makes it grow (*ye-gaddēl*)" (Isa. 44.14); in connection with a disjoined quantity, "An exceeding great host" (Ezek. 37.10). When it is found in reference to time [it signifies] an addition of years as, "And the boys grew" (Gen. 25.27). In a qualitative sense [we find] "The two great lights" (Gen. 1.16), where it (i.e., the greatness) refers to their light. "The great wonders", with respect to wondrousness. With regard to distinction and honor, "A great woman" (II Kings 4.8). It also refers to elevation and dignity as associated with certain acts as, "Moreover the man Mosheh was very great" (Exod. 11.3). In the latter signification it is employed in reference to God, "O LORD, My God, You are very great" (Ps. 104.1); "For you are great and doe wondrous things" (Ps. 86.10). Whenever the term greatness is applied to God it has this latter sense, i.e., [great] by virtue of His wondrous works not that it indicates a quantitative addition.

CHAPTER 22[310]

The Hebrew *ṣelem* is a term adapted to every form that sustains a thing as regards either its properties or its essence. This form that sustains the properties of a thing may be either a natural or an artificial form. It is in the sense of an artificial form that an idol is called *ṣelem*. Similarly, "the forms of your emerods" (I Sam. 6.5) refers to their artificial forms. A natural property (form) is alluded to in the statement, "and the form of his visage changed" (Dan. 3.19), i.e., the natural properties of his face. For it was stated previously that, "he was filled with fury" (*Ibid.*) ,and it is well known that the face of one who is filled with fury and has become angered will not have its usual form during a period of anger. This is in agreement with the statement of the Philosopher who has asserted that the accidents of the soul when they are active in the soul also produce a certain effect upon the body such as pallor in the coward and redness in one who is ashamed.[311]

When Scripture states, "O LORD, in its city You will despise their form", (Ps. 73.20) it alludes not to the properties of the organs of their bodies, but to their soul which sustains them in their existence and guides them. For contempt can only concern the most elevated part that is found in a being. [The soul of the wicked] is likened to a dream for at the time of the dream it appears to be an actuality, but after awakening it seems to disappear and from its end it becomes clear that it is really a nonexistent. Similarly the form of the wicked is despised while yet in its city–which is a simile for its body–as attested by its end which takes place after its separation from the body, i.e., because of the punishment destined to befall its soul, namely, excision. This is the contempt that will overtake the soul while in its body. For not through the righteousness of its deeds has it attained peace in the present world, but because it has directed all its attention towards the maintenance of the body, its pleasures and desires and it has not concerned itself with its own perpetuation which is its existence in the future world. It is therefore rightly said, "O LORD, in its city You will despise their form", i.e., since it has directed all its attention towards the maintenance of the body, consequently contempt will overtake it for it will not enjoy immortality after death.

It is to this intellectual constituent [of man] that Scripture refers in stating, "Let us make man in our form, after our likeness" (Gen. 1.26), "In His own form, in the form of God created He him", (Gen. 1.27). For [when Scripture speaks of] all the creations that were brought into being during the act of creation it refers not to the outward appearance of every creature, but to that essential element by means of which it is distinguished from other creatures. Thus, "Let the earth put forth grass" (Gen. 1.11) alludes only to the vegetative soul, not to its outward form. "Let the waters swarm..." (Gen. 1.20) refers to the animal soul as does the verse, "Let the earth bring forth the living creature (Gen. 1.24). By virtue of this (i.e., the animal soul) it is distinguished from plant life. Similarly, when it states, "Let us make man in our form", it refers to the intellectual constituent by virtue of which he is distinguished from the lower animals. For if this were not so what distinction is presented between man and animal comparable to that between animals and plants, the former of which are distinguished by the animal soul, when it states, "A living soul". This demonstrates that the signification of the term *ṣelem* is only the intellectual soul by virtue of which man is distinguished.

It is possible that since *ṣelem* is a homonymous term therefore Scripture adds, "In our likeness" (Gen. 1.26). For the connotation of, "In our *ṣelem*" does not bring to light its full meaning since all man's acquired forms are his images (*ṣelāmīm*). Therefore, it states, "After our likeness", i.e., a *ṣelem* that exists *per se* without requiring a body, similar to Him–following the opinion of one expositor. This [interpretation] is not necessary, however, for we can ascertain by scientific investigation that it (the intellectual soul) exists *per se*.[312]

It is known that the term *demūth* is a noun derived from the verb *dāmāh*, "he is like". It is not a substantive noun like the term *ṣelem*, but suggests a likeness between one thing and another as regards either their essences or some other factor in which one resembles the other. Hence, we must reject the notion that these are repetitious terms; that what the term *ṣelem* denotes is also the signification of the term *demūth*. Similarly incorrect is the opinion which holds that *ṣelem* is [to be understood as a form] similar to Him; i.e.; one that exists *per se*. For it was not really intended to make a comparison with the creation of the form alone, but with form joined with body, as it states, "Let us make man in our form", and the word man (*'ādām*) is a descriptive term derived from

137

'ādāmāh (earth). Now, when it states, "After our likeness", it refers to both, not to the form alone since it does not say, "Let Me make a form after My image". And the letter *beth* of the word b̲eṣalmēnū is the *beth* denoting "by of". Likewise the opinion of him[313] who holds that the term ṣelem denotes form and the term *demūth* its activities, which are [effected] without the use of any organ like the acts of God, is to be rejected like the first [view] that associates *demūth* with form alone. The same applies to the contention that the term ṣelem denotes form and the term *demūth* signifies matter; for what meaning could be associated with the *kaf* of similitude in the term *ki-demūthēnū*?

The real intention is to establish a comparison of leadership, i.e., as we are leaders so shall he, by virtue of his rank, be a leader over the creatures below him. This is the meaning of the verse, "And let them have dominion over the fish of the sea; And over the fowl of the air" (Gen. 1.26) which refers to the scope of his reign and authority over them by virtue of his being a leader; for every leader is a ruler. Thus, it states, "Yet You have made him but little lower than the angels, and have crowned him with glory and honor. You have made him to have dominion over the works of Your hands; You have put all things under his feet" (Ps. 8.6, 7). This is also the connotation of the verse, "In the likeness of 'elōhīm (angels) made He Adam" (Gen. 5:1), i.e. ; perfect in leadership; for he (Adam) was not like those born of woman who had not as yet come into actuality. Proof of this is the statement, "In the day that God created Adam" (Gen. 5:1). In accordance with this interpretation, the letter *beth* of the word *bi-demūth* is correctly employed, since it denotes a comparison with the dominion of the angels. Proof of this is the use of 'elōhīm, a homonymous term. But in connection with the term *ki-demūthēnū* the *kaf* of similitude is employed since there is included the First Cause. When it states, "In our form" this is an actual faculty, consequently the *kaf* of similitude is employed in the term *ki-demūthēnū* to obviate [absolute] equality. In the statement, "And he begot a son in his own likeness (*bi-demūthō*), after his form (*keṣalmō*)" (Gen. 5.3) the term *demūth* is used with a *beth* since both leaderships are alike; but the term *ṣelem* is used with a *kaf* for the form (*ṣelem*) of Adam was not the same as that of Seth.[314] Now, if the term *ṣelem* did not indicate the intellectual soul but the outward shape it would follow that the other sons born to him were not similar in shape to Adam. As for him who contends that [*ṣelem*] refers to a physical form and explains it as the image, "in which I appear in a prophetic vision", how can he compare what is perceptible to the senses and is possessed of solid existence to that which has no existence save in the imagination. Similarly, he who explains[315] that it (*ṣelem*) refers to an attribute of the Glory regarding which it is stated, "as the appearance of a man upon it above" (Ezek. 1.26), this is also impossible for it is necessary that one element of a comparison be primary so that the other may be compared to it, but here each element is primary permitting the other to be compared to it. This is inadmissible. Furthermore, it is stated in the vision of the chariot as a metaphor, as will be explained below.[316] Similarly untenable is the opinion that Mosheh said [the words *be-ṣalmēnū ki-demūthēnū*], in connection with himself and the people of his generation [to explain] that Adam had the same physical appearance as we. For if the people of his generation were in doubt regarding the form of Adam this statement would not clarify their doubt.

CHAPTER 23[317]

The Hebrew *temūnāh* is a noun adapted to the shape and figure of an object; cf., "A graven image, nor any manner of likeness (*temūnāh*)" (Ex. 20.4). It is also applied to the properties of any thing even though it is incorporeal, as, "but you saw no form (*temūnāh*); only a voice" (Deut. 4.12). In stating, "only" it can be inferred that the term *temūnāh* applies to voice. Proof of the fact that it applies not merely to a physical shape is that after the phrase, "A graven image, nor any manner of likeness (*temūnāh*)". Scripture does not end there, but proceeds to explain the signification of the term *temūnāh*, viz., "Any thing that is in heaven, or, that is in the earth", referring to its physical form. This implies that the noun *temūnāh* applies to things other than physical forms. Since this is so then any thing perceptible to any of the senses may be termed *temūnāh* and would denote the qualities of the said perceptible even if it is perceived by the imagination, although it has no existence outside of the intellect. Thus, it is stated, "It stood still, but I could not discern the, appearance thereof; a form was before mine eyes" (Job. 4.16), and previously it had said, "In thoughts from the visions of the night" (Job. 4.13). Now, most certainly, the true form of an object which is perceived by the intellect should be designated by the term *temūnāh*, and this is its signification in the words "And the, similitude (temunah) of the LORD does he behold" (Num. 12.8), i.e., it denotes an intellectual perception.[318] Maimonides was more correct in asserting that the homonym of this term (*temūnāh*) is employed in an absolute sense than Samuel ibn Tibbon, who contended that its homonymy is figurative in the phrase, "And the, similitude of the LORD does he behold"; for an absolute homonym is cognate with the adapted homonym.

It is in this sense that we must understand "I shall be satisfied, when I awake, with Your likeness (*temūnāh*)" (Ps. 17.15). For this awakening is not that which follows dozing since there is no mention here that he was asleep. Rather, the reference is to that constituent of man that remains after death when it has undergone the transition from pot6ntiality to actuality, and intellect is perceived by pure intellect. Not, as the preceding verse indicates, regarding those people whose portion is in this life and who do not admit that there is a part of man that remains in existence after death. The former notion is also the perception which Mosheh perceived while his soul was yet within his body of, "And the similitude of the LORD does he behold".

The explanation of the verse, is then, as follows, "As for me, I shall behold Your face in righteousness" (Ps. 17.15), i.e., by means of the acts of righteousness which I shall do I shall perceive Your existence, that is, by granting to each his due and enabling the potential to come forth into actuality. The noun *pānīm* (face) is a homonymous term that signifies "existence". This will lead me, after death, to be satisfied with Your true essence. This is the sense of the verse, "I shall be satisfied, when I awake, with Your likeness" (*Ibid.*).

CHAPTER 24[319]

The term *mar'eh* (appearance) signifies that which is perceived by the sense of sight; e.g., "of fair appearance". (I Sam. 17.42); "and he looked (*wayyar'*) and behold, a well in the field". (Gen. 29.2). It is also used to denote that which is perceived by the intellect or the heart; "has seen much of wisdom" (Eccles. 1.16), for wisdom is perceived not with the eye, but by the understanding of the heart. In the latter sense "seeing" is applied to God, i.e., as an intellectual perception and understanding; e.g., "And they saw the God of Israel" (Ex. 24.10); "Even manifestly (*mar'eh*), and not in dark speeches" (Num. 12.8), i.e., the comprehension of intellect through intellect. Similarly, whenever the terms *re'iyyāh* (seeing); *habbatah* (looking) or *haziyyāh* (beholding) are ascribed to God, they are to be understood as intellectual perceptions; e.g., "And they saw the God of Israel" (Ex. 24.10); "And they beheld God" (Ex. 24.11); "And the similitude of the LORD does he behold" (Num. 12.8). For we find [employed in the latter sense] *re'iyyāh* in the passage, "yea, my heart has seen (*rā'āh*) much of wisdom" (Eccles. 1.16)'; *haziyyāh*, in the statement "The word that he saw (*hazāh*)" (Isa. 2.1)–since words are understood, not seen; and *habbatah*, in the verse, "And that can not look on mischief" (Hab. 1.13)–since mischief cannot be seen. Not so [are we to understand] "In a vision. (*mar'eh*) shall I make myself known unto him" (Num. 12.6) for here the term *mar'eh* is associated with the riddles perceived in prophetic vision through the imagination–which He removed from the perception of Mosheh–which are the intermediates between God and the prophets. And the statement, "My servant Mosheh is not, so... with Him do I speak mouth to mouth" (Num. 12.7,8) signifies "with but intermediates", but through the intellect. The term *mar'eh* is employed in the sense of "of the mirrors (*mar'ōth*) of the serving women" (Ex. 38.8), i.e., by means of a mirror (*mar'eh*) one perceives things.

Now, whenever you find the term "seeing" applied to God and it can be understood as an intellectual perception then it should be taken as such. But if this does not apply in every passage, and in certain instances refers to sense perception, then it signifies a phenomenon created to indicate His mighty Providence. This is called "the glory of God". Scripture has revealed this matter in certain passages while elsewhere it has concealed it. Thus, it states, ",for today the LORD appears unto you" (Lev. 9.4); and in another passage, "And the glory of the LORD appeared" (Num. 16.19). The same sense applies to, "And they saw the God of Israel" (Ex. 24.10), i.e., the glory of the God of Israel–according to one of its interpretations, viz., that it refers to the perception of God through His Providence; and Scripture has applied the term "feet" to the Providence associated with the sublunar world; as it is said, "and there was under His feet the like of a paved work of sapphire stone" (Ex. 24.10). This will be explained below.[320]

CHAPTER 25[321]

The term *qōl* (voice) is adapted to signify what is perceived aurally; cf., "And when the voice of the born", (Ex. 19.19). It also denotes the content of a statement, e.g., "And the report (*qōl*) was heard in Pharaoh's house" (Gen. 45.16). Similarly, in the passage, "And it shall come to pass if they will not believe you, neither listen to the voice of the first sign" (Ex.4.8), it means "statement". Likewise, "And they shall listen to your voice" (Ex.3,18), i.e., "to try statement" for it does not refer to the perception of sound.

In like manner we must understand the verse, "And they heard the voice of the, LORD God walking in the garden". (Gen. 3.8). It does not signify "the sound of His walking" for God is incorporeal. Rather, it refers to the statement which preceded His admonition when He said, "Of every tree of the garden you may freely eat; but of the tree of the knowledge of good and evil, you shall not eat of it" (Gen. 2.16). The meaning here is that he should not confine his eating to the tree of knowledge alone, but should eat from the fruits of both trees.[322] "Walking" is predicated of *qōl* as, "And when the voice (*qōl*) of the horn waxed louder and louder" (Ex. 19.19); and the sense of the term "walking" is the admonition "spread forth and became an actuality" in the garden as a result of what had occurred. The entire matter should be understood as follows: when Adam and his wife were beguiled and they ate from the tree of knowledge alone, without considering that they must eat from both trees, they disregarded the prohibition and as a result of their eating from the tree of knowledge they perceived their nakedness. But they remained unmindful until the sun of desire had set at the time when the day's wind was becoming cool, as it is said "toward the cool of the day" (*Ibid.*). Then they said, "What can be the significance of this thing which we did not apprehend prior to our eating of the tree of knowledge and now, after confining our eating to the tree of knowledge alone, we do apprehend it?" It can only be that previously the intellectual part of us prevailed when we engaged in corporeal matters for the perpetuation of our kind for the sake of necessity and we needed not to regard the principles of apparent truths (morals), i.e., to define the meanings of "good" and "bad"; in other words, to consider certain things contemptible and others praiseworthy; the prophets, too, attest to the effects of prevailing intellectual influence.[323] However, since we confined our eating to the tree of knowledge and we gave way to the gratification of bodily functions for the sake of pleasure alone without regard for necessity, it is this which lead to the recognition of apparent truths as "bad" or "good". By apprehending the inferior they perceived the value of what they had lost. Immediately afterwards their hearts were struck with the thought of the admonition. Only then did they comprehend its import; and at the time when the admonition struck their hearts it was as though at that moment they hearkened to it: cf., "You will return to the LORD your God, and listen unto His voice" (Deut. 4.10). Now, since the matter of the admonition struck their hearts, they concealed themselves for shame. But immediately "The LORD God called unto the man" (Gen. 3.9). This hiding did not take place because they were naked as might be inferred from, "And I was afraid, because I was naked" (Gen. 3.10), for they had sewn fig-leaves for themselves. Furthermore, why should they have concerned themselves with this matter now when previously they had not been censured for the fact that they were naked. The real meaning of the phrase "because I was naked" is to be dissociated from the words "I was afraid"; and when it states, "because I was naked", it means: my present knowledge that my nakedness constitutes something shameful is a fact which I did not perceive previously; this is my offense, that I turned aside after the knowledge of apparent truths and the cause of my knowing them was only my disobedience. For I was disobedient and confined my eating to the tree of knowledge, consequently I was compelled to censure and praise, which is the signification of "good" and "bad", and I did not extend my eating to both trees. It is as though he said, "I am ashamed for I was found to be a transgressor. Therefore, I hid myself".

Thus, it has been made clear that the phrase "the voice of the LORD God" refers to a statement ascribed to God. And wherever you find the term "voice" applied to God it is not to be likened to the sound emitted by a human being, for He is not a body possessed of lungs that cries out and its voice is heard. Rather it is something separate from His essence which is ascribed to Him; cf., "with the rod of God" (Ex. 17.9).

We shall have occasion to elucidate this matter below.[324]

CHAPTER 26

The reason for our efforts in expounding these terms has been mentioned in previous chapters.[325] The reason is to adapt the plain meaning of Scriptural verses to the end that they will not stand in conflict with what the intellect has demonstrated to be true in connection with the removal of corporeality and its properties. There are also other advantages, namely, if the intellect demonstrates the negation of corporeality by means of proof and we find a prophetic statement which, in its plain meaning, stands opposed to this it is impossible that the prophet intended that his statement be understood according to its plain meaning, which would place it in conflict with the intellect. Rather the connotation of that statement is something other than its plain meaning so that its intended sense will not be in conflict with the intellect. Three advantages may be derived from this:

1.   The rectification of what the intellect teaches so that no contradiction will arise from prophecy.

2.   If we are convinced that a prophetic statement in its plain meaning is opposed to the intellect and it is inadmissible that its connotation should follow this plain meaning, but it must contain

another sense, then it is necessary to determine the true sense that was intended. For all our efforts are directed to discover the truth and we find ourselves constrained to do so in view of the fact that it is a prophetic statement. It is necessary then to expound it so as not to conflict with any fact taught by the intellect and to ascertain its true sense.

3.   If we are enlightened regarding the real intention of a prophetic statement which is a matter distinct from its plain meaning there is revealed a hidden and concealed aspect of the Torah and by its elucidation we shall derive great benefits through the secrets of our faith.[326]

CHAPTER 27[327]

The Hebrew *nefesh* (soul) is a homonymous term. It signifies, first, the spirit of vitality which is common to all sentient beings, e.g., "to every thing wherein there is a living soul" (Gen. 1.30). It denotes also the "reason" of man, as in, "And the soul of man" (Num. 31.35). Another signification is the part of man that remains after death;[328] comp., "But the soul of my LORD shall be bound in the bundle of life" (I Sam. 25.29).[329] It denotes also "rest" after exertion and toil, as in, "And the son of your handmaid, and the stranger shall rest" (Ex. 23.12). Lastly, it signifies "will"; comp., "And deliver not You him unto the will of his enemies" (Ps. 41.3). In this latter sense, i.e., denoting "will", the term *nefesh* is employed in reference to God. E.g., "My soul could not be toward this people" (Jer. 15.1), i.e., My desire and goodwill could not be [toward them]; "They shall do according to that which is in My heart, and in My will" (I Sam. 2.35).

Maimonides mentions, in connection with the meaning of "will", the verse, "He ceased from work *way-yinnāfash*" (Ex. 31.17), i.e., that which He desired was accomplished and what He wished had come into existence.[330] Similarly he explains the phrase, "And His will (*nafshō*) to trouble Israel ceased" (Jud. 10.16), i.e., His will desisted from afflicting Israel further. In like manner H. Yehudah the Mourner, may his soul rest in peace, explains:[331] His will and desire refrained

149

from afflicting them any further when He beheld the affliction and toil of the Israelites who were enslaved and subjected to hard labor by the Ammonites.

It appears to me, however, that these two terms are both employed figuratively following the fourth signification (i.e., "rest"). Now, since cessation is ascribed to Him in a figurative sense–although it is not the cessation which follows exertion and toil, as though He were affected [by rest]; for it has been made clear that the universe was created by God's word and we find cessation applied to words, as in, "And Job's three friends ceased". (Job. 32.1),[332] so must we understand the term *way-yinnāfash* as a cessation from speaking. Thus, it states, "He rested and He ceased [to speak]". (Ex. 31.17), not a resting after exertion and toil but a figurative usage denoting His cessation from speaking. This "speaking" refers either to His will or it is actual speech attributed to Him as will be explained below.[333]

The passage, "And there ended *nafshō* because of the miseries of Israel", (Jud, 10.16), is now to be understood thus: There came an end to His cessation and resting with respect to the miseries of Israel, i.e., with regard to having mercy on them. Comp., "For Zion's sake will I not hold My peace, and for Jerusalem's sake I will not rest" (Isa. 62.1).

CHAPTER 28[334]

The term *ḥayyīm* (life) is a homonym which describes every creature that is nourished and is sentient; e.g., "of every living (*ḥay*) thing" (Gen. 6.19). It also denotes "recovery"; "And he was recovered (*way-yeḥī*) of his sickness" (Isa: 38.9). Another signification is "uncooked flesh" as in, "But raw" (*ḥay*) (I Sam.) In addition it refers to flowing water that is sweet, "Living (*ḥayyīm*) waters shall go out" (Zach. 14.8); "that they may be healed and live (*ḥay*)" (Ezek. 47.9), i.e., that they may become sweet. Wisdom, too, is termed *ḥayyīm* cf., "For they are life unto those that find them" (Prov. 4.22). Now, just as we people, are called "living" because we are sentient beings, so wisdom is termed "life", because it perceives things, since 'it is able to perceive. But the perception of the faculty of sensation is not like, the perception of the intellect. The term *ḥayyīm* (living) is employed homonymously in reference to both of them ambivalently.[335] In the last mentioned sense *ḥayyīm* (life) is ascribed to God.

CHAPTER 29[335]

The term *neshamah* (breath) signifies the force by which man breathes, i.e., the vital spirit by means of which man moves; this is the sense of "in whose nostrils was the breath (*nishmath*) of the spirit of life" (Gen. 7.22). It is also stated "And his heart died within him so that there was no breath left in him;[336a] "neither was there breath left in me", (Dan. 10.17). It denotes also, "speech"; cf., "and whose neshamah came forth from you?" (Job. 26.4), i.e., "whose speech". It signifies, in addition, the "intellect" through which man attains intelligence as, "The intellect (*nishmath*) of man is the lamp of the LORD, Searching all the inward parts", for this "searching" applies only to the intellect.

We find this term (*neshamah*) ascribed to the human species alone. The passage, "All in whom was the breath (*nishmath*) of the spirit" (Gen. 7.22) refers to man. Now, it appears to me that this term signifies the "Intellectual soul". Nevertheless, by virtue of its signifying the spirit of vitality within man as well as his speech, which is the particular property of man, i.e., it distinguishes him from the animal faculties, therefore it is designated by the term neshamah. It also denotes the flow of intelligence which influences man and causes the transition of his intellect from potentiality to actuality; cf., "And the influence (*nish-*

math) of the Almighty that gives them understanding".
(Job. 32.8)

It is always in this latter sense that the term ne-*sh*ama*h* is ascribed to God and occasionally in the second meaning, i.e., signifying "speech". The passage, "By the breath (ne*sh*ama*h*) of God they perish" (Job. 4.9) denotes then "by the word of God"; "By the breath (ne*sh*ama*h*) of God ice is given". (Job. 37.10), i.e., "by His word". The melting of the ice is also effected by His word, as it is said, "He sends forth His word, and melts them" (Ps. 147.18).

CHAPTER 30[337]

The term *rūah* is a homonym for many things. It signifies "elemental air", cf., "And the air of God moved" (Gen. 1.2). It denotes also, "direction". E.g., "toward the four directions of heaven", (Dan. 8.8). Next, it signifies "vital breath" c.f., "All in whom there is the breath of life in his nostrils" (Gen. 7.22).[338] It signifies also the constituent of man which remains after his death; cf., "And the spirit shall return unto God Who gave it" (Eccles. 12.7). Another signification of this term is "knowledge"; cf., "A man in whom is knowledge" (Num. 27.18).[339] It denotes, in addition, "prophetic inspiration"; e.g., "And the inspiration rested upon them" (Num. 11.26). Finally, it signifies "will" as, "My will abhors my life" (Job 19.17); "Wherever the spirit was to go" (Ezek. 1.20), i.e., the will [was to go]; similarly, "They have eased My will" (Zech. 6.8) Whenever the term *rūah* is ascribed to God it is employed in either of the two last senses, namely, "prophetic inspiration" or "will".

CHAPTER 31[340]

The verb *rā'āh* (he saw) signifies, first, perception by the sense of sight; cf., "I had not thought to see your face" (Gen. 48.11). It is also used figuratively in the sense of intellectual perception; e.g., "My heart has seen much of wisdom" (Eccles. 1.16), for wisdom is perceived not by the eye, but by the intellect. Furthermore, it states, "my heart", and the term "heart" is a homonym for the intellect, as has been explained above.[341] "See you the word of the LORD" (Jer. 2.31), means "understand His word". "I have seen with my heart" (Ps. 66.18), but the heart does not see, rather it understands.

It is in accordance with the nature of things that "seeing" is ascribed to them; if it is the nature of that which is perceived that it be perceived by ocular perception then "seeing" denotes visual perception, but if it is a thing which is understood, then "seeing" signifies intellectual perception, as has been stated above. We do not mean to imply that since certain things are perceived by the sense of sight then God possesses eyes; for God is incorporeal. What we do mean is that, in connection with the knowledge of perceptibles, whatsoever He perceives this perception is termed "seeing". But our perception cannot be compared to the perception of the Almighty, for we perceive by means of physical organs, but not so God. Hence, "seeing" is applied to us and to God only homonymously and there is no comparison between the two perceptions. This will be explained in the following chapters in connection with Providence.[342]

Similarly, the terms haza*h* (he saw) and *hibbīt* (he saw) [are employed figuratively in the sense of intellectual perception]. With the meaning of "understanding" the verb *rajah* is used in the passage, "I will go down now, and see" (Gen. 18.21). The meaning is, "I will understand", for it speaks of, "the cry of it".

CHAPTER 32[343]

The Hebrew ʿayin is a homonymous term: a fountain (ʿēyn) of water; the eye (ʿēyn) of a seer, the appearance (ʿēyn) of what is seen. It denotes also "aid"; cf., "And you shall be to us an aid (ʿēynāyim)" (Num. 10.31). Another meaning of the word is "visual perception", e.g., "and set your eyes upon him" (Jer. 39.12); "And I shall set mine eyes upon him" (Gen. 44.21), i.e., I shall see my sight, which is perception.

When the term ʿayin is ascribed to God it signifies "aid", e.g., "Behold, the eye of the LORD" (Ps. 33.18), i.e., the aid of God, and also "perception", e.g., "And Mine eyes and My heart shall be there" (I Kings 9.3); "The eyes of the LORD are toward the righteous" (Ps. 34.16). This is made clear by the verse, "His eyes behold, His eyelid try, the children of men" (Ps. 11.4). Similarly, "Open your eyes, and behold" (Dan. 9.18) signifies that the perception be stimulated to perceive. Far be it from Him to possess eyes, for He is incorporeal. Perception is designated in accordance with the nature of that which is perceived since a seen thing is perceived only by the sense of sight.

CHAPTER 33[344]

The term *shmī'āh* is a homonym. It signifies "to hear" as, "the noise of them that sing do I hear" (Ex. 32.18); "and they heard the voice of the young man the Levite" (Jud. 18.3). It denotes also "to obey", e.g., "And it shall come to pass, because you obey (*tishme'ūn*)" (Deut. 7.12); "But if you will not listen (*tishme'ū*)" (Lev. 26.14). Another meaning of the word is "to understand", as in, "Give Your servant therefore an understanding (*shōmē'ah*) heart" (I Kings 3.9). The term *shemī'āh* used in reference to God must be understood in the first signification, that of "perception" by which He perceives those things that are heard through sound, i.e., their quality. This is designated by the term "hearing", although the Almighty is incorporeal and possesses no ears. It is also ascribed to God in the sense of "to receive:" e.g., "Hear the right, O LORD" (Ps. 17.1); "The LORD has received my supplication" (Ps. 6.10); "I will not receive" (Isa. 1.15). Finally, it is used in reference to God with the meaning "to understand:" cf., "I attended and understood" (Jer. 8.6). All that we have explained in connection with the term *re'iyāh* (seeing) may be asserted regarding the word *shemī'āh* (hearing); for "hearing" must be understood in accordance with the nature of the things of which "hearing" is predicated. If it is a sound that is heard then hearing must be taken literally. This does not mean that He perceives hearing by ear, for God is incorporeal. Rather in whatever manner He perceives sound that perception is designated by the term "hearing". There is no comparison, of course, between our hearing and His hearing save in the name "hearing" alone.

When it (*shemī'āh*) denotes "to receive", it implies that He answers the request of man or does not answer it. It signifies also intellectual perception, e.g., "I attended and understood (*wa-'eshma'*), but they spoke not aright" (*Ibid.*).

All that we have explained concerning the sense of hearing applies equally to the sense of smell, neither more nor less.

The meaning of '*ōzen* (ear) is well known. It is employed figuratively in the sense of hearing, cf., "Who among you will give ear (*ya'azīn*) to this?" (Isa. 42.23), i.e., "will hear". Similarly, "Give ear, O my people, to my teaching". (Ps. 78.1). Whenever the term '*ōzen* is applied to God it is used figuratively in the sense of the perception by means of which He perceives that which is audible,[345] e.g., "Incline Your ear" (Ps. 17.6); "Nor gave He ear" (Deut. 1.45), i.e., "Nor did He hear".

CHAPTER 34[346]

The primary meaning of the term *yāshab* is "he sat, "cf., "And the king sat upon his seat" (I Sam. 20.25); but since "sitting" indicates the permanence and unchanging character of a thing better than any other aspect of corporeality it is employed figuratively in the sense of anything that is constant and permanent even though it is not a body. E.g., "And you cause the seat of violence to come near". (Amos 6.3), i.e., the permanence of violence; similarly, "And righteousness shall abide (*tēshēb*) in the fruitful field" (Isa. 32.16). Following this figurative use it is employed in the passage, "But Yehudah shall abide for ever" (Joel 4.20), i.e., it shall remain constant and permanent.

Whenever "sitting" is ascribed to God, as in, "But the LORD abide (*yesheb*), for ever" (Ps. 9.8) it signifies constancy and permanence. Now, since all sublunar existents are interrelated[347] and all activities cease with the outermost sphere, the former are transient and the latter is perpetually in motion and demonstrates the permanence of His existence. Therefore, His permanent existence is associated with the heavens through the term "sitting". Comp. "O You that sit in the heavens" (Ps. 123.1)";He that sit in heaven" (Ps. 2.4). Similarly, in the passage, "It is He that sits above the circle (*ḥūg*) of the earth" (Isa. 40.22) Circle refers to the sphere, as it is stated "And He walk upon the circle (*ḥūg*) of heaven" (Job 22.14).

This signifies that the activities of the earth are dependent upon this circle (sphere) and the circle demonstrates the permanence of His existence, praised be He, Who is the Dispenser of all things, in contradistinction to the opinion of the scholar[348] who holds that the term hug refers to the transient things of the earth that come and go. For the earth is associated with God only. as His footstool, as it is said "And the earth is My footstool" (Isa. 66.1).

Now, as regards the statement "The LORD sat above the flood" (Ps. 29.10), the "flood" indicates corruption and change and the term "sat" denotes that He abides for ever and is not subject to any change. Consider that it states, "above the flood not "in the flood". This indicates that although all things change, He remains immutable. Aced the term "sat" is related to "And in His temple, all say: Glory" (Ps. 29.9). Note this well.[349]

CHAPTER 35[350]

The term *kissē'* (throne) signifies that upon which one sits; cf., "And the king sat upon his throne (Esther 5.11). Since the word "throne" indicates the greatness and rank of him who sits upon it then anything that indicates the rank and greatness of a thing is designated by the term "throne". In this sense we must understand the words "Then the king sat on the throne of the LORD", (I Chron. 29.23); here it (the throne) indicates the rank of authentic judgment as alluded to in the statement "for the judgment is God's' (Deut. 1.17); and in the verse, "For there were set thrones for judgment" (Ps. 122.5). Similarly, "And he shall be for a throne of honor to his father's house" (Isa. 22.23) signifies that this man will be so elevated that he will indicate the dignity and greatness of his father's house as the throne indicates the dignity of him who sits upon it.

Again, greatness and rank are not attributes that can be predicated of matter, and in this way we must conceive the relationship between the throne and God, as in, "The heaven is My throne" (Isa. 66.1) and similar statements, i.e., the heavens indicate His essence and His greatness, not that He is a corporeal being borne upon a throne. Maimonides, however, explains: the term "throne" in the passage, "For the hand is upon the throne of God" (Ex.17.6) as an attribute denoting His Essence and Greatness; the noun "throne" indicates His essence. He asserts further that it is inadmissible to consider the throne as something separate from His essence for if we admit this, viz., that it is separate from His essence, it would appear that God exists at certain times with the throne and at other times without the throne. Such a belief would constitute heresy. It is evident from his words that it would not be heretical to explain that the term "throne" does not indicate His Essence. He only refers to one who believes that God exists at times with and at times without the throne. Arid he desires to find Scriptural proof that the term "throne" indicates His Essence, so as not to believe that He exists at different times with and without the throne; for if the term "throne" constantly indicates something separate from His Essence it would appear that He existed only at a certain time with the throne since any thing other than He is considered as nonexistent. But the might and rank described by the throne must be predicated of God at all times. Hence, whosoever believes that God existed both with the throne and without the throne is a heretic. Maimonides supports his opinion with the verse, "You, O LORD, remain for ever; Your throne from generation to generation" (Lam. 5.19). This verse indicates the permanence of the throne, hence it is His Essence.

I contend, on the contrary, that if it is impossible to describe God as having existed both with the throne and without it then this notion is heretical. For if rank and might are described by the throne it is because the throne is in existence and indicates these attributes; and all the time that they are described by the throne it would necessitate the existence of the throne. This is undoubtedly heretical for it indicates the eternity of the heavens, since it is impossible that

He be described by a throne that is nonexistent. Furthermore, even if. His Essence is termed "throne" the signification of "throne!" always indicates the elevation of something separate from itself. Indeed the scholar, Samuel ibn Tibbon, states that Maimonides has made an assertion in this reference which he fails to comprehend.351

The true meaning of the words "For the hand is upon the throne of God" (Ex. 17.16) alludes to the constellations of the zodiac352 and it denotes that a time will come in the disposition of the heavenly bodies when the foot of Amalek shall slip; comp. "Vengeance is Mine and recompense, against the time when their foot shall slip" (Deut. 32.35). But then, in the days of Mosheh, the *Mazzāl* of Amalek prevailed; cf., "And the Canaanite was then in the land" (Gen. 12.6). Now, if you possess understanding you will comprehend the meaning of "And it came to pass, when Mosheh held up his hand " (Ex. 17.11). And the verse, "And You, O LORD, remain for ever; Your throne from generation to generation" (Lam. 5.19) signifies, even with respect to the relationship between the revolutions of the constellations and the inhabitants of the sublunar world; cf., "from generation to generation" (*Ibid.*). For it is stated "For it is time to be gracious unto her, for the appointed time is come" (Ps. 102.14;. The meaning is then that although things change in accordance with the constellations "You, O LORD, remain for ever",' i.e., You are eternal, permanent and immutable.

CHAPTER 36

The term *shākhan* signifies, first, the continued staying of a person in a place whether he sits there or moves about in any manner of motion; e.g., "And he was dwelling (*shōkhēn*) in the plains of Mamre" (Gen. 14.13). It is also applied metaphorically to a thing that is incorporeal and does not occupy space; cf., "to cause His name to dwell there", (Deut. 12.11), for a name is not a thing that occupies space.

In the latter sense we must understand the term *shekhīnāh* when it is ascribed to God, as in, "And I will dwell (*we-shākhantī*) in the midst of you" (Zach. 2.14_), for this "dwelling" does not signify occupying space, rather it denotes the continuance of His Providence. Occasionally it refers to a created object that indicates the might of God's Providence, e.g., the created Light that dwells in the Sanctuary comp. "And the glory, of the LORD abode (*way-yishkōn*)" (Ex. 24.16), this alludes to an object that indicates the might of His Providence. It is for this reason that the Tabernacle is termed mishkan.

CHAPTER 37[354]

The term *qām* signifies, first, the act of rising after having been seated, as in, "And he rose up (*wa-yāqam*) and went his way", (Gen. 25.34). It is also employed figuratively to denote that which has been removed from its previous status and the term *qīmāh* is applied to it although in actuality it continues as it is, e.g., "So the field of Ephron was made sure (*wa-yāqam*)" (Gen. 23.17); "Then the house shall be made sure" (Lev. 25.30); "And that the kingdom of Israel shall be established in your hand". (I Sam. 24.21).

In short, the term *qīmāh* is applied to that which is removed from its previous status. Whenever the term *qīmāh* is applied to God it is employed in this figurative sense, whether it be for a good dispensation or an evil one, as though one status were changed for another, e.g., "You will arise (*tāqūm*) and have compassion upon Zion", (Ps. 102.14); "And I will rise against the house of Yerovoam", (Amos 7.9). It does not signify that He is a corporeal being that rises after having been seated.

CHAPTER 38[355]

The verb *amad* is a homonymous term. It denotes, first, "to stand upon one's feet", c.f. "Son of man, stand (*'amōd*) upon your feet" (Ezek. 2.1). It further signifies "cessation" as, "and she ceased (*wat-ta'amōd*) to bear" (Gen. 29.35); "but they stood still and answered no more", (Job 32.16), i.e., they ceased to speak. Another signification is "to be everlasting and enduring", e.g., "And His righteousness endures for ever", (Ps. 111.3). It is possible that the passage, "'And His feet shall stand (*we-'āmdū*) in that day", (Zach. 14.4) is a metaphor employing the first meaning [of the verb *'āmad*], for every act that requires strength for its execution is accomplished by man while he stands upon his feet. Hence, because of the wondrous things that were to be wrought at that time and in that place the phrase "standing upon His feet" was ascribed to Him in a figurative sense. Or perhaps it is employed in the third signification as denoting", to be enduring and everlasting, with the proviso that the phrase "His feet" is a homonymous expression indicating the knowledge of God relative to the sublunar world.[356] The meaning would then be that because of the wondrous things that would be wrought it that place the knowledge of God would be spread abroad and be everlasting.

167

CHAPTER 39[357]

The term *yāṣab* a homonym signifying in the first instance "to stand upon one's feet., e.g., "You are standing (*niṣṣābīm*)" (Deut. 29.9); "They came out, and stood" (Num. 16.27). It is also employed in reference to the leadership of those who are appointed over the people; cf., "besides the chief officers. (*han-niṣṣābīm*)" (1 Kings 5.30). In the latter sense we must understand the verse, "Your word establishes (*niṣṣāb*) the heavens" (Ps. 119.89), i.e., it guides them and establishes them, as, "By the word of the LORD were the heavens made" (Ps. 33.6). It is always with this signification that the verb *yaa'* is employed in reference to God; cf., "And, behold, the LORD stood (*niṣṣāb*) upon it"[358] (Gen. 28.13), i.e., he did not conceive God upon the summit of the ladder save by virtue of His acts with respect to it.[359] For this reason Scripture makes use of the term *nissa'* as it does in the verse, "The LORD stands up (*niṣṣāb*) to plead", (Isa. 3:13).

On the other band, in the verses "And you shall stand upon the rock" (Ex. 33.21), and "And the LORD descended in the cloud, and stood with him there it denotes a standing of cognition. This is a figurative usage of its first signification. It is also correct to interpret the verse, "And, behold the LORD stood (*niṣṣāb*) upon it" (Gen. 28.13) in a different manner so that it will be a figurative usage of the first signification. According to this interpretation the term "ladder" does not include the heavens; as it states, "And the top of it reached to heaven", (Gen. 28.12), i.e., heaven is separate from the ladder. Now, the heaven is the seat of Glory and the earth is His footstool. Thus, the top of the ladder is the pedestal. Note this.

CHAPTER 40[360]

The verb *hālakh* denotes "to go". Its primary signification is the motion of living beings from one place to another as, "And he went into the land of Canaan (Gen. 11:31),[351] "And whatsoever goes upon its feet"[362] (Lev. 11.27). It is also found to signify "spreading abroad", cf., "The sound thereof shall spread abroad like the serpent's" (Jer. 46.22), "And their tongue spreads abroad through the earth" (Ps. 73.9) i.e., their talk is drawn forth and spread abroad. In the latter sense we must understand the versa "The voice of the LORD God walking (*mithha lekh*) in the garden" (Gen. 3.8), i.e., [the voice] was drawn out and spread abroad.[363] Similarly, "After the LORD your God shall you walk" (Deut. 13.5) means you shall follow and :pursue His will. It is in this figurative sense that the spreading forth of God's Providence is termed "going", as in, "Let the LORD go in the midst of us" (Ex. 34.9), i.e., [let] His Providence spread forth.[364] And when the Providence departs to return to its place this is also termed "going",' as in, "I shall go and return to my place" (Hos. 5.15). Similarly, "And the anger of the LORD was kindled against them and He went" (Num. 12.9); for it states above "And the LORD came down in a pillar of cloud". Thus, it could not signify a corporeal going.

CHAPTER 41³⁶⁵

The primary signification of the verb *'ābar*, "to pass", 'refers to the motion of living beings in space, as in, "Pass over before me" (Gen. 32.17). It denotes next "to pass beyond one's limit", e.g., "And like a man whom wine has overcome (*'aḇārō*) (Jer. 23.9). It is also applied to the passage of sound as, "And they caused a sound to pass throughout the camp" (Ex. 36.6). In a figurative sense it refers to that which is incorporeal as, "And my right is passed over from my God" (Isa. 40.27); "And let pass over me what will" (Job 13.13), i.e., evil occurrences. It is also applied figuratively to thought that is transferred to one's mouth, e.g., "That I have a thought which should not pass my mouth" (Ps. 17.3). It is in this figurative sense that we must understand the verse, "For I will pass through the land of Egypt" (Ex. 12.12), i.e., His decree and His word shall pass through. However, in the verse, "And the LORD passed by (*way-ya'aḇōr*) before his face" (Ex. 34.6) the verb *'d'ar* refers to the abundantly mighty conception which Mosheh conceived. The expression "before his face" alludes to "the face of Mosheh" and signifies "before his inner face" (i.e., his intellect). Similarly, we must take the verse, "And it shall come to pass, while My glory passes by and I will cover you with My hand until I have passed by". Now, when [Mosheh] perceived it (the conception), it was passing by; not standing still or seated. For that which passes by is seen at one time and at another is hidden.–The same interpretation cannot be applied to the verse, "I will make all My goodness pass by" (Ex. 33.19), for since Scripture specifies "ell" it elucidates the matter.

But Maimonides[366] interprets the phrase "before His face", (Ex. 34.6) as referring to God and he explains the verb *way-ya'aḇōr* as it is employed in the verse, "He shot an arrow, causing it to miss the aim (*le-ha'aḇīrō*)" (I Sam. 20.36) [where the verb *'āḇar* denotes:] to abandon one aim and turn to a different aim and object. It is as though Scripture said that Mosheh had made two requests. First, "Show me now Your ways", (Ex. 33.13). This was answered by "I will make all My goodness pass before you", (Ex. 33.19). But He withheld the answer to the second question in stating, "You can not see My face" (*Ibid.* 20). And the verb *way-ya'aḇōr* [in Ex. 34.67] signifies it is as though He made him to turn (*he'eḇīr*) from the question of "the conception of the Divine face" into a conception of a lower degree, viz., "the conception of the back". In this sense He deflected His aim for the purpose of teaching that "the conception of the Divine face is by its nature inaccessible to the human intellect".

Maimonides also explains that the verb *'āḇar* may be understood as applying to a prophetic vision,[367] as in, "And behold a smoking furnace, and a flaming torch that passed (*'āḇar*)" (Gen. 15.17). But it is well known that Mosheh did not prophecy through the imaginative faculty as it is explicitly stated, "Even manifestly, and not in dark riddles", rather, as one man speaks to another.

Others explain the verb *way-ya'aḇōr* [in Ex 34.6] as requiring an additional word[368] and it would then denote: And a voice passed by. But how will they explain the phrase "until I have passed by" (Ex. 33.22)? Still others suggest that "the object which passed by" was a created Glory.[369] But what shall be done with the verse, "And I will cover you with My hand until I have passed by" (*Ibid.*)?

And now we should affirm that in truth Mosheh did make two requests: first, "Show me now Your ways" (Ex. 33.13); and second, "Show me, I pray You, Your Glory" (*Ibid.* 18). But scholars are divided in their opinions as to whether He answered both these requests or merely one of them. Maimonides contends that He answered both. With regard to the question of "Show me now Your ways" (*Ibid.* 13) Mosheh was told "I will make all My goodness pass by" (*Ibid.* 19), i.e., you will comprehend the existence of My universe concerning which it is stated "And God saw every thing that He had made, and, behold, it was very good" (Gen. 1.31). For it is through [God's] acts that one can comprehend the "ways" that are implied in the verse, "Show me now Your ways" (Ex. 33.13). But in answer to the question "Show me, I pray You, Your Glory" (*Ibid.* 18) he was told, "You can not see My face" (*Ibid.* 20), i.e., the true nature of My existence. Rather He vouchsafed to him a conception inferior to this by asserting "And you shall see My back" (*Ibid.* 23). Through this, he says, Mosheh attained a conception that no man, before or after him, has attained. I have seen that several expositors of Maimonides associate the last mentioned phrase with the conception "I will make all My goodness pass by" (*Ibid.* 19). They appear to hold that Maimonides never intended that he (i.e., Mosheh) was answered at all with regard to his second request. But they have not considered the matter carefully. He (Maimonides) states further that with regard to "the conception of the back" He promised him (Mosheh) that he would conceive it by means of divine assistance, in the words "And I will cover you with My hand until I have passed by" (*Ibid.* 22). But this does not appear to be so, for in connection with "the conception of the back" it is stated "And I will take away My hand" (*Ibid.* 23).

Again, it appears from his words that Maimonides explains the phrase "My back" as denoting " he knowledge of the acts that are ascribed to Him", and he interprets the words "All My goodness" to signify that He alluded to indicating to him all existents, as it is written "And God saw everything that He had made, and, behold, it was very good" (Gen. 1.31). Now, it seems that both these ideas are included under one beading, viz., the relationship of existents, despite the fact that he (Maimonides) associated the phrase "My back" with the request "Show me, I pray You, Your glory", (*Ibid.* 18), and the phrase, "All My goodness" with the request "Show me now Your ways" (*Ibid.* 13). I do not know, however, whether he has divided these (ideas) according to the divisions of existence; viz., that "All My goodness" is an allusion to those works through which [God's] attributes are ascertained respecting which it is stated "Show me now Your ways" (*Ibid.* 13), and this is also the meaning of "And I will proclaim the name of the LORD before you" (*Ibid.* 19); i.e., "I will make known"; and that the phrase "My back" refers to the emanations of God that perform His will, since Maimonides interprets 'the words "My back" as denoting[376] "that which follows Me is similar to Me, and is the necessary result of My will". However, it appears, from Scripture, which states regarding this conception". And I will take away My hand", (*Ibid.* 23), that in connection with this conception he (Mosheh) did not require divine assistance. However, when it states, "And I will cover thee with My hand" (*Ibid.* 22) it signifies that he will require divine assistance, as is alluded to in the words "and you shall stand upon the rock. And it shall come to pass, while My glory passes by" (*Ibid.* 21, 22), for it is inadmissible that "passing by" be predicated of an object unless it is conceived, as will be explained.[371]

It is also to be wondered why this scholar (Maimonides) did not feel it, necessary to point out why it was that when Mosheh made the petition "Show me now Your ways" (*Ibid.* 13) He did not reply immediately "I will make all My goodness pass by" (*Ibid.* 19), but He withheld the reply until he (Mosheh) would request something far more difficult, nay impossible! Still more astonishing, and we must offer some explanation, is that when Mosheh asked "Show me now [Thy ways]" (*Ibid.* 13) and he saw that He did not answer him, how did he ask a question that is even more profound! Some explain that Mosheh asked for something impossible, which even those of weak intellect comprehended as being inconceivable. They were required to justify this request in view of the fact that it is unattainable; but they were unsuceessful.[372] I see that all the expositors, have hidden their eyes from this difficulty, but I do not know whether they did not realize it or whether they were aware of it, but were unable to offer any explanation.

Now, some scholars have upset the order of the verses by representing the first petition as last and vice versa for the reason that I have mentioned and also because Mosheh had inquired concerning who will go with him, in saying "And You has not let me know whom You will send with me" (*Ibid.* 12); and he was told "My presence shall go" (*Ibid.* 14) after he had asked "Show me now Your ways" (*Ibid.* 13). But how is it possible that, before God replied to his first petition he should ask a second! It is possible to explain, however, that both requests were made together and God replied to the one, but not to the other. Indeed, what compelled them to entertain this notion is that respecting the petition "Show me now Your ways" (*Ibid.* 13) Mosheh desired to know how to lead the people of Israel; and respecting the petition "Make known to me, I pray You, Your glory" (*Ibid.* 18), since it is withheld from man's intellect so long as his soul is 3ontained within his body—it is inadmissible that Mosheh was ignorant of this and held it to be possible—they assert that Mosheh desired the separation of his soul from his body. But it is inconceivable that he asked first to lead the Israelites and afterwards that his soul be separated from his body. Now, since this is inadmissible they agreed to consider the first petition as second and vice versa. But these arguments are inconclusive.

I have seen that ibn Ezra[373] considers the words "I will make all My goodness pass by" (*Ibid.* 19) as a reply to "Make known to me, I pray You, Your glory" (*Ibid.* 18) and the phrase "My goodness" is an allusion to the Divine face which is compared to the most elevated conception (i.e., God's essence). He interprets the verb *'a'aḇīr* as in, "He shot an arrow, causing it to miss the aim (*le-ha'aḇīrō*)" (I Sam. 20.36); or the allusion contained in, "Until I have passed by" (*Ibid.* 22) is to be understood in the same manner as "You can not see My face" (*Ibid.* 20). To be sure, He vouchsafed to him a conception of a lower degree, viz., "the conception of the back". He (ibn Ezra) explains the verse, "I will make all My goodness pass by (i.e., miss) your face" (*Ibid.* 19) as referring to the inner face of

Mosheh, that is, the inner face of his heart. He also refers the words "And I will be gracious to whom I will be gracious" (*Ibid.* 19) to Mosheh and identifies them with the passage, "And I will cover you with My hand until I have passed by" (*Ibid.* 22). In other words, since it is beyond the power of the human intellect to conceive this extraordinary conception, 'viz., the perception of the Divine face, as has been explained, then how will it pass by the conception of Mosheh intellect so that his soul will not become separated from him'! [This will be accomplished] when I will cover him with My hand; and this is the meaning of "And I will be gracious to whom I will be gracious" (*Ibid.* 19). But with regard to the conception of My back I will r6move My hand; and this is the meaning of "And the similitude of the LORD does he behold" (Num. 12.8). In the opinion, of this scholar, Mosheh could not conceive God, since He is different from all things, dissociated from all things, and independent of all things. This is the significance of "But My face shall not be seen" (*Ibid.* 23); and, respecting this, Mosheh required the covering of God's hand. Nevertheless, Mosheh did conceive God in so far as He is all things, His glory fills all things and from Him all things derive, this is the "conception of the back". It further appears from his views that the words "And I will proclaim the name of the LORD before you" (*Ibid.* 19) constitute a reply to "Show me now Your ways" (*Ibid.* 13). Again, according to his opinion, Mosheh' petition "Make known to me, I pray You, Your glory" (*Ibid.* 18) is of an inclusive nature, and God informed Him what was impossible to conceive and what was possible. Regarding that which he could not perceive— for it is impossible to conceive this so long as the soul is united with the body, unless it becomes separated— He indicated to him in what manner this conception will pass by him, in the words "And I will cover you with My hand until I have passed by" (*Ibid.* 22).

This is inadmissible, however, for the significance of the covering of His hand is not to prevent Mosheh from conceiving the true nature of God lest his soul thereby become separated from his body. For even the Separate Intelligences cannot conceive Him as He is, and certainly not a separate soul. Furthermore, what is impossible *per se* does not require an external factor to render it impossible. On the contrary, the words "And I will cover" may signify divine assistance. If this be so, then it must needs be an extraordinary conception, which is beyond man's intellect to conceive, and consequently he required divine assistance to conceive it; this is the significance of "And it shall come to pass, while My glory passes by, that I will put you in the cleft of a rock" (*Ibid.* 22). The homonymity of the term *'ābar* indicates the remarkably extraordinary conception that Mosheh conceived, for if Mosheh had not conceived this it would not have been proper to describe the Glory as passing before him. Now, ibn Ezra has not examined these difficulties nor has he regarded the difficulties, which we mentioned above.

I shall now commence to elucidate the intention [of Scripture] by its plain meaning through an extraordinary analysis. It is known that God said to Mosheh "And I will send an angel before you" (*Ibid.* 2) whereupon Mosheh replied "But You has not let me know whom You will send with me" (*Ibid.* 12). i.e., if this be the angel alluded to in, "For My name is in him", (Ex. 23.21). The meaning is not that he wished to know which angel this is, rather it is a manner of introduction. For he said "Yet You have said: I know you by name and you have also found grace in My sight!' (Ex. 33.12), hence what need have I that You should send an angel with me. And together with this petition Mosheh said, "Show me now Your ways" (*Ibid.* 13). Now, the reason that Mosheh made this request is that his conception of the knowledge of God is that He is the Righteous One (*Ṣaddīq*) and the term *ṣaddīq* is a derivative from the noun *ṣedeq* "justice" which denotes that He will give unto each one what is his due according to law. Consequently, when he beheld that the Israelites had sinned in connection with the Calf and should be condemned to annihilation according to law yet God urged him to make supplications for them, then the ways of God's thoughts were too profound for Mosheh and he desired to comprehend this. Hence, he asked "Show me now Your ways" (*Ibid.*). With respect to the first request, God replied, "My presence shall go" (*Ibid.* 14), i.e., I, Myself, will go—"I will give rest only to you" (*Ibid.*). Thereupon Mosheh rejoined, "If Your presence go not amongst all of us, carry us not up hence" (cf., *Ibid.* 15). And Mosheh continued, "For wherein now shall it be known that I have found grace in Your sight, I and Your people, is it not in that You go with us...". (*Ibid.* 16). Then God answered, "I will do this thing also that you have spoken" (*Ibid.* 17). But when Mosheh beheld that although his request was for knowledge of the ways by which he could know Him, since these are the intermediaries between God and himself, and although his request was possible (i.e., it could be answered) nevertheless God tarried and did not answer him, Mosheh thought that God tarried and did not answer his request for information regarding His ways only for the purpose of arousing him to a more elevated conception than that which he had first requested. Hence, he asked, "Make known to me, I pray You, Your glory" (*Ibid.* 18). For it would not suffice him merely to know the ways of God save if he comprehended Him through His true essence by means of which the knowledge of His ways could be verified and he would understand that just as His essence is distinct from our essence so is His conduct distinct from our conduct. Then He replied to the first question first; with regard to the petition, "Show me now Your ways" (*Ibid.* 13) He replied to him, "I will make all My goodness pass before you" (*Ibid.* 19), i.e., I shall cause to pass before you all the existents that emanate from Me, for they are My goodness, as it is stated "And God saw everything that He had made, and, behold, it was very good" (Gen. 1.31). I shall cause them to pass before your intellect and when. you comprehend the nature of My universe with perfect comprehension then you will recognize the relationship of My guidance respecting it. This is the significance of "And I will proclaim the name of the LORD before you" (Ex. 33.19), i.e., you will comprehend the truth concerning My ways and you will know Me. The passage, "And I will be gracious to whom I will be gracious" (*Ibid.*) will be explained in another chapter of this treatise.374

Now, with regard to the second petition He replied, "You can not see My Face" (*Ibid.* 20); and He made known to him the impossibility of seeing the Divine face. The reason for this impossibility is not due to Mosheh's soul being bound up with his body and were he to behold it his soul would be separated. For the words "My face" denote "the true nature of His existence" and this He alone comprehends, no one other than He. Cf., "Behold, He puts no trust in His holy ones" (Job 4.18). This is also implied in the term *wa-ḥay* (nor angel), i.e., "Man will not see me, nor angel (*wa-ḥay*)" (*Ibid.* 20) for this is the sense of the noun *wa-ḥay*. The meaning is not that Mosheh did not understand that this conception is impossible [to be comprehended] and he, considering it possible, inquired; for the impossibility of conceiving His essence is understood even by those possessed of weak intellects. On the contrary, after Mosheh perceived the delay in replying to a matter that was possible and he was aroused to petition for a more elevated concept than what he had previously requested–you know, of course, that beyond the knowledge of His ways is the conception of His essence– hence he said, "Show me, I pray You, Your glory" (*Ibid.* 18). This is an inclusive petition and Mosheh requested that with which he had not been graced since he did not know the extent of the knowledge that He desired to grant him. Then God answered him and desired to inform him what is impossible to be comprehended and what is of a lower degree that may possibly be conceived with the assistance of God, and finally that which can be conceived even with out Divine aid. Therefore, He states, with regard to the conception that is impossible., "You can not see My face" (*Ibid.* 20). It is not that Mosheh was ignorant of this and requested it, rather it is a manner of introduction in order to point out to him a conception that is inaccessible to the human intellect without the help of God. And Mosheh was told, regarding this conception that requires Divine aid, "Behold, there is a place by Me, and you shall stand upon the rock" (*Ibid.* 21). The term "rock" is a homonym[375] and signifies in this context "the source of existents". Similarly, "The Rock, His work is perfect" (Deut. 32.4); He is called "Rock" by virtue of the acts which derive from Him, cf., "Look unto the Rock whence you were hewn" (Isa. 51.1). The expression, "Behold, there is a place by Me" (Ex.

33.21), signifies that degree of scientific insight into the essence of the Glory that he would conceive. It states further, "And you shall stand upon the rock", (*Ibid.*), this refers to a standing of cognition and comprehension. The passage, "And it shall come to pass, while My glory passes by" (*Ibid.* 22), i.e., the conception of the Rock, which denotes the commencement of existence, signifies it shall pass by before your intellect. In other words, you shall stand upon the rock, but I will indicate to you the hollow source of the rock, i.e., I, Myself, shall indicate to you the essence of all beginnings, how there were originated and there emanated from Me all existing activities. For the meaning of "I will put you in a hollow of the rock" (*Ibid.* 22) is not, as many have thought, the same as "to come into a hollow of the rocks" which implies a place of concealment. ,for after He said to him, "And you shall stand upon the: rock" (*Ibid.* 21)– in the opinion of the readers who see only the plain meaning of this passage it would be more proper to say to him, "You shall come into a hollow of the rock", rather than "I will put you in a hollow of the rock" (*Ibid.*22). The real meaning here is as we have explained. Rhetorically stated, cf., "Look unto the Rock whence you were hewn, and to the hole of the pit whence you were digged" (Isa. 51.1), and the words "1 will put you in a hollow of the rock, and will cover you with My hand until I have passed by" (Ex. 33.22).

The prophet Eliyahu covered his face with his cloak, but Mosheh was covered by the hands of God. The revelation came to Eliyahu through fire, storm and wind, and after them a thin, still voice. In the case of Mosheh, however, this was not so. Rather he was aroused to this conception by the Glory itself when He said "I will put you in a hollow of the rock", (*Ibid.* 22).

The essence of this conception consists of the relationship between the Agent and His acts, and this conception is so lofty and inscrutable that it almost approaches the knowledge of His essence. It is for this reason that He promised him the covering of His hand. Hence, it states, "And it shall come to pass, while My glory passes by, that I will put you in a hollow of the rock, and I will cover you with My hand until I have passed by" (*Ibid.*). This glory is not an attribute that is ascribed to Him, for it states, "Until I have passed by", (*Ibid.*).

With regard to "the perception of the back" He promised that He would remove His hand, as it is said "And I will take away My hand, and you shall see My back" (*Ibid.* 23). The noun *āhōr* (back) is a homonym, as will be explained. It denotes "the emanations from Him that follow after Him"; these are also separate from matter. Knowledge of this kind is attainable, i.e., after he conceived the relationship between the Agent and His acts. When he attained this degree, i.e., when his knowledge was derived from the Agent and what effects He produced, then he comprehended the bond of His leadership in the knowledge of His ways. The conception that Mosheh attained was not attained by any man either before or after him. This was the acme of his conception. For Mosheh desired that He make His ways known to him in order that he should comprehend Him through them, but God aroused him to know Hit ways by comprehending His glory from which there emanate activities. Then he would realize that just as His essence is different from our essence so is His leadership different from our leadership.

We have departed from the subject of this chapter in order to elucidate this awe-inspiring sight. According to the order of this exposition there will be clarified the meaning of the verse, "And the LORD descended in the cloud, and he stood with Him there". (Ex. 34.5). This is the same "standing" referred to in, "And you shall stand upon the rock'" (Ex. 33.21), i.e., the conception with which he was endowed as a reply to his second request. Consequently, it states, "And the LORD proclaimed His name" (Ex. 34.5) which refers to the previously mentioned concept. And then the Glory passed by, as is stated "And the LORD passed by before him" (*Ibid.* 6), He aroused him regarding his first petition which was answered by "I will make all My goodness pass by" (Ex. 33.19). This is the knowledge of His ways, which is contained in the words "The LORD, God, merciful and gracious" (Ex. 34.6).[376]

Blessed be He, Who has taught us wondrous things from His Torah.

CHAPTER 42377

The verb *shūḇ* (to return) signifies primarily the motion of a body from a place to the place whence it came, as, "Going and returning (Gen. 8.3.). It was next employed figuratively to denote the changing of a man's notion to the notion he held previously without involving any motion whatever, e.g., "Return, O Israel, unto the LORD your God" (Hos. 14.2). The meaning is, to remove the false beliefs in order to hold the true beliefs, which they held previously. It is also applied to what is incorporeal, as, "So shall My word be that goes forth out of My mouth: it shall not return unto Me void". (Isa. 55.11). Scripture further extends the meaning of *shuvah* (returning) to include the author of a statement himself, i.e., when his word comes to pass it is as though he returned, cf., 'I will certainly return unto you when the season comes round" (Gen. 18.10). Now, we do not find that he actually returned, but when his word became a reality it is as though he returned.

In this figurative sense you will find the term *shībah* applied to the departure or appearance of God's Providence, e.g., "I will go and return to My place", (Hos. 5.15); "And I will return unto you", (Mal.3.7), i.e., My Providence will appear in order to deal well with them as in the beginning. But, in the verse, "*Shūḇāh*, O LORD, the ten thousands of the families of Israel" it is to be understood as in, "Then the LORD your God will bring back again (*we-shāḇ*) your captivity" (Deut. 30.3). Wherever you will find the verb *shūḇ* ascribed to God with the meaning of "to rest" it is to be taken as a transitive verb, lest the effects of action be attributed to Him. On the other hand, if it is employed as an intransitive verb it should be understood figuratively following our explanation as denoting the departure or appearance of Providence; not that He is a corporeal being which moves from one place to another.

CHAPTER 43³⁷⁸

The primary significations of the verbs *yārad* (he went down) and *'ālāh* (he went up) are as follows: when a body moves from a lower to a higher place *'aliyyāh* (going up) is used; and from a higher to a lower place *yerīdāh* (going down) is employed, as, "Go up to the hill country" (Hag.1.8); "We came indeed down at the first time" (Gen. 43.20). The terms *''aliyyāh* and *yerīdāh* are next employed figuratively with regard to greatness and lowness, cf., "The stranger that is within you shall get up above you very high, and you shall come down very low", (Deut. 28.43).

These terms are also applied to conceptions, i.e., when one conceives a. lowly matter he is described as "coming down and when he apprehends an elevated concept he "goes up", as it is stated, "The dissembler in heart shall have his fill from his own ways (*mid-derākhāw*);.and a good man shall be satisfied *mē'ālāw"* (Prov. 14.14). The sense is to have one's fill from lowly things is to be a dissembler in heart since lowly things are termed "ways" (*derākhīm*) by analogy, from the term *middrākh* (a treading-place), i.e., they are lower than, he. On the other hand, a good man is satisfied from what is elevated and honorable. Hence, the term *ūmē-'ālāw* (and from what is elevated) is used. Thus, one who apprehends what is elevated is termed "ascending" and he who conceives "ways" is termed "descending". For Scripture alludes to intellectual processes when it speaks of "the dissembler in heart"; and the words "elevation" and "ways" are descriptive terms for intellectual concepts.

It is in this figurative sense that we must take the, verbs ascending and descending wherever ascribed to God. When He is described as conceiving lowly things, He is termed "coming down" as it states, "And I will come down and speak" (Num. 11.17); "And the LORD came down upon mount Sinai", (Ex. 19.20). Furthermore, whenever He endows a prophet with inspiration this is termed "coming down, and when this departs it is termed "going up, "e.g., "And God went up from Avraham" (Gen. 17.22). If, in certain passages, it is possible to apply the "descending" to some object in addition to Him then it refers to the created Light[379] that manifests the might of Providence and is termed "Glory"., Hence, "The LORD descended", would indicate the might of Providence. It is possible through this Light for one to apprehend wondrous concepts respecting knowledge of the Divine.

CHAPTER 44[380]

The primary signification of the words *bī'āh* (coming in) and *yeṣī'āh* (going out) is as follows: the motion of a body from one place to another is termed *bī'āh* and its departure from that place is called *yeṣī'āh*, as, "And he was yet scarce gone out (*yāṣā*)..... that Esau his brother came in (*bā'*) from his hunting" (Gen. 27.30). These terms are also applied metaphorically to what is incorporeal, e.g., "That when your words come to pass (*yāḇō*) we may do you honor (Jud. 13.17); "For out of Zion shall go forth (*tēṣē'*) the Law" (Isa. 2.3); "Let there go forth a royal commandment", (Esther. 1.19). Again, "going in" and' coming out", are employed in a figurative sense with regard to certain subjects even though these verbs do not apply to the subjects themselves, but to their attributes, as, "And all countries came into Egypt" (Gen. 41.57); "The city that went forth a thousand" (Amos 5.3). With this metaphorical meaning *yeṣī'āh* and *bī'āh* are ascribed to God referring to something in addition to Him, as in the preceding metaphor, viz., His revelation or His appearance, e.g., "Behold, the LORD comes forth from His place" (Isa. 26.21); "And the LORD my God shall come" (Zach. 14.5), that is to say, His word or decree shall come.

CHAPTER 45[381]

The primary signification of the words *rām* (high) and *nāśō* (to lift up) is height and elevation in space as, "Raise you on high your rod" (Ex. 14.16); and in connection with the latter term, "That bore (*nōśē*) burdens". (I Kings 5.29). They are also employed to denote rank and greatness. With regard to height, cf., "But the horns of the righteous shall be on high" (Ps. 75.11); "And he was exalted with my tongue" (Ps. 66.17), this refers to the praise and laudation of His dignity and greatness. And with reference to elevation, cf., "And that He had elevated his kingdom". (2 Sam. 5.12), this applies to might and greatness, not elevation in space. The terms *rām* and *nišśā* appear to be synonymous, but they are different. The word *rām*indicates the might and greatness of His essence by itself, not by virtue of any thing else; whereas *nišśā* indicates His rank and greatness because of the acts which demonstrate His might and greatness. We shall have occasion later on to explain the relationship of these attributes.[382]

CHAPTER 46[383]

The verbs *qārōb* (to come near) and *rāḥōq* (to be far) are primarily applied to a body that draws near or moves away from another body, as, "and the one came not near the other all the night" (Ex. 14.20). "Coming near" is next used in connection with time, e.g., "The seventh year is near" (Deut. 15.9). It is also employed in the sense of imparting knowledge, comp. "You shall bring (*taqribūn*) it unto me, and I will hear it", (Deut. 1.17). In line with this figurative meaning we must understand the term "near" whenever applied to God as, "The LORD is near" (Ps. 34.19); "Through them that are near unto Me I will be sanctified" (Lev. 10.3). It refers to intellectual conception, not corporeal proximity. The opposite of what we have stated is the sense of *rāḥōq* (to be far). "And they were far from the Zidonians" (Jud. 18.7), here it signifies physical distance. In the following verses it is applied to time, "From afar the LORD appeared unto me (Jer. 31.3); "Afar off" (Ezra 3.13). It is also employed in connection with incorporeal things, e.g., "Therefore, is justice far from us" (Isa. 59.9). Finally, it is used to denote "distant with regard to knowledge", as, "but have removed their heart far from Me" (Isa. 29.13.); similarly, it states, "For lo, they that go far from You shall perish" (Ps. 73.27). In this figurative sense we must also take the verse, "The LORD is far from the wicked" (Prow. 15.29), i.e., He does not regard them. Now, whenever proximity or distance is used to describe the relationship of God to His creatures or of His creatures to God it is to be understood in an intellectual sense.

Kindred to *qārōḇ* (to come near) are the verbs *nāga'* (to touch) and *nāgōsh* (to approach) which are applied to material objects as, "Stand (*gesh*) back" (Gen. 19.9); "And she touched the top of the scepter (Esther 5.2). They are also used in connection with matters that are not corporeal concepts, e.g., "Forasmuch as this people drew near, and with their mouth" (Isa. 29.13); "And the tidings reached the king (Jon. 3.6). Similar is the explanation of "Touch the mountains, that they may smoke" (Ps. 144.5), i.e., His word touched; also "And touch his bone" (Job. 2.5), i.e., with reference to bringing a plague upon him.

The verb *sāmakh* is a homonym used primarily as in, "And he shall lay (*we-sāmakh*) his hand" (Lev. 1.4). It is next employed to signify proximity, cf., "Your wrath lies hard upon me" (Ps. 88.8). It also applies to giving strength, as, "And His righteousness it strengthened Him" (Isa. 59.16); "They are strengthened for ever and ever" (Ps. 111.8). In this sense we must under stand "The LORD supports (*sōmēkh*) all that fall" (Ps. 145.14); not as a physical support.

CHAPTER 47[384]

The accepted meaning of the noun *regel* is the foot of a living being, as, "Foot (*regel*) for foot" (Ex. 21.24). It was next applied figuratively to any object upon which something stands and this object is termed "root", e.g., the feet of the table. It is also employed metaphorically in a verbal sense to signify an action by which something is made to stand even though this action is regarded as a "foot" only with respect to the manner in which the thing stands. Thus, it states, "end I, I sustained (*tirgaltī*) Ephraim, taking them by their arms (Hos. 11.3), i.e., I have given feet to Ephraim and they stand upon them. In what way? By My taking them by their arms in order to uphold them, like an infant that is enabled to stand by holding its arms since an infant is unable to stand by itself unless it receives assistance. This is the interpretation of my teacher and uncle, H. Yehudah, may his soul find peace. The meaning of the verse, "But they know not that I healed them (*Ibid.*) is as follows: Healing can be predicated only of one who is ill, and since illness did not befall them, for they are continually assisted by Me and are thus accustomed to standing, it appears to them that this is due to their merits; hence, "They knew not that I healed them" (*Ibid.*).

In accordance with this figurative meaning we must understand the term "foot" as applied to God, not in the sense that He stands upon it, but in connection with the relationship of place. Thus, if the heaven is the throne upon which the Almighty sits and the earth is His footstool then the earth is the place of His feet,[385] i.e., His essence and greatness which are acquired by the intellect from the nature of the sublunar world are described by the term "feet: if you have understanding, you will comprehend that the universe is divided into three parts. And, in accordance with the degree of knowledge concerning His essence which each of these three divisions imparts, God's relationship to His universe is figuratively described by the upper and lower parts of" man's body.[386] If you desire to understand this, reflect upon the visions of Ezekiel concerning the divided man. Then you will comprehend the truth.

In accordance with the above, we can understand the verse, "And there was under His feet as it were a work of a stone (*libnath*) of sapphire" (Ex. 24.10). The term *libnath* in this passage does not denote "whiteness", for in that case it would have stated, "as it were an appearance" rather than "as it were a work"., It is of the same meaning as the word *lebēnīm* (bricks). In another passage we find the phrase "A stone (*eben*) of sapphire" (Ezek. 1.26); it is also stated, "And they had brick (*lebēnāh*) for stone" (Gen. 11.3).

In the opinion of Maimonides the meaning of it (*libnath*) is "transparency",[387] and transparency is not a color, although it is described by the term "white", for it receives all the colors; [388] hence it states, "as it were a work". It is comparable to matter, which removes one form and assumes another. His view, however, is not logically sound; ,for in a comparison, matter should be compared with matter, not matter with accident., On the other hand his observation that transparency receives colors just as matter receives forms one after the other is quite correct. Ibn E.zra[389] asserts that he is compelled to explain the term *libnath* as being cognate with *lebēnīm* (bricks) since the sapphire is reddish which he ascertains from the verse, "They were more reddish in body than rubies, their polishing was as of sapphire" (Lam. 4.7), hence it appears that it (the sapphire) is red. But this is not true. Rather, since the sapphire is transparent and receives all the colors and Scripture places the sapphire near rubies, which are reddish, therefore the sapphire also appears reddish. Nor can we accept the view of H. Aharon[390] that the term *lebēnāh* (brick) is in the construct state relative to the noun "sapphire"; and that the sapphire is distinct from the brick, since the firmament is compared to a sapphire. For in the nature of making comparisons one compares certain aspects of an object, whereas there it states, "as the appearance", (Ezek. 1.26), and here as., the work". (Ex. 24.10). Note this well.

This is similar to what is stated in connection with the' dream of Ya'aqov, namely, "And, behold, a ladder set upon the earth, and the top of it reached to heaven (Gen. 28.12), and after these words it states, "And, behold the LORD stood upon it". (*Ibid.* 13).[391] Reflect upon the expression "stood upon it". The essential characteristic of standing is to stand upon one's feet; and the real nature of "ladder", is expressed in the words, "as it were the work of a stone of sapphire", (Ex. 24.10), for the prepositions "under" and "upon" are correlative terms. The allusion is that they (the nobles of the children of Israel) conceived God from the nature of the sublunar world, not from a higher vantagepoint. Hence, it states, "And upon the nobles of the children of Israel He laid not His hand" (*Ibid.* 11). The noun "hand" refers to prophecy in accordance with the homonymity of the term "hand.". By means of prophecy one conceives the middle world which is comprised of the Separate Intelligences through which prophecy is communicated, and the visions of prophetic sight confirm this. For this reason Scripture states, "And they beheld God, and did eat and drink". (*Ibid.*), for their conception was merely reflective, not of a prophetic character. Their conception was not so mighty that its intellectual aspect should prevail without their inclining to perceptibles, as was the case with Mosheh Who became pure intellect as a result of his mighty conception. Thus, it states, "And Mosheh alone shall approach unto the LORD" (Ex. 24.11), this "approaching" was of an intellectual character. Consequently, he remained forty days "without having to eat bread, nor drink water" (Ex. 24.28).

The interpretation of the verse,[392] "And His feet shall stand in that day upon the Mount of Olives", (Zach. 14.4), is as follows: As a result of the wonders that will be wrought in that place there will be spread abroad in great measure the knowledge of God, which is compared to His feet in its relationship to the sublunar world.

CHAPTER 48

The verbs *pā'al* and *'āśāh* are applied, in the first instance, to work done by hand, e.g., "He makes (*yif'al*) a god" (Isa. 44.15); "And he made (*wa-ya'aś*) the table (Ex. 37.10). They are also employed in connection with matters that do not require any physical contact and in this context denote "to establish", as, "And he shall establish justice and righteousness in the land" (Jer. 23.5); "That have established His ordinance (Zeph. 2.3). In the latter, figurative sense we must take these two terms whenever ascribed to the Almighty, e.g., "Who has wrought and done it?" (Isa. 41.4).

The verb *bārā'* (to create) is free from any stain of corporeality since it succeeds privation, for it states, "I make peace and create evil" (Isa. 45.7); and similarly, "In the beginning God created" (Gen. 1.1), since this creation is *ex nihilo*.

The verb *yāṣar* (to form) is found, in its primary signification, in the expression "a maker (*yōṣēr*) of earthenware" (Jer. 19.1), this being a work done by hand. We also find it applied to things that are incorporeal, as in, "Who frames (*yōṣēr*) mischief by statute" (Ps. 94.20). The meaning of this verse is: the wicked man devises evil thoughts all day long and it is his law to do so. Evil desire is termed *yēṣer*, as it is stated, "For the inclination (*yēṣer*) of man's heart is evil from his

197

youth" (Gen. 8.21), this refers to the devising of evil thoughts. It is also applied respecting good thoughts in the verse, "The mind (*yēṣer*) stayed on You keep in perfect peace" (Isa. 26.3). It is in accordance with this figurative meaning that the verb *yāṣar* (to form) is ascribed to God. This term is also found in connection with something incorporeal, according to one explanation, in the passage, "And formed (*weyoser.*) the spirit of man within him" (tech. 12.1).

CHAPTER 49[393]

The noun *yād* (hand) is a homonymous term.
Its first meaning is found in the passage, "That one
put out a hand" (Gen. 38.28). Next, it denotes "jurisdiction" as, "Take in your hand (i.e., under your
jurisdiction) ten men";[394] similarly, "Let us fall now
into the hand of the LORD (2 Sam. 24.14). It is also
employed to signify "statement", cf., "Is the hand of
Yoav with you", i.e., his command or word; similarly,
"According to the direction of David" (2 Chron. 23.18)
Kindred to this usage is the verse, "Your hands have
framed me and fashioned me" (Job. 10.8), for in
reality the Merciful cannot be conceived as stretching
forth His hand, only His word or decree. Another
signification is "stroke", e.g., "My stroke (*yādī*) is
heavier than my groaning" (Job. 23.2); "My sore
(*yādī*) ran in the night" (Ps. 77.3). In this category
belong also the following, "Behold, the hand (i.e., the
stroke) of the LORD is" (Ex. 9.3); "Because of Your
hand" (Jer. 15.17). It is also employed in the sense of
"means" as, "This has been by your hand" (Mal. 1.9),
i.e., by your means; similarly, "Is the LORD's means
(*yād*) waxed short?" (Num. 11.23); again, "Behold, the
LORD's means is not shortened", (Isa. 59.1). And it is
used to signify "aid", cf., "Let your hand be ready to
help me" (Ps. 119.173). Finally, it means "prophetic
inspiration", e.g., "The inspiration (*yād*) of the LORD
was upon me" (Ezek. 37.1); "And the hand of the LORD

was strong upon me", (Ezek. 3.14); not that He is a corporeal being possessed of these organs.

CHAPTER 50[395]

The term *kaf* denotes the "palm" of the hand as, "I will spread forth my palms" (Ex. 9.29). Next, it signifies "cloud", e.g., "With clouds He covers the light" (Job. 36.32); comp. "Behold, a cloud as small as a man's palm" (I Kings 18.44). It is also used figuratively in connection with incorporeal things, cf., "And he led them by the skillfulness of his hands (*kapāw*)", for skillfulness is incorporeal and it states previously, "So he shepherded them according to the integrity of his heart" (*Ibid.*). It is termed *kaf* since thoughts are completed by the hands and palms. The expression "And I will cover with My palm" (Ex. 33.22) is a figurative usage of its first connotation referring to strength and aid, i.e., divine aid, which is described by the term *yād* (hand). It is also termed "palm" since the latter is round and covers on all sides. Thus, it states, "You bast laid Your palm upon me" (Ps. 139.5) since it had said "You bast hemmed me in behind and before" (*Ibid.*). Similarly, the passage, "The place of the soles (*kapōth*) of My feet" (Ezek. 43.7) alludes to the wisdom which encompasses the sublunar world which is spherical.

CHAPTER 51³⁹⁶

The noun *zerō'a* (arm) is a well-known term, e.g., "The sodden shoulder (*zerō'a*)" (Num. 6.19); "His arm shall be clean dried up" (Zach. 11.17). Now, since strength is found in the arm, cf., "And he works it with the strength of his arm" (Isa. 44.12), therefore strength is denoted by the term "arm" as, "And as a man of might (*zerō'a*), who has the earth (Job 22.8); "And the might of the flood shall be swept away (Dan. 11.22); "And the arms of the south", (*Ibid.* 15), i.e., its strength and its might. In this sense we are to understand the verse, "The eternal God is a fortress, and underneath are the everlasting arms", (Deut. 33.27), i.e., the eternal God shall be your shield and buckler, He who rides upon the highest heavens of yore; and beneath the heavens you shall have "everlasting arms", i.e., strength and might. The same applies to the expression "By the greatness of Your arm" (Ex. 15.16), i.e., by Your might; it does not mean the greatness of an arm of flesh.

CHAPTER 52[397]

The term *yāmīn* (right) is applied to a bilateral body. That side which is the honored side is termed "the right", cf., "And upon the thumb of 'his right hand" (Lev. 8.23). Now, since strength is found in the right side therefore strength is denoted by the term "right", as in, "And their right hand (*yemīnām*) is a right hand of lying" (Ps. 144.8); this refers to their strength and their might. It does not refer to the right side, since that is a corporeal object. Similarly, we must understand the verses, "Your right hand, O LORD, glorious in power", (Ex. 15.6), and "The right hand of the LORD is exalted", (Ps. 118.16).

CHAPTER 53[398]

The noun *'eṣba'* (finger) is well known. Since every act that man does is effected by means of his fingers, consequently the acts of God are described in a figurative sense as being produced by His fingers as, "When I behold Your heavens, the work of your fingers" (Ps. 8.4). But in another passage it states, "By the word of the LORD were the heavens made" (Ps. 33.6)! From this it becomes clear that the heavens were brought into existence by His word[399] and that the latter is termed "finger". Similarly, in the verse, "written with the finger of God", (Ex. 31.18), "finger" refers to the desire of God. Since the act of writing is the function of the fingers therefore the writing of the tables is associated with His finger, i.e., His will. The creation of this writing by the divine Will should not seem more extraordinary than the creation of the universe. And if we were to say that the "finger" is a certain thing ascribed to God there would be no harm. Reflect, too, on the use of *"elohim"* (*Ibid.*), which is a homonymous term, and not the word "God". For one who authorizes the doing of a certain act is as the one who actually does it. Hence, it states, "Which I have written that you may teach them" (Ex. 24.12).[400]

CHAPTER 54[401]

The three nouns *peh* (mouth), *śāfāh* (lip) and *lāshōn* (tongue) are commonly accepted as referring to physical objects. Nevertheless, since they are organs of speech the latter is referred to by these same terms, e.g., "Behold, they are one people, and one language (*śāfāh*) (Gen. 11.6); "And with joyful lips (*śifthēy*)" (Ps. 63.6). The meaning of *śāfāh* in either instance is "speech". In the verses" Whosoever he be that shall rebel against your commandment (*pīkhā*)" (Josh. 1.18), "A man of evil speech (*lāshōn*) shall not be established upon the earth" (Ps. 140.12) and "With a lying tongue (*lāshōn*) (Ps. 109.2), these terms also denote "speech". Similar to the aforementioned figurative usages are the phrases, "The commandment (*pī*) of the LORD" (Ex. 17.1), "Mouth to mouth", (Num. 12.8), "And open His lips against you" (Job 11.5), "And His tongue is as a devouring fire" (Isa. 30.27). In all these examples the terms signify "speech" or "statement".

CHAPTER 55[402]

The accepted meaning of the, verbs *'āmar* (to say) and *dibbēr* (to speak) denotes "the separation of letters by clear enunciation and proper articulation". They are also used to signify "thinking" as, "I said in my heart" (Eccles. 2.1); "I spoke with my own heart" (Eccles. 1.16.), in each instance the meaning is, "I thought". In both these senses "speech" is ascribed to God. With regard to the first meaning, however, speech is attributed to God not in the sense that it comes from Him, for speech requires a physical source and God is removed from any corporeality, but that speech is a created thing that has been brought into existence by Him and is ascribed to Him. This is the belief of the scholar H. Yosef, as will be explained in one of the chapters of this treatise.[403] It is not far fetched to believe that speech, not originating from the essence of God although created by Him, should be ascribed to Him. For we find, "And the LORD said unto Ahaz" (Isa. 7.10), and although this was said by a prophet it is attributed to God. Certainly, then, it can be attributed to Him when He creates speech by itself. The matter of speech existing *per se* without any intermediary will be explained in its proper place when we consider the question of prophecy.[404] If you desire to verify the fact that at times speech is ascribed to God in the first sense, consider the fact that at one time He is described as "saying" and at another as "speaking". The types of speaking are well known, they are: command, narration, menace, etc. The term "saying" is not employed without an object. Hence, one is correct in saying: a living being that speaks; and he is incorrect in saying: a living being that says.[405]

CHAPTER 56[406]

The noun *pānīm* (face) is a homonymous term. Its first meaning is found in the passage, "And all faces are turned into paleness". (Jer. 30.6). The accidents of the soul, namely, mercy and anger, when they produce any effect upon the soul also produce a reaction in the body, as pallor in fear and redness in shame. And when mercy or anger affect the soul the face also evinces a certain effect. For this reason anger and favor are described by the term "face", as in the verse, "And her anger (*pānehā*) was gone" (I Sam. 1.18)., In the same sense it is employed in the verse, "The anger (*penēy*) of the LORD is against them that do evil" (Ps. 34.17). Similarly, respecting mercy, cf., "Cause Your face to shine upon Your servant" (Ps. 80.20);[407] "The LORD lift up His countenance". (Num. 6.26). Another signification of the word is "existence", e.g., "And in the presence (*penēy*) of all the people I will be glorified" (Lev. 10.3); "In the presence of Aharon their father" (Num. 3.4). With the same meaning it is used in the verse, "You shall have no other gods before Me (*pānāy*)" (Ex. 20.3); the meaning is: You shall not join any other god to My existence. Similarly, the words "But My face shall not be seen" (Ex. 33.23) refer to "the true nature of My existence", when He was petitioned, "Show me, I pray You, Your glory" (*Ibid.* 18).[408] Since one man recognizes another by the latter's face therefore the true nature of His existence is described by the term "face".

Similarly, in the verse, "And the LORD spoke unto Mosheh face to face". (*Ibid.* 11), it means Existence to existence without any intermediate between them, although His face was not seen.

The Hebrew term *'āḥōr* is a homonym signifying "back", e.g., "Behind (*'āḥarēy*) the tabernacle"
(Num. 3.23) It is also an adverb of time; cf., "after
(*'āḥarēy*) these things" (Gen. 48.1). For "before" and
"after" are the reality of time.[410] This term is also used
in connection with the pursuit acrd the profession of
faith. Comp. "You shall walk after (*'āḥarēy*) the LORD,
your God", (Deut. 13.5), "And they shall not walk after
the stubbornness of their own evil heart, and after the
Ba'alim which they taught them" (Jer. 9.13).

The word as employed in the passage, "You
shall see My back" (Ex. 33.23) denotes those existent
beings which were created by Me first.[411] "But My face
shall not be seen" (*Ibid.*) refers to the true nature of
My existence; the front is prior in rank and existence,
and that which is made always comes after its maker.
For this reason Scripture states, "And you shall see
My back" (*Ibid.*). This constitutes the highest conception that the human intellect is able to attain. Merely a
little higher than that is the relationship of the Agent
to the act which is alluded to in the verse, "I will put
you in a cleft of the rock" (*Ibid.* 22) as is explained in
connection with the homonymity of the term
"rock".[412] Regarding, this conception, however,
Scripture asserts, "And I will cover you with My hand"
(*Ibid.*)[413]

CHAPTER 58[414]

The noun *lēḇ* (heart) is a homonymous term with meanings of a figurative character. It denotes in the first place "the corporeal heart".

And since the heart is the seat of wisdom the latter is termed "heart", cf., "Your word have I laid up in my heart" (Ps. 119.11); "Consider it in your heart" (Deut. 4.39j. The expression, "In my innermost parts" (Ps. 40.9), signifies "in my heart", for the heart is one part of the inner organs, as it states, "The yearnings of Your heart (innermost parts)" (Isa. 63.15); "My heart moans within me" (Jer. 4.19). Another signification of this term is "will", e.g., "Is your heart (i.e., will) right' (2 Kings 10.15). Similarly, we find, "According to that which is in My heart and in My mind" (I Sam. 2.35); "And I shall give you shepherds according to My heart", i.e., according to My will.

Next, it denotes "thought" as in, "Whose heart (i.e., though) turns away" (Deut. 29.18) It also signifies "counsel", cf., "All Israel was of one heart (i.e., counsel)" (I Chron. 12.38). Finally, since the heart is the primary component of the body and from it there originate all the faculties, accordingly all these faculties are described by the term "heart". In a figurative sense the qualities of the heart such as joy, grief and similar emotions are applied to God; comp. "And it grieved Him at His heart" (Geri. 6.6.); "Let the LORD rejoice in His works (Ps. 104.31).

CHAPTER 59[415]

The verb *yālad* is a homonym signifying in the first instance "to bear". e.g., "The woman with child and her that bears (*yōledeth*) together", (Jer. 31.8); "Behold, you are with child and shall bear a son" (Gen. 16.11). This verb is next employed in connection with coming to be and origination, as in, "Before the mountains were brought forth (*yullādū*) (Ps. 90.2). And since time "brings forth" events the latter are termed "children", cf., "What a day may bring forth (*yēled*) (Prov. 27.1). Thoughts and ideas are also termed "children", as it is stated, "And they please themselves with the brood (*yaldēy*) of strangers", i.e., with the learning of strangers. It is for this reason that the disciples of the prophets are called "sons of the prophets", by virtue of their learning. In this sense we must also understand the passage, "And he begot a son in his own likeness, in his form", i.e., Adam taught him (Seth) and he followed his direction. For if this referred to the physical form of man, did Adam not previously beget Cain and Abel? And it is impossible to conceive that they were not endowed with the physical form of man. Rather, the term "form" denotes "the intellectual soul", which is the perfection of man.

In keeping with the second meaning (i.e., bringing forth) we must take the verse, "Of the Rock that begot you were unmindful", (Deut. 32.18), i.e., you forgot the cause that brought you forth from nothingness and instructed you in the perfection of man by the giving of the Torah.

CHAPTER 60[416]

The noun *kānāf* {wing) is a homonym. In its first signification it is employed in the verse, "Any winged (*kānāf*) creature", (Prov. 1.17). This term is next applied figuratively to denote "extremity", e.g., "upon the four-corners (*kanfoth*) of the vesture" (Deut. 22.12); "That it might take hold of the ends (*kanfōth*) of the earth", (Job 38.13). It is also used as a metaphor to signify "spreading", comp. "With healing in its wings". (Mal. 3.20), i.e., by the spreading of its light; "And because of the spreading of detestable things" (Dan. 9.27). Another signification is "concealment", as in, "Yet shall not your Teacher be concealed any more" (Isa. 30.20). In this sense we must also understand the verses, "To take refuge under His wings". (Ruth 2.12); "And under His wings shall you take refuge" (Ps. 91.4), i.e., under His protection and concealment. Or we may take them as instances of its first meaning in a figurative sense, i.e., since divine Providence covers like a wing, His covering is described figuratively by the term "wing".

CHAPTER 61⁴¹⁷

The term *menūḥāh* (rest) is a homonym having three figurative meanings. It is first applied to the resting of an object in space, e.g., "in the quiet resting-places (*menūḥōth*)". (Isa. 32.18). It also signifies resting after fatigue, as in, "3 am weary with my groaning, and I find no rest" (Jer. 45.3). Finally, it denotes "to cease", as in, "They spoke to Nabal according to all those words in the name of David, and ceased (*way-yānūḥū*)", (I Sam. 25.9). It does not indicate here that they had been weary, nor had they spoken so much as to become fatigued; for the utterance of two or three statements could not have produced such pain that the term *way-yānūḥū* would refer to resting from pain. Therefore, it denotes "ceasing to speak". In this third sense we must understand the verse, "And He rested (*way-yānaḥ*) on the seventh day", (Ex. 20.11), i.e., He ceased to utter the Word whence there issued forth His acts.

The same applies to the verb *shābath* (to cease) in the verse, "And He ceased (*way-yishbōth*) on the seventh day", (Gen. 2.2), i.e., He ceased to speak; for fatigue cannot be predicated of Him since the universe was created by His word. We also find this verb in connection with speaking, e.g., "And the three friends of Job ceased to answer (*way-yishbethū*)' (Job 32.1).

CHAPTER 62[418]

The word ṣūr (rock) is a homonym. It is applied to a certain kind of stone, as in the verse, "And the rocks are broken asunder before Him" (Nah. 1.6). Now, since rock is strong it is also employed figuratively in connection with what is strong, e.g., "knives of flint (ṣūrim)" (Josh. 5.2); "Then Zipporah took a flint" (Ex. 4.25). With the meaning of "strength" it is also ascribed in a figurative sense to God in the verse, "The God who is my Rock (ṣūrī), in Him I take refuge", (II Sam. 22.3). And since rock is the origin of the composites, viz., minerals, plants, animals and humans, when Scripture desires to explain one thing as the source of another it compares that which is the source to a rock. Thus, it states, "Look unto the rock whence you were hewn" (Isa. 51.1) and then it continues; "Look unto Avraham your father", (*Ibid.* 2).

It is in this sense that the term "Rock" is ascribed to God, i.e., as the origin whence all existents have come into being, as it is stated, "He is the Rock, His work is perfect" (Deut. 32.4); "Of the Rock that begot you are unmindful" (Deut. 32.18); "The Rock of Eternity" (Isa. 26.4); "There is no Rock like our God" (I Sam. 2.2). This means that He is the principle that has brought into being all that exists and He does all that He desires; He makes poor and He makes rich; and He causes the barren woman to beget abundant offspring. It is to this matter that the following passage alludes, "And you shall stand upon the rock" (Ex. 33.21), i.e., you shall attain a conception of the origin whence all this existence is derived. The latter is alluded to in the words, "Behold, there is a place by Me" (*Ibid.*).[419]

CHAPTER 63[420]

The term *mālē'* denotes, in the first instance, that one body enters another and fills it, e.g., "Fill four jars with water" (I Kings 18.34). Next, it is applied to the completion of a period of time as, "For my days are completed" (Gen. 29.21). It is also associated with the idea of perfection, cf., "Them has He perfected (*millē'*) with wisdom of heart" (Ex. 35.35). In the latter sense we must understand the verses, "The whole earth is full of His glory" (Isa. 6.3); "And all the earth shall be filled with the glory of the LORD" (Num. 14.21), i.e., the world is perfected by His existence for He provides the world with sufficiency. With reference to the verse, "And the glory of the LORD filled the tabernacle", if we say that it refers to the "created light"[421] which indicates the might of God's providence, this would be correct.

The noun *kābōd* (glory) is a homonym. It is applied to the essence of God in, "Blessed be the glory of God from His place" (Ezek. 3.12). It is inconceivable that it refers here to some created thing; for how could one possibly worship any creature, which is something other than the essence of God! Similarly, when it states, "And it shall come to pass, while My glory passes by" (Ex. 33.22), it refers to His essence. For it states afterwards, "until I have passed by" (*Ibid.*). This term is also applied to the "created light" which God causes to dwell within a certain place in order to exalt

219

it as, "And the glory of the LORD abode" (Ex. 24.16); "And the glory of the LORD filled the tabernacle (Ex. 40.34). In the verse, "The whole earth is full of His glory"" (Isa 6.3) it refers to the dissemination of His providence throughout the sub-lunar world. The term "glory" also denotes "the glorification" which is employed by one who praises, e.g., "Give glory (i.e., glorification) to the LORD your God" (Jer. 13.16.); "And in His temple all say, "Glory" (Ps. 29.9). And now, since there is a certain extraordinary aspect respecting the homonymity of this term, listen to words of wisdom.

It is necessary to comprehend that the entirety of existence, that is, the three divisions of existence, are interrelated. Consequently, divine Providence extends to every individual thing of this world, from its units to its classes. For He perceived with His wisdom that His Providence should apprehend all the works of His hands. And he established the universe in proper fashion so that no other establishment is better than this, in accordance with the perception of His wisdom. Thus, it states, "The LORD by wisdom founded the earth; by understanding He established the heavens", (Prov. 3.19). And for this reason Scripture states, "And God saw every thing that He had made, and, behold, it was very good", (Gen. 1.31). Through this establishment of the universe His Providence is bound up with high and low, even with the lowliest of things. Hence, His glory fills the world. And this is the reality of His Providence forever.

The prophets have called attention to the form of existence as it is bound up with Providence; cf., this entire matter as referred to in the account of the Chariot:[422] the *ōfannīm* and their work, the *kēruvīm* and their appearance, their faces and their wings, the firmament that was above them, above the firmament the likeness of a throne, and above the likeness of the throne a likeness as the appearance of a man divided (Ezek. Chap. 1). In this order are included the three divisions of existence.[423]

Now, when the Almighty desired to distinguish the people of Israel by means of a special measure of Providence, He established them in a manner corresponding to the universe as a whole, cf., "His majesty is over Israel, and His strength is in the skies" (Ps. 68.35), to the end that they shall be distinguished by an extraordinary Providence. Thus, Israel is composed of twelve tribes, which constitute four standards corresponding to the four faces of the chariot.[424] Similarly, the tribe of Levi is divided into four family-groups. The four standards thus correspond to the four living creatures (ḥayyōth) each of which possesses four faces, so as to be similar to the Chariot. Similarly, the arrangement of the Tabernacle, the Ark with its kērūvīm, the Table, the Candlestick and the Altars contain extraordinary allusions respecting the order of the mighty universe for him who will investigate.[425] Comp. "You throne of glory, on high from the beginning, You place of our sanctuary" (Jer. 17.12); this refers to His glory which abides amongst the people of Israel to care for them with respect to both good and evil dispensations, as it is stated, "You hope of Israel, the LORD! All that forsake You shall be ashamed" (Ibid.13). Likewise, there are great wonders associated with the arrangement of the vestments of the High Priest.[426] For it was not commanded that they be made in this particular manner merely by chance, God forbid! Anyone ignorant of this fact may be likened to a herbivorous creature. It is for this reason that

Mosheh placed upon these vestments the Urim and the Thumim so that he who wears them and directs his heart heavenward will be imbued with a spirit of understanding, he will comprehend the highest knowledge and foretell things to come; the service below being like the service above. All this is due to the fact that the mighty Providence of the people of Israel has prepared them and established them after the fashion of the order of the universe, this Providence continuously extending over them. This is the glory that dwells among the children of Israel. Consequently, you will find the reference to the man described as sitting upon the throne alluded to in the words "This was the appearance of the likeness, of the glory of the LORD", (Ezek: 1.28), and concerning the glory, which he saw in the plain, it is stated; "as the glory which I saw by the river Chebar!' (*Ibid.* 3.23). And when Ezekiel was brought to the temple in a prophetic vision it is stated, "And, behold, the glory of the LORD was there, according to the vision that I saw in the plain" (Ezek. 8.4). It states also, "And the glory of the LORD mounted up from the *kērūv* to the threshold of the house", (Ezek. 10.4). And the sages assert that this is one of the *kērūvīm* which Solomon had made; for the Ark had been concealed at the time when the scroll of the Torah was found in the Temple, cf., "I have found the book of the Law in the house of the LORD"! (II Kings 22.8). Hence, the glory abode upon the *kērūv* of Solomon. Samuel ibn Tibbon, however, refers the words "up from the *kērūv*" to the statement, "And I knew that they were *kērūvīm*" (Ezek. 10.20). And "the threshold of the house" is an allusion to the universe concerning which it states, "He is trusted in all My house" (Num. 12.7). The threshold alludes to the intermediates between the middle and sub-lunar worlds corporeal angel that is imperceptible to the eyes. For since Scripture ascribes to it motion and limitation within the confines of space and these are qualities of corporeality it is impossible that it should allude to God. And while the glory dwelt in the Sanctuary, it states, "Then hear You in heaven Your dwelling-place" (I Kings 8.39); "And Mine eyes and My heart shall be there perpetually" (*Ibid.* 9.3).[428] Maimonides teaches that it does not allude to God, but is a created object associated with God, who is above the whole chariot.[429] For it is described by the words, "From the appearance of his loins and upward; and from the appearance of his loins and downward" (Ezek. 1.27), but God is incomparable and beyond description; on the contrary, it refers to the divided figure of a man whose upper part alludes to the kind of angel that does not speak with man, that is called *Ḥashmal* and is enclosed by fire round about; and whose second part is a kind of angel called *'Ēsh* having brightness round about it, that does speak with man. Samuel ibn Tibbon includes God in that part which is likened to *Ḥashmal*, although in the visions of Isaiah it distinguishes Him from the angels, as it states, "I saw the LORD sitting upon a throne high and lifted up, and His train filled the temple. Above Him stood the *seraphīm*" (Isa. 6.1, 2). Thus, the prophet separates them from God. How is it possible, then, that He be included under the name *Ḥashmal*, so that the latter indicates God, and *'Ēsh* includes both the angels that speak with man and those that do not? It is inadmissible that God be described by the words "from the appearance of his loins and upward" which include many different organs.

But this matter still appears difficult. How does the Prophet refrain from alluding to God when his desire is to authenticate Providence and to indicate that all the works that have come to be are dependent upon Him? Furthermore, the dream of Ya'aqov, the vision of Isaiah and the account of Ezekiel are all three of one nature, namely, to ascribe all the works that come into existence to the Almighty even though their genesis is effected by intermediaries. Thus, Ya'aqov mentions God and remains silent regarding the kinds of intermediaries; Isaiah mentions God and explains the kinds of intermediaries by general allusions. Ezekiel, however, presents an exhaustive clarification of the kinds of intermediaries, as I shall explain. How, then, can he omit an indication of the existence of the Prime Agent?

Now, the account of Ezekiel with regard to the divine Chariot follows. The prophet beheld "a stormy wind coming out of the north, a great cloud" (Ezek. 1.4), as it is stated, "Out of the north the evil shall break forth" (Jer. 1.14). This was a reference to the domination of the ignorant peoples. He also beheld in a vision that all this was in accord with the divine Will. For Israel had denied the existence of God and hence was obliged to suffer an evil dispensation, as it is stated, "With a fire flashing up, so that a brightness was round about it; and out of the midst thereof as the color of electrum, out of the midst of the fire" (Ezek. 1.4). All these are symbols of God and His angels. From this vision he comprehended general Providence, as it is stated, "And out of the midst thereof came the likeness of four living creatures" (*Ibid.* 5). This is an allusion to the middle world. Following after them are the four *ōfannīm* "for the spirit of the living creature was in the *ōfannīm*, as it is stated "when they mounted up, these mounted up" (Ezek. 10.17); "And when those were lifted up from the earth, the *ōfannīm* were lifted up beside them" (*Ibid.* 1.21). All

224

this indicates the might of the ignorant nations through the might of God. It is this that the prophet reveals in the words "And over the heads of the living creatures there was the likeness of a firmament, like the color of the terrible ice And above the firmament was the likeness of a throne; and upon the likeness of the throne was a likeness as the appearance of a man... from his loins and upward there was as the color of electrum and from his loins and downward there was a likeness of fire and a brightness was round about him" (Ezek. 1.2228). And then he states, "This was the appearance of the likeness of the glory of the LORD" (*Ibid.* 28). This then is the glory that appeared to the prophet at the time of the departure of the glory. And the import of the dwelling and departure of the glory is the appearance of Providence and its going away through His angels; not that motion or limitation is applied to Him, God forbid! That the acts of the Almighty are put into effect by His angels is stated in the verses, "For He shall give His angels charge over you" (Ps. 91.11); "And the LORD my God shall come, and all the holy ones (angels) with you" (Zach. 14.5). Thus, the prophet has shown that Providence returned to its place so that its influence is bound up with the lower things by means of intermediaries. And, for this reason, the ignorant nations became sufficiently mighty to prevail over Israel. The former are the four kingdoms which are identical with the four chariots which Zachariah saw when he exclaimed, "And again I lifted up mine eyes, and saw, and behold, there came four chariots out from between the two mountains; and the mountains were mountains of brass" (Zach. 6.1). Similarly, it states, "Blessed be the glory of the. LORD from His place" (Ezek. 3.12), corresponding to the verse, "And one called unto another, and said: Holy, holy, holy" (Isa.

6.3). Likewise, the passage, "And the house was filled with smoke" (*Ibid.* 4) is similar to "And, behold a stormy wind, a great cloud" (Ezek. 1.4). Hence, the prophet was appalled at this vision; cf., "and I went in bitterness, in the heat of my spirit And I remained there appalled seven days (Ezek. 3.14, 15), so that in the second vision he explains how the glory departed from the Chariot designated for Israel to the Chariot of the universe.

What our father Ya'aqov beheld in his dream, however, purported to indicate the superiority of the Land of Israel in that there is a special Providence for the Land of Israel, as it is stated, "How full of awe is this place! This is none other than the house of God", (Gen.'28.17); "And he called the name of that place Adonai-yireh (i.e., the LORD seeth)", (Gen. 22.14). All this is because He promised the patriarchs to give this Land to Israel. Hence, it desire's to explain their excellence, namely, that although the Almighty abides in the highest of heights nevertheless His Providence is upon the earth and is especially concerned with the Land of Israel. Here there was built the eternal Temple, which indicates the might of His Providence when it states, "And Mine eyes and My heart shall be there perpetually", (I Kings 9.3); "The eyes of the LORD your God are always upon it" (Deut. 11.12); "Awful is God out of your holy places" (Ps. 68.36).

The vision of Isaiah, on the other hand, indicates that the wrath of the LORD was kindled against Israel because of the wickedness of their deeds after the death of Uzziah, and the ways of Ahaz are well known and when God desired to punish them He punished them only by means of tyrannical nations to whom He gave success. For this reason the prophet desired to describe God as "sitting upon a throne high and lifted up and His train filled the temple", (Isa. 6.1). The meaning of *seraphīm* is "intermediaries". These called one to another, "Holy, holy, holy" (*Ibid.* 3). The passage, "And the posts of the door were moved at the voice of them that called", (*Ibid.* 4) alludes to the middle world, and the words, "And the house was filled with smoke" (*Ibid.*) alludes to the lower world. This is the meaning of "The whole earth is full of His glory" (*Ibid.* 3); "For God is judge; He puts down one, and lifts up another" (Ps. 75.8). As a result of this the prophet exclaimed and said, "Woe is me! for I am undone" (Isa. 6.5). For he beheld in a prophetic vision the retribution that was destined to come and because of it he refrained from rebuking them. This is the prevention of repentance, as it is stated, "Make the heart of this people fat" (*Ibid.* 10). Then God aided him and there came upon him a prophetic inspiration, cf., Then flew unto me one of the *seraphīm*", (*Ibid.* 6). Thus, the chapter continues until he does rebuke them. "Then the prophet, out of great astonishment over the vision and the severity of this dispensation, exclaimed "O Lord, how long?" (*Ibid.* 11). And he was answered, "Until cities be waste without inhabitant, and houses without man, and the land become utterly waste (*Ibid.*). All this came about because of the departure of the Providence which was especially designated for Israel and its return to the universal Providence, so that there should overtake them every evil retribution from the strength of the nations of the world, which are the share allotted to the constellations, as it is stated, "Which the Lord your God has allotted unto all the peoples under the whole heaven" (Deut. 4.19). Despite all this, however, He promised them, "Although I have removed them far off among the nations, and although I have scattered them among the countries, yet have I been to them as a little sanctuary... (Ezek. 11.16). This is because of His Providence over them that He should not destroy them completely; but He shall save them at the time when the ignorant nations will conspire to bring harm to Israel. This is the meaning of the verse, "And yet for all that, when they are in the land of their enemies, I will not reject them, neither will I abhor them, to destroy them utterly... (Lev. 26.44).

Now, after the departure of the glory, the people of Israel remained under the supervision of the middle powers, as it states, "And there is none that holds with me against these, except Michael your prince" (Dan.10.21), and it states further, "And at that time shall Michael stand up, the great prince", (Dan. 12.1). Similarly, it states, "Lo, the prince of Greece shall come", (Dan. 10.20); "But the prince of the kingdom of Persia withstood me", (*Ibid.* 13). For at that time God's Providence will not be mighty over Israel, and hence you will find God described as the "Lord of hosts" until the return of the glory, that is, the mighty Providence respecting which it states, "And, behold, the glory of the God of Israel shall come from the way of the east" ((Ezek. 43.2); "Now, let them put away their harlotry, and the carcasses of their kings, far from Me, and I will dwell in the midst of them forever" (*Ibid.* 9). It is utterly conceivable that it (the glory) should refer to a created object. Some suggest various interpretations for the meaning of the term *bārūkh* [in the verse, '*Bārūkh* the glory of the Lord from His place",] but these are not derived from its plain meaning. On the contrary, wherever Scripture mentions the dwelling of the glory or its departure it refers to His Providence. Indeed, His Providence is described from the viewpoint of the various organs of man, his upper and lower parts. Consequently, since the man's sitting upon the throne with his loins, and that which extends from the height of the concavity of the throne until the center of the earth, all these constitute works of God which indicate the might of His power therefore his appearance is "the appearance of fire, and there was brightness round about him". (Ezek. 1.27), because of the majestic splendor of His Providence over them. Knowledge of Him is acquired by means of these by those who can comprehend. This is the meaning of "And you shall see My back" (Ex. 33.23). But, "from the appearance of his loins and upward!' it was "as the color of electrum (*ḥashmal*), as the appearance of fire round about enclosing it", (Ezek. 1.27), the true nature of which is inconceivable. This is the meaning of "but My face shall not be seen", (Ex. 33.23). It is termed *ḥashmal* because even those who stand in His presence refrain from telling (*ḥāshīm mile-mallēl*) the true nature of His essence since this conception is withheld from the human intellect. The allegories of prophecy are familiar. The words, "The whole earth is full of His glory (Isa. 6.3) refer to His Providence, which extends over the sub-lunar world. The terms awakening, rising, visiting, and remembering are employed in a figurative sense in connection with the extension of Providence; and the terms sleeping and repentance for the departure of Providence. All this refers to the effect upon the receiver; not that there is any change in His essence. For it states, "And also the Glory of Israel will not lie nor repent" (I Sam. 15.29); "For I the LORD change not", (Mal. 3.6). Maimonides asserts that we do not find in Scripture the term "sleep ascribed to God, but H. Mosheh, my teacher and father-in-law, cites the verse, "Awake, why sleep You, O LORD? Arouse Thyself" (Ps. 44.24). We have already explained the metaphorical use of the terms "awakening" and sleeping; when Providence extends it is termed "awakening" and when it departs it is described as "sleeping". But there is no change in the essence of God in that at one time He supervises and at another He does not. Change takes place only in the recipients of His supervision, but He is far from corporeality and the qualities of corporeality. He is One and truly unique and He undergoes no manner of change whatsoever, praised and exalted be His name, because of His true perfection.

All that we have explained in connection with the removal of certain meanings of terms from God is true beyond doubt. In explaining the intended meaning of these nouns and verbs, however, we have followed as closely as possible one of the three methods[430] which we provided in the preceding chapters; either that of the absolute homonym, or the metaphor, or the addition of a word in order to expound that passage to the end that no contradiction will arise to what has been demonstrated by the intellect.

CHAPTER 64[431]

Now, that it has been demonstrated to us by forceful proofs that God exists and that He is neither corporeal nor a power residing within a body it behooves us to establish the proof for the unity of God. You must know that the term "one" is applied to many things, nevertheless our investigation in this place will confine itself to three principles:

FIRST, that God is one simple essence, that He is not composed of parts, and that His essence is indivisible. **SECOND**, to believe that God's unity is in truth unique and that the true nature of His essence exists in none other than He. **THIRD**, to believe that God alone is a necessary existent and that no being other than He is a necessary existent. We must demonstrate the truth of these three principles by proof resulting from rational investigation.

That He is a necessary existent has already been made clear and established by forceful proof to which no one can object:[432] And the fact of His being a necessary existent demonstrates that His essence is not composed of parts. For the composition present in a particular object is the cause of the existence of that object. Hence, its parts *per se* are possible existents and consequently the necessity of its existence is only by virtue of its composition and the latter is the cause of its existence. But any object the existence of which is due to a cause is *per se* a possible existent whereas we are considering an essence that is a necessary existent that has no cause for its existence. The form of this proof is then as follows: God is a necessary existent, No necessary existent is composite, Therefore, God is not composite. In any case, we must remove from Him anything that leads to composition.

It is also inadmissible that His essence is potentially divisible; for it is inconceivable to predicate potentiality of a necessary existent. Furthermore, division is found only in bodies and that which is not a body is divided when the body, which is its substratum, is divided. But, since it has been made clear by forceful proofs that God is neither a body nor a power residing within a body, no division can be conceived in Him.

It is further impossible that there is a second to Him. For the concept of a necessary existent has led us to believe in an essence without composition respecting which we have denied all imperfection and have affirmed every perfection. Now, if we believe in a second deity then he must also be a necessary existent and all that we believe regarding the first must also apply to the second. And if they are identical essences, how can we conceive their being divided so that number is applied to them, seeing that their essence is free from corporeality. Consequently, it is inadmissible that although their natures are identical there should not be in the essence of each one an added element by means of which one is distinguished from the other. Thus, each would be possessed of two elements. But this we deny, for it is inconceivable that in a necessary existent there be the possibility of composition, nor can there be any plurality in its essence. Even if one were distinguished from the other by some element added to its essence the result would be that one is a necessary existent since it is not composite and the other, distinguished by an added element, since it is composite, is a possible existent. For since they ire included under the species of divinity it is necessary to distinguish between them. For every species is divided into individuals and in each individual there is a feature by means of which one is recognized and distinguished from the other. Consequently, that element through which one is recognized and distinguished from the other together with the element of divinity constitutes two elements.

FIRST ARGUMENT FOR THE UNITY OF GOD: It is known that from the nature of the universe we have comprehended the existence of God. Now, if we were to find division in the acts (i.e., in the nature of the universe) we would understand the existence of as many agents as there are separate acts. But, since all existence may be likened to one man, in that each part is closely joined to the other, and the forces on high extend over the lower beings, how is it possible that each act should have a separate agent for itself? Furthermore, since they would be identical with respect to their divinity they would produce identical acts. Hence, the one agent would be identical with the other.

ANOTHER ARGUMENT FOR UNITY:[433] If there were two deities, we should have four possibilities: (a) either both act simultaneously, (b) or the one deity is active at one time, the other at another time, (c) or that one engages in one activity and the other in another activity, (d) or that one deity is active while the other desists. It is inadmissible that they both act simultaneously. For this alternative may have two reasons: Either the act can be accomplished only by both since one alone is not able to accomplish this act, or one alone is able to accomplish the act and the other is superfluous. Now, neither of these reasons is acceptable. For if the act cannot be accomplished save by both it follows that each of them is defective in that he has need of the other, whereas an independently necessary existent must be of consummate perfection. And, since they are both of identical essence, it is proper that the acts of both be of one kind. Now, it is inadmissible to assert that the inability of the one to complete the act and his requiring the cooperation of the other signify the utter impossibility of the first to complete the entire act, and, hence, we could not ascribe any imperfection to the latter, since the intrinsically impossible does not imply any imperfection, as the impossibility of combining two opposites in one substrate. For, since this inability applies to the one, and they are both of the same essence, it should properly apply to the other also. This could not be described as an impossibility, but as an imperfection since the impossibility does not derive from the act, but from the agent. For what is absolutely impossible cannot at any time whatsoever become an actuality, either by one agent or by another. And, since this act is possible of accomplishment by both, but is impossible for one, this perforce implies imperfection—which is inconceivable in the nature of a necessary existent. It is also inadmissible to assert that the act can be effected by the one and that the other is superfluous For if the nature of this act finds it sufficient to demonstrate the existence of one agent what evidence is there to indicate the existence of a second? We believe only in what has been ascertained by an investigation of the nature of things.

It is also impossible that the one acts at one time and the other at another. For this possibility can have only two alternatives: either it is possible for this act to originate from the one at all times, or it is impossible. It is inconceivable that this act is an intrinsic impossibility, for since both are of identical essence then at the moment that the act originates from the one it is proper that it should originate from the other. Hence, the act is possible, and if so it is proper that the act should originate from the other at any one time, as well as at another. And since the one deity acts at one moment, not at another, and all moments are identical to him, although he is not confined by time,[434] there must be some cause which constrains the one deity to act at one time and the other at another. But it has previously been made clear that the Eternal is not subject to cause.[435] Furthermore, since both are of identical essence the cause of either must be the same at all times, and at the time that it constrains one it should constrain the other; for there is no superiority in the one over the other at any particular moment. Consequently, it is inadmissible that the cause should act at one time, not at another, and hence both deities must act simultaneously. But this has already been refuted.

Again, it is impossible that the one deity act upon one thing and the other upon another thing. For they are both of identical essence in respect of divinity and if they are divided in their acts there must be a cause in addition to each one for this division of acts. But it has already been demonstrated that the Eternal is not subject to cause. And if there be no cause for each for the division of their acts seeing that they are identical in respect of divinity it is evident that the acting of the one is the same as the acting of the other.

Finally, it is impossible that one deity acts and the other desists. For we have comprehended the existence of God only as a result of acts, but if he does not act how can his existence be ascertained. Besides, this possibility would be inconceivable without a cause that compelled the one to act and the other to desist. But the Eternal is not subject to cause.

ANOTHER ARGUMENT FOR UNITY: Our sages have pointed out the possibility of the occurrence of cancellation.[436] That is, if there were two deities and one desired that a body be at rest while the other desired that it be in motion—a body must perforce be either at rest or in motion—the desire of both could not take place, only the desire of one of the two. Consequently, when the desire of one and not the other takes place, then the one whose desire did not take place is defective.[437] Nor can it be objected that both deities will desire with the same will either that the object be at rest or in motion since they are both wise. This is no objection at all. For we are considering the possibility of such an occurrence, namely, if one desired the opposite of what the other did this cancellation would occur between them and this would indicate a weakness in one of them. Consequently, it has been demonstrated by all the foregoing proofs that God is one and unique as a necessary existent; that there is no second god beside Him; and that His essence is indivisible, as has been taught to us by proofs which lead[438] to truth.

CHAPTER 65[439]

Even as intellectual proofs have demonstrated the unity of God, so do the words of our prophets bear witness to His unity. Cf., "Hear, O Israel: The LORD our God, the LORD is one" (Deut. 6.4); "There is none like unto You, O LORD; You are great, and Your name is great in might", (Jer. 10.6). "You, O LORD, are alone" (Isa. 37.20); "20 whom then will you liken God" (Isa. 40.25); "To whom then will yet liken Me, and make Me equal" (Isa. 46.5), and other passages similar to these. These verses have not been adduced as proof for His unity because we are in doubt regarding knowledge of His unity as derived from intellectual reasoning, since His unity has already been made clear to us by apodeictic proof through rational speculation.[440] For the verses which indicate His unity are not more than those pointing to plurality. Rather these verses are to serve as evidence of His unity for him whose intelligence is incapable of comprehending His unity through ratiocination. He must be supported by the word of the prophet.

How pleasant are the words of the scholar H. Yosef HaMaor[441] when he asserts that one who is enjoined to believe may dispense with rational evidence that He is living, that He perceives and that there is none beside Him but it is impossible for the enjoined, lest his knowledge be weak, to comprehend that the LORD is God, Omnipotent and Omniscient.

The significance of his words is: If one who has been enjoined neglects the pursuit of investigation and relies upon prophetic utterances to as certain that He is One, and to determine other facts similar to those he mentions there is no harm in this; because there is no necessity to obtain a knowledge of these prior to belief in the prophets. On the other hand, with regard to the latter two attributes, viz., Omnipotent and Omniscient, it is impossible for one to be lax in rational investigation and rely upon prophecy. For the knowledge of God is prior to the belief in prophecy and we cannot ascertain the knowledge of God through these two attributes, namely, Omnipotent and Omniscient. How, then, is it possible to obtain knowledge of them from the prophets? The meaning is not that because this scholar perceived the weakness inherent in the proofs derived from intellectual investigation which demonstrate His unity, therefore, he relied upon the statements of the prophets. For when he states, "one who is enjoined may dispense with" it does not signify that he will perceive the weakness of intellectual proof; rather because of the weakness of his own intellect or as a result of his laxity in examining the proofs he relies upon the prophets. For if this scholar intended to say that because of the keen intellect of the investigator the proofs are weak, why does he call attention to what is even weaker than the latter, i.e., the statements of the prophets? How is this possible, seeing that the above mentioned scholar has clearly demonstrated the unity of God by intellectual proof? Could this outstanding scholar be ignorant of the difference between opinions based upon weak knowledge and opinions founded on firm knowledge! The view of this scholar can only be as I have expounded it, because there is no necessity to comprehend the denial of a second deity beside Him prior to believing the words of prophecy. And if the enjoined will rely upon prophecy for the fact that there is no second deity beside Him there can be no harm in this. This is not so, however, with regard to knowledge of His essence; for knowledge of His essence is prior to belief in the, prophets, although from the knowledge of His essence, one can ascertain His unity.[442]

Regarding the statement of the scholar H. Aharon to the effect that H. Yosef did not declare Scriptural statement to be evidence for His unity, the opposite appears to be true.[443] In reality, the view of H. Yosef is that even as rational proofs demonstrate the unity of God so do the statements of the prophets; both serve as evidence for His unity. Of course, you are aware of the superiority of intellectual proof over that obtained from tradition, and it is impossible for one to forsake the intellectual and to grasp the traditional.[444] The aforementioned scholar called attention to tradition only for one whose intellect did not enable him to succeed in ascertaining His unity by intellectual means. He must rely upon tradition and there is no harm in this.

My teacher and father-in-law, the scholar H. Mosheh, has offered a beautiful interpretation, cast in the mold of H. Yosef HaMaor's view, of the verse, "Hear, O Israel". He asserts that the verb shāmaʿ (to hear) is found to have various meanings. We find it to signify the hearing of a report, e.g., "And the report thereof was heard (nishmaʿ) in Pharaoh's house" (Gen. 45.16). We also find that it denotes "to assemble", as in, "Call together (hashmīʿū) the archers against Babylon", (Jar. 50.29). Again, it is found to signify "acceptance", e.g., "And they shall accept (we-shāmeʿū) your words". (Ex. 3.18). Next we find that it means, "to understand", as in, "Give Your servant therefore an understanding (*shōmēʻa*) heart" (I Kings 3.9). Finally, it denotes "guardianship", cf., "And David set him over his guard (*mishmaʼtō*)" (II Sam. 23.23) The proper interpretation of this term in this particular context includes the meanings, "acceptance on authority" and "understanding". And because the nation of Israel contains two classes of persons: those who are fit for understanding, and those who are fit for tradition, the term *shemaʼ* includes both sign dictations. Thus, one who is fit to comprehend the unity of God by intellectual proof shall learn it by intellectual proof and one who is fit to ascertain His unity by tradition shall learn it by tradition.

CHAPTER 66[445]

In connection with the removal of plurality from the essence of God it is to be noted that just as it happened with regard to the removal of corporeality because of Scriptural passages which stand opposed to the intellect so it happened with regard to the removal of plurality because of the literal sense of Scripture. And not only because of the literal sense of Scripture has this happened, but also because of the human intellect this error has taken place. The reason for this is as follows: When people beheld many different actions proceeding from God they ascribed to Him a multiplicity of elements in relation to His acts. It is this that led to the ascription of attributes to God.[446] That which we find among the utterances of the prophets we shall have occasion to elucidate in a separate chapter when treating of providence.[447]

Now, the attributes that the intellect dictates as necessary and through which God is known are the following: Omnipotent, Omniscient, Living, Acting with Will, Existent. Our knowledge of these is obtained in the following manner: When we see a person doing an act we ascribe to him the attribute "able". Similarly, when we comprehend that God created the universe we describe Him as Omnipotent. And when we see a person doing an act correctly we ascribe to him "the attribute "knowing". Hence, when we perceive that God has made a perfect universe, we describe Him as Omniscient. Likewise, we see a person doing a thing in one way instead of another and we term him "willing". So when we behold that God executes acts in one particular way rather than another we describe Him as Acting with Will. When we realized that these three attributes, viz., Omnipotent, Omniscient, Acting with Will, cannot exist save in an essence that is alive, and we found them in His essence, we speak of Him as Living.[448] Again, when we comprehended that only what is in existence can properly be described by attributes, and we found that God is described by attributes we call Him, Existent. These are the attributes in which our intellect constrains us to believe as constituting the essence of God, and it appears that there is a plurality of elements in His essence. But the necessity of His existence forces us to believe that God is a simple essence without composition, and not possessed of a plurality of elements. Thus, we have arrived at two narrow passages and it behooves us to ascertain the path that will lead to the truth.

CHAPTER 67[449]

Although the concept of necessary existence has led us to believe in one simple Essence, we conceive Him in manifold ways of different aspects. This is due to the fact that His acts, through which we conceive Him, are different from one another. Besides, since perfection includes many elements and we desire that this Essence be of consummate perfection, we had no method of attributing perfection to Him seeing that He is a simple Essence. Hence, we characterized Him by many predicates to the end that we shall conceive Him in consummate perfection despite His being a simple essence.

We have now before us three alternatives: either we believe that there are elements in Him in addition to His essence, or that His essence is composed of many parts, or that His essence is one simple entity from which there axe seen to proceed many forces although He is one essence and we do not believe that there is a plurality of elements in His essence. The first alternative, viz., that there are additions to His essence, signifies that God is living through life, Omniscient through knowledge, Omnipotent through power, Acting with Will through a will and Existent through existerice.[450] This is inadmissible; for these attributes must perforce be either eternal or created. Now, if each of these is eternal then that which reasoning has led us to believe regarding the category of eternity of a particular one we must also believe concerning the eternity of the other. Thus, as we conceive God with these attributes so must the Omnipotence added to His essence be conceived as eternal, possessing these attributes since the principle of eternity abides in it. Hence, this Omnipotence would possess Omnipotence, Omniscience, Will, Life and Existence. The same would also apply to knowledge. But, if the knowledge of Omnipotence suffices for Him, what need has He of other knowledge. It is improper to believe in such a theory as this. We have mentioned this view because, if the concept of necessary existence leads us to believe certain facts to be true about one essence then we must believe the same regarding any other essence that is a necessary existent. Furthermore, if there is a plurality of elements added to His essence not one of these would be perfect *Per se*. But reason demands that one who is a necessary existent should be perfect *per se*. Now, if we assume that it is the combination of these elements that must needs be perfect it follows that the Eternal is caused, for the combination is the cause of His existence. Besides, while these causes are existent in Him He is perfect, whence it also follows that He is caused. But the Eternal is not subject to cause. Again, it would be necessary for these elements to reside in something and this residing cannot take place save in a substrate. But God is not substance that is the subject of accidents. It has also been made clear in the section on unity that what is composite in its essence is not a necessary existent *per se*; for composition is the cause of its existence and that which has a cause for its existence is not a necessary existent *per se*. But we are seeking an essence that is a necessary existent *per se*. On the other hand, it is inadmissible that these added elements are created. For if they were created they would require a creator and this creator would need ability and knowledge in order to create them. And if in this instance these elements are also created they would require another creator who could not create anything unless he possessed ability and knowledge, and thus it would continue *ad infinitum*. But infinite regress is impossible.

The second alternative, viz., that there are many elements in His essence so that His essence is composed of many things different from each other and still He is a necessary existent, is impossible. For the composition of an aggregate is the cause of the existence of the aggregate. Each of its parts *per se*, however, is a possible existent. But we are seeking an essence that is not caused, an entity in whose essence there is no possibility whatsoever. Then it will be a necessary existent.

The third alternative, viz., that God is one, a simple essence without composition and without a plurality of elements, as reasoning has compelled us to believe, is our true conviction. For the one essence may be described in many ways in accordance with different relationships, but not because of the latter must there be ascribed to Him a plurality of elements. On the contrary, He is one simple Essence comparable to the human intellect that conceives many things that are different and contradictory and yet it is one faculty. And we do not assert that because it conceives these many variegated things therefore it is composed of a multiplicity of elements. Similarly, fire melts, hardens, blackens, bleaches, burns and warms, and all these acts are wrought by one quality not by many elements. Thus, God is one Essence to which is ascribed many aspects of perfection in accordance with the relationship of those acts which proceed from His essence. Consequently, we believe that Omniscience, Omnipotence, Life, Will and Existence are He; they constitute His essence, and His essence is identical with them, i.e., one simple essence without composition. Now, we have not conceived His essence by our intellects so that we should differentiate in our conceptions the omniscient essence from the omnipotent essence and the living essence in order to ascertain their quiddity. It is only through the relationship of His acts that we have justified the words of our language in our intellects in order to teach the true nature of His existence. We compared His acts with our acts and we ascribed the names of those forces that execute our acts to God when He produces these same acts. But there is no real comparison between ourselves and Him, nor can one category include both. Rather by virtue of His acts we call Him Omnipotent and by virtue of the perfection of His work we describe Him as Omniscient. The same applies to the attributes: Living, Acting with Will and Existent, not that we have conceived His essence.

How esteemed is the expression of our sages, peace be on them, when they describe these attributes as "essential" attributes, that is, they are His essence and His essence is identical with them. They are not elements separate from His essence. Our sages do not mean that if they are the same as His essence then each of the attributes is a different essence, i.e., the essence of Omnipotence is distinct from the essence of Life. How can this be their view seeing that they themselves asserted that if omnipotence is an element added to His essence they would reduce it to either the category of the eternal or that of the created. And they have established the proof that it is not an element added to His essence, but is identical with His essence, as has been explained. The same holds true if the essence of Omnipotence is different from the essence of Omniscience, namely, each of these essences will be reduced either to the category of the eternal or that of the created. And proof will be established that He is not composed of many essences just as it has been ruled out that there be elements added to His essence. Thus, it is clear that their opinion is not to classify the attributes as qualities, but to consider them essential attributes that are identical with His essence, i.e., God is one simple essence, there are no elements added to His essence and His essence is not composed of many essences. That is, His essence is one and simple even though there are, perforce, many aspects of perfection in His essence. This is tie perfect faith in which there take pride the assembly of Monotheists, scholars of truth.

CHAPTER 68[451]

I now desire to present an easier clarification of the truth of the fact that these elements which are conceived in His essence are one entity. You are aware of what has been explained in connection with the homonymity of the term ḥay (animal), viz., that the accepted meaning of the noun ḥay is "a nutritive, sentient body". It is due to the addition of the sentient quality over the nutritive that it is termed ḥay.[452] The essential characteristic of sentience is perception yet the essence of life (ḥayyīm) is not something separate from this perception; for "animal" is a concept and its divisions are: nutritive and sentient. Now, if the lowest of perceptions, i.e., sensation, is termed "living", then the true intellect which conceives authentic conceptions should certainly be termed "living". Would it then enter any one's mind that the intellect is possessed of a life that is something distinct from its essence? Thus, it has been made clear that we do not speak of "Living as an entity separate from the essence of "Omniscient". With regard to Will, you realize that among the essential characteristics of intellect is just action, and just action is Will. Hence, it is clear that intellect and will are one. Similarly, the attribute "Omnipotent" is not different from the essence of perception for the essential nature of an intellectual act is perception and every act indicates that its agent has the power to perform the act. Thus, it becomes evident that the essence of perception is identical with

248

"Omnipotence". The fact that He exists not through existence as an attribute, but His essence is identical with His existence is well known. For everything whose existence is conceived as distinct from its essence has a cause for it's existence, from which it follows that whatever has no cause for its existence has no existence distinct from its essence. It has now been made clear from this extraordinary and recondite explanation that He is identical with Omnipotence, Life, Existence, Will and Omniscience. These constitute one simple essence without composition. It might appear at first thought that God is described by the attributes Omnipotence, Omniscience and Will with respect to extraneous things such as indicate His power, knowledge and will, whereas the attributes Life and Existence describe His essence, and thus there appears to be a difference between the various attributes But the fact will not appear so after minute investigation. For it is necessary to examine the essence of that force *per se* and perforce all the attributes will be included in His essence for they are one essence without composition.

CHAPTER 69

With reference to all that we have explained in connection with attributes, one should not think that we have inclined to an overreaching passion in order to maintain certain views, from which we desired to remove all objections, and we have thus imposed upon our intellect abstruse opinions that are properly incredible, for he would misconstrue our endeavors in this respect. Rather, it is incumbent upon a person to see, investigate, and examine the truth by itself. He should not impose his notions upon us and decree *a priori* that our opinions are objectionable. In the chapter following this, there will appear explanations, respecting the differences of opinion with regard to attributive appellations, through which you will arrive at the truth. Your soul will find peace in our refutations and arguments which will remove every objection and every difficulty, and will bring to light the pretenses of several of those who claim that we are in error, and will indicate how they themselves are found to be in error. For what is objectionable to our views is likewise objectionable to theirs from the viewpoint of argumentation. Nor will their justification be of any avail to them since it is only an utterance of the lips, not the result of speculative investigation.

CHAPTER 70[453]

The opinions of scholars respecting the designation of names to God can be classified into three divisions. The first category consists of those who refuse to subsume God under the category of language and describe Him by no other term than the Cause. For they believe in the eternity of the universe and that the universe owes its existence to Him as its Cause, that God is a Cause and the universe has resulted from cause. I have already shown previously, however, that the universe is created.[454] The reason which renders it impossible to bring God under the category of language is that all existents perceptible to us are included under substance, and the nine categories, and all terms of language conform to one of these ten categories. However, our intellect has demonstrated that God is none of these ten even though He is included in the category of substance. Hence, what term could properly be applied to Him seeing that we have no accepted terms save those included in the ten categories? We shall now present their arguments.

FIRST ARGUMENT: Since it is known to us that all terms are accepted as denoting one of the ten categories, i.e., substance and nine accidents, and God is distinct from these ten categories in that He is absolutely unique it follows that if we describe Him by a certain term, even though we designate Him exclusively by this term, nevertheless we associate Him with other connotations of this same term and He would not be truly unique; for we would thus subject Him to comparison which we have endeavored to avoid.

SECOND ARGUMENT: Since we comprehend not His essence, but merely the fact of His existence, how can we subsume Him under the category of language and assert that He is the opposite of any quality? If we do assert that He is the opposite of a quality it would indicate His essence, whereas the conception of His essence is concealed from the eyes of our intellect.

THIRD ARGUMENT: Any term by which we might describe Him would necessarily be one of two kinds: either this term would include His essence, or it would designate a certain part of the essence in question. It is impossible to assume that this term includes His essence since there would be many terms indicating things of various essences and hence it would be impossible for this particular term to include all their meanings. On the other hand, if it were to indicate a part of the essence in question it would follow that His essence is composed of several elements and is not truly one, whereas we desire absolute unity.

FOURTH ARGUMENT: Every attribute indicates a subject and predicate and is distinct from the object that it describes. Hence, He would be composed of two elements of different essence, viz., subject and predicate, whereas we desire absolute unity.

FIFTH ARGUMENT: Every attribute indicates an element superadded to substance, this element being an accident borne upon it (substance), and accidents are always borne upon bodies. But God is not a body that bears accidents by which He might be described.

The second division consists of those Scholars who describe God by negative attributes, saying: He is not ignorant; He is not feeble and employing similar terms that negate deficiencies. It appears to them that with this approach they will not be affected by the preceding arguments. And when they found that the literal sense of Scripture did not follow the method of negative attributes, but that of positive attributes, their intellects constrained them to assert that these terms are not intended as positive attributes save where the term is the quality of an action or they serve to negate any defect in Him. In other words, we describe Him as knowing only in order to deny that He is ignorant; we designate Him as Omnipotent only to negate any weakness with respect to Him. Hence, these terms are employed in a negative sense, not as positive attributes. The same applies to our describing Him as: Living, Acting with Will, Existent, First and One. These words are merely uttered in self-justification, however, and the truth will become clear subsequently in the following chapter.

The third division is the view of our own sages, may they rest in peace, who have truly elucidated by pure reason the propriety of ascribing names to God. They have adduced rational proofs fox this and have refuted every argument, every objection, and every deception that was charged by the preceding views. Following are the proofs adduced by the true scholars to demonstrate the propriety of ascribing names to God, exalted be He.

FIRST PROOF: The great and outstanding scholar H. Yeshu'ah, may his soul rest in peace, made the following statement: Know that the same reason that leads us to ascribe names to beings other than He also applies to Him. And were we to assert that it behooves us to attribute names to Him more so than to other beings it would be quite correct. For God is not visible to the eye, nor is He perceived by any other sense. Hence, we could not allude to Him by any one of our organs and we have no other way of making known to others His essence and His nature save by means of language. This is the gist of the words of this eminently praiseworthy scholar.[455a] He also asserts: It should be added that it behooves us [to attribute names to Him more so than to other beings because we are required][455b] to substantiate proofs with regard to Him, etc.

SECOND PROOF: Since it is generally agreed to employ certain terms for certain relationships, e.g., when we see an act proceeding from a man we describe him as "able"; and when we perceive an act issuing from God we also describe Him as "Able", this analogy is associated merely with the acting, not with the essence of the agent. For we have not perceived Him nor have we apprehended Him so that we might make Him subject to comparison.[456] It is only by virtue of the occurrence of the act that we describe both agents by the term "able", regardless of the manner in which each acts, seeing that their essences are different from each other.

THIRD PROOF: Since we find that God applies names to Himself and it is proper for Him to ascribe names to Himself it is likewise proper for us; for the ascription of names either by Him or by us is for the same purpose, namely, to make known to others His will by the ascription of a particular name. If the ascription of names were to be withheld from us it would also be withheld from Him without distinction, as has been truly proved by H. Yeshu'ah's discussion of the propriety of divine attributes in his book "On Forbidden Marriages". He argues there against those who claim that God's knowledge is greater than that of others regarding the application of names. He contends that the purpose of ascribing attributes is merely to make known His will and with respect to making His will known there is no distinction between Him and us. Since then the ascription of divine attributes is proper for Him it is also proper for us.

CHAPTER 71[457]

In this chapter we must show that just as the first view imposes objections upon us, so it is proper to impose these same objections upon the advocates of the second view. Even though the followers of the second view appear to justify themselves, holding that these objections do not affect them, their justification will avail them nothing. They assert, in connection with God's unity, that it is preferable to describe it by a negative attribute rather than by a positive attribute, even though either one designates His unity, e.g., if you see a man from a distance, and upon inquiring of someone what it is, you are told it is neither a plant nor a mineral. This is more correct than if he were to say that it is a living being; for this would describe it and indicate a part of the generalization that is sought.[458] Thus, a negative attribute designates an object by that which it negates, whereas, a positive attribute associates with that object other things [that are included] in that attribute.

We shall explain, nevertheless, that whether we accept negative attributes or positive attributes in both instances the resulting connotation will be the same. Besides, just as the positive attribute cannot escape from association so the negative attribute cannot escape from association, for negation begets affirmation. Thus, when they assert that it is not a plant, nor a mineral, it must necessarily be a living being. For the species in existence are four in number: mineral, plant, animal, human, and animals include human beings. Hence, by negating plant and mineral there remains the animal species. Likewise when they assert that He is neither feeble, nor ignorant they perforce affirm that He is Omnipotent and Omniscient. This is necessarily so especially since these statements are negations and affirmations; there is no third alternative between a negation and an affirmation as there is between two positive assertions. As an illustration, when we say Re'uven is in Jerusalem or in Egypt it is possible that he is neither in Jerusalem nor in Egypt, but in Hebron. On the other hand, when we say Reuven is in Jerusalem or he is not in Jerusalem, there is no alternative other than these two. In the science of logic a difference is made between the two negative terms *'ayin* and *lō*; the term *lō* affirms something, but the term *'ayin* does not affirm. We need not concern ourselves, however, with this distinction in this context.

Again, they contend that the negation that we employ is not as though we were to say regarding Reuven, he does not see. For it is in his nature that he sees. Rather it is the negation of a certain quality of a thing which does not naturally possess this quality, e.g., we say regarding a stone, it does not see, for sight is not found in a stone. They have gone to such an extent in order to escape from positive assertions. Now, when they say regarding a stone, it does not see, one can negate its opposite and say, it is not blind. But when they say of God, He is not ignorant, they cannot also say, He is not omniscient. For they, themselves, have asserted that He is identical with Omnipotence, Omniscience, Life, etc.

Furthermore, it is more decorous to employ positive attributes than negative attributes, especially in view of prophetic utterances that describe Him with positive attributes such as Omnipotent and Omniscient. But they cunningly answer that we describe Him thus in order to negate feebleness o r ignorance from Him. It follows from this that when we negate feebleness and ignorance from Him there will remain omnipotence and omniscience. But, even if a positive quality is not evident from a negative attribute, it is conceived in the ideas of the intellect, and of primary significance is the rational idea, not the word. ,for the word follows after the rational idea, not the rational idea after the word. Words are not natural things that do not depart from their natures; they are conventional phenomena, and convention follows after ideas of the intellect which turns the meaning of words into whatever direction it pleases.

I have presented you here with a key by means of which you can open many closed doors. Let it remain ever engraved upon your mind in connection with anything that I shall explain with regard to attributes. With it you will untie many knots. And now that we have indicated the identity of those who accept negative attributes and those who accept positive attributes with respect to the objections urged against us by the first view, let us turn to the refutation of these views.

CHAPTER 72[459]

The first objection has affirmed that the conception of His essence is concealed from the eyes of our intellect, but if we describe Him by an attribute and assert that he is its negation it follows that His essence is conceivable to our intellect. For the ascription of an attribute perforce has one of two meanings: either by this attribute we apprehend His essence *per se*, or apart of His essence. Now, it is inadmissible that by this attribute we should apprehend His essence *per se* because He is possessed of other attributes different from this attribute and it is false to assume that the latter includes them all. On the other hand, if we assert that we apprehend a part of His essence it follows that His essence is composite, one part being conceivable, and the other not. But this we have denied since His essence cannot be composite.

Our reply would be that in reality the conception of His essence is concealed from the eyes of, our intellect and we comprehend merely the fact of His existence. Nevertheless, in whatever manner we have conceived the fact of His existence through His acts we have described His existence in. conformance with His relationship to these acts. Thus, when we perceived that He executed an act we described Him as Omnipotent and Omniscient and through these attributes we comprehended His existence. Now, in applying to Him the appellations Omnipotent and

Omniscient, which are essential attributes, we know only the fact of their existence, but the conception of their essence is concealed from the eyes of our intellect. In reply to the assertion that an attribute encompasses His entire essence, or a part of His essence which would indicate that He is composite, it has already been ahown⁴⁶⁰ that one essence can execute various acts and yet this essence will be described in accordance with its relationship to each particular act. Plurality and composition would be involved in this essence if one act were to indicate something that the other did not indicate. This matter will be further clarified in our reply to the fourth objection, through the words of the scholar H. Yosef, as to what should constitute our true belief regarding this.

In reply to the objection which asserts that [the ascription of attributes subjects God] to comparison it can be answered that if it was our intention in describing one of us as able and God as able to include them under one category it would be incorrect and convey the idea of comparison. How could it possibly be our intention to include them under one category when we believe that in respect of God these are essential attributes which do not require a substrate while in connection with other beings they are descriptions of causes and these causes are accidents which are borne by these beings; how could one category include both so as to subject God to comparison? It follows then that our ascription of the terms "able" and "knowing" to God and to beings other than He is an instance of absolute homonymity where the homonymity is in the term exclusively, not in its signification; and hence these terms could not possibly be comparable in meaning.

How worthy are the words of the scholar H. Yeshu'ah who asserts that appellations are of two kinds: the first of these is a broad general term, the name of a thing, which includes substance and accident and there is nothing at all that is not included under the name of a thing; our sages term this "the name of no advantage"; the second division indicates a category or a part of a category. The appellations of God, he continues, are not of the second division for the latter indicate belonging to a particular classification; for if the appellations of God were of this kind it would subject God to comparison. Rather, they are of the first kind, i.e., the name of a thing, which includes variegated and contradictory things. And if we describe Him by one appellation it would not, bring several things under comparison; on the contrary, this one appellation would include things of variegated essence. Thus, we have also refuted this objection conclusively.

If anyone among our own people objects to the ascription of attributes as bringing God into comparison it should be noted that the prophets themselves who applied attributes to God declared Him to be incomparable, cf., "To whom will you compare God" (Isa. 46.5.), and similar passages. Now, if attributes were to lead to comparison the words of the prophets would be contradictory, which is utterly impossible.

The third objection affirms that a plurality of appellations indicates the existence of elements of different essence from which it follows that His essence is composed of many elements and that He is not truly unique: Our reply is that in truth a plurality of appellations implies a plurality of elements. Yet although we grant this, the fundamental doctrine of our faith becomes Clear, viz., that all these appellations point to one essence that is simple and not-composite.[461] But, since God is comprehended through His acts and all of the latter are of different types, we designate Him by many characteristics in relation to His acts. Despite all this, speculation has compelled us to believe that He is one simple essence. The fact that one force executes different acts has already been demonatrated.[462]

How extraordinary is the statement of H. Yosef in connection with this very reply when he states:[463] Know that an author's meaning must be known and understood, then his words, will be understood correctly. For he must employ words and in doing so he might be led to an inexact term. My opponent should have considered the intention of my words and then he would not have inclined his heart to the destruction of my words in their superficial meaning. Thus, you should have from him inquiring: Is God's attribute of Omniscience identical with Him or is it other than He, and his attribute of Omnipotence, is it the same as His Omniscience or is it other than this? My opponent should have discussed the matter with me fully.....

The gist of H. Yosef's statement is as follows: Is the essence of the attribute of Omniscience identical with the essence of God? And is the essence of the attribute of Omnipotence the same as the essence of the attribute of Omniscience, or not? If we were to concede the last it would be incorrect: On the contrary, the foundation of our belief is that all the attributes constitute one essence. The real intention of this scholar is to justify his position, i.e., that even if our words appear similar to those of the Kalabiya[464] the ideas are not the same. For the Kalabiya teach that there are elements in addition to and different from His essence, but we do not believe so. For this reason the scholar asserts that one should not attack us on the basis of words. Rather it is incumbent upon a person to see, to investigate and to examine the rational notions regarding the foundation of our faith since it is particularly difficult for one to express in words the nature of our faith which is implanted in the notions of the intellect. For that which is conceived b y the intellect is most recondite and a conception cannot be similar to a word. There is no remedy for this save to facilitate the approach of word to thought as closely as possible.

In reply to the two objections, the fourth and the fifth–the objection which asserts that attributes imply a substratum and what is borne upon it, and the objection which contends that an attribute is a kind of quality and the latter is an accident which requires a body as a substrate–our answer is that the accepted terms employed as names of God are not in conformance with conventional usage. It would behoove the objector to reflect upon the term "essential" by which we describe attributes; the signification of this term denotes the "essentiality" of attributes.

Nouns are of five kinds: The first kind is a noun by which one merely recognizes an essence, e.g., Reuven, Shimon, redness, and whiteness. The second is a noun that maintains the existence of an essence, as plant, animal, human. The third is that which is maintained by means of the essence, i.e., an accident. The latter is of four types: The first is an accident associated with matter because of its quantity, e.g., length, and shortness. The second is associated with matter because of form, as cold, heat, appearance, and taste. The third is associated with form, e.g., opinions and traits of character. The fourth is an accident. associated with form by virtue of the latter's union with matter, such are the five senses. Some of these accidents are related to quantity, others to quality. Then there are nouns of relationship such as father and son. And finally there are verbal nouns, e.g., a builder, a writer. Of all these kinds of nouns we refer only to the first and last, in speaking of the names of God since they do not imply any plurality or composition in His essence.

You must know that because of this matter the scholar H. Yosef opposed [the Kalabiya] and termed them (i.e., the names of God) "appellatives", rather than attributes so that our belief should not appear similar to the belief of the Kalabiya. For when this sect calls them attributes it believes them to be added elements. Hence, our scholar fled from this name and changed the term, calling them appellatives, lest his belief appear similar to their belief, i.e., the belief that they are added elements. On the contrary, when he speaks of an essential appellative, it is as though he termed it an essential name; and when we say, He knows in His essence it is as though we said, blackness in its essence, i.e., it indicates only the essence of blackness not an additional element, and whenever the essence changes the name also changes. Hence, when we say, He is able or He knows it is as though we said, He is identical with ability or He is identical with knowledge; the meaning is not, He and His ability, pie and His knowledge. Our desire in employing these terms is to use simpler language for the knowledge of God.

H. Yosef has made the following statement:[465] God is to be distinguished from those that have no ability and no knowledge since it has been established that He is Omnipotent and Omniscient. And because we know and comprehend the distinction with respect to the qualities mentioned we have extended these terms and have spoken of other distinctions that are known and understood as "appellatives", applying this name to them. He states further: Were we to speak to our opponent in the matter of attributes, were we to make them known to him and make him comprehend what we mean and what we refer to in this matter he would be unable to utter anything regarding this save what we ourselves have uttered and with the words that we have employed or similar ones. Reflect now, you investigator, can there remain any complaints in this regard after the words of this man? And it is not more objectionable to speak of God as Omnipotent, which indicates two things—namely, He and His Omniscience—than to speak of Omnipotence and Omniscience, which also indicate two things. This is all the more so when it is explained that these are essential attributes, which do not indicate the existence of any additional element, save the essence

Thus, we have refuted the objection that asserts that essential attributes of God indicate a substratum and what is borne upon it. And by the refutation of this it is also refuted that that which is borne is an accident requiring a body as its substrate. In fine, you must understand that our ascription of these appellations to God follows their accepted meaning in accordance with the notions of our intellect, not in accordance with the conventional meaning of these terms.

H. Aharon the Elder, may his soul find peace, has straightened this path by explaining the inadmissibility of attributes conceived in accordance with the accepted meanings of terms. He states I do not present this matter in order to destroy the words of our sages, of blessed memory. For they have asserted that His attributes are essential. They are neither eternal nor created, but constitute His essence. Their purpose was to straighten our thoughts so that we shall not be in doubt in this regard. It was not their intention to ascribe qualities in addition to His essence. They were merely unable to find the exact words to describe their ideas, but their meaning is known. This is the essence of this scholar's words.[466]

CHAPTER 73[467]

In this chapter we must consider the following matter which I shall recount. Our sages call the divine appellations "essential attributes", and describe the name *yod hē waw hē* as the "essential name", i.e., the name which indicates the Divine Being. For the meaning of this name is "the Existence" since the signification of "to be" is identical, with "to exist", and the Existence is the essence of God. They have denied, however, that His name is identical with His essence, as the scholar H. Yeshu'ah asserts: Know that the divine name is not to be identified with that which it describes, for the name is a matter of expression, which cannot properly be applied to that which it describes. Glory and its opposite should be ascribed to God, but since the divine name has become almost like that which it describes, i.e., the Divine Being, Scripture ascribes glory and its opposite to the former. Hence, it states, "To fear the name" (Deut. 5.26); "So that you profane the name" (Lev. 19.12). What we derive then from the preceding statement is that His name is different from His essence. In support of this contention is the passage, "You are great, and Your name is great in might" (Jer., 1.0.6); since it states, "great" twice. From the statements of the renowned scholar Maimonides, however, it appears that His name is the same as His essence and His essence the same as His name. H. Aharon the Elder also maintains this view when he states that His name is He, and He is His name.[468] It appears from the contents of these divergent statements that the views of these two groups are different. But it is not so, as will be known after reflection. In reality, their opinions are identical relative to the fundamentals of our faith, as I shall explain. The difference between these two groups is to be found in the following matter, which I shall clarify. And you, reader, direct your heart and you will comprehend the truth.

The scholar (i.e., Maimonides) asserted that 'shim (name) is a homonymous term having three sigaificationa.[469] It refers to the letters uttered by tee's lips which allude to that which is described by them. It also applies to His essence, as in the passage, "They shall say to me: What is His name? What shall I say unto them?" (Ex. 3.14) i.e., What is His essence? Finally, it stands for "His word", e.g., "'For My name is in him" (Ex. 23.21). Now, when he states that the term "name" applies to His essence he refers to the meaning [of the term "name"] which explains the matter of His essence; and this meaning is explained by the name, hence this meaning is termed "name", which is identical with His essence. Maimonides does not refer here to the spoken letters; that, they constitute the essence of God, as it has entered the thoughts of those who did not comprehend the real signification of these words and believed that these scholars (i.e., those in accord with Maimonides) referred to the letters. Indeed some people thought that in saying, His name is identical with Him, it means that the letters *shin* and *mem* are the essence of God; others thought that they mean the letters of the Tetragrammaton are the essence. Finally, they presumed to offer refutations that even the least intelligent recognized as absurd. What these scholars really intended to express in speaking of the Name is the meaning of the Name, which is identical with the essence of God, not the letters shin and mem nor the letters *yod hē waw hē*. Now, the correct meaning of the letters of the Tetragrammaton is to be identified with God's essence and it is to this that they refer when saying: He is His name. This is the accepted view of our sages in this matter and they need not depart therefrom. Nevertheless, the grounds for their view in rejecting this assertion (that He is His Name) are based upon a definition of terms. It is their opinion that the accepted meaning of the term "name" refers only to its letters that are pronounced, not to its meaning. Hence, if we assert that His name is identical with Him it follows that the letters are the essence of God, which we do not believe. It should rather be affirmed that the *meaning* of His name is His essence, and His essence is the *meaning* of His name. Thus, the differing viewpoints of these two groups are based on their disagreement with regard to the term "name". One group asserts that the term "name" is applied both to its letters that are pronounced and to the meaning that the name indicates. In this latter sense they are correct in stating: His name is identical with His essence. Our sages, on the other hand, contend that the term "name" does not apply to its meaning, but to its letters alone. According–to this view it cannot be asserted that his name is identical with His essence. It should rather be asserted that the meaning of His name is the same as His essence. In this instance our sages are more correct in that their language is more specific. If you consider this carefully you will comprehend that the meaning of the Divine name which indicates His essence is identical with what they describe by the expression "essential attribute". Note this.

Now, the error which arises as a result of adding a name to Him which indicates the existence of two elements and implies that He is not unique is the same error as when we assert that He is Omnipotent; for this is an attribute which indicates the existence of a substratum and what is borne upon it, and implies that lie is not truly unique. Consequently, just as it was insufficient for us to assert merely that He is Omnipotent—lest we be in error—until we added "through His essence" and explained that by searing. He is Omnipotent. It does not indicate a substrate and its object, but that He is truly unique. Likewise, it was insufficient for them to speak of His name—lest they err by the ascription of an element to His Essence—without stating that His Name is identical with His essence, thus explaining that He is truly unique.

The Philosopher (Aristotle) states that identity can be predicated of substance and of accidents.[470] We shall consider here only the identity which is predicated of substance, i.e., which is predicated of all that is described by the term "one". For things that are fundamentally one in number or in form can be considered identical; the same applies to things that have one form. Identity is predicated of that which has two names, e.g., Ya'aqov is identical with Israel. It also applies to a name and its definition, e.g., a human being is a rational animal. What is other than the first cannot be identical with it. Now, when we assert here that His name is He and He is identical with His name we mean it in the same sense as Ya'aqov is identical with Israel. One should not object against the necessary error that derives from the inadequacy of language. But despite this one should endeavor to simplify his language so as to approach the concept of unity to the best of his ability. Such a one approaches God, praised be He.

CHAPTER 74[471]

The Divine name consisting of the letters *yod hē wow hē* is called by the sages: the Tetragrammaton. This is the name of God's essence; it is the most elevated of all the appellations ascribed to God, and is described by the sages as the name applied exclusively to God. Thus, they say respecting the passage, "This is My name" (Ex. 3.15), that it means: This is the name that is peculiar to Me. For this reason it is called *shēm ham-mefōrāsh*, i.e., this name is distinguished and set apart (*mefōrāsh*) exclusively for God.. Similarly, it is termed the Name of Worship, as it is written, "For then I will turn to the peoples a pure language, that they may all call upon the name of the LORD, to worship Him with one consent" (Zeph. 3.9).

You must know that the term *ḥāyāh* (to be) is an intransitive verb that is sufficient for itself and does not depart from itself (i.e., it does not pass over to an object) so as to require the addition of an explanatory word. Now, all the names of God are derived from His acts; e.g., He is called *shadday* (the Almighty) since He directs the opposition of the stars, as is stated in connection with Avraham, "I am God Almighty" (Gin. 17.1). Likewise the name *'elōhīm* (God) denotes "judgeship". The Tetragrammaton, on the other hard, is not derived from any activity, rather it indicates existence; and His existence is identical with His essence. There is no doubt that the patriarchs were cognizant of this name, as is attested by Scripture. When at states, "I appeared unto Avraham" (Ex. 6.3) it means: 1 appeared unto them as an Agent that is fittingly described by the name God Aımighty, but I did not appear unto them as an Agent that is fittingly described by the Tetragrammaton. Nevertheless, they (the patriarchs) were aware of this name. Hence, it follows that this name has a double signification; it indicates the existence of God and it indicates that He brings acts into being. The first signification was known to the patriarchs, namely, that it is a name that indicates the existence of God. But they were unaware of the second signification, i.e., that God brings acts into being. It is with regard to the latter signification that Scripture states, "But by my name *yod hē wow hē* I made Me not known to them" (*Ibid.*).

When Mosheh states, "Behold, when I come unto the children of Israel,... and they shall say to me: What is His name? what shall I say unto them? (Ex. 3,13) he is referring to the second signification by which God was not known to the patriarchs.[472] The verse means: they will say to me: By virtue of what power have you come to deliver us from Egypt? For in accordance with its power a name is determined, and hence he framed their question around God's name. Otherwise, what advantage could they derive from requesting His name. For if they knew it by tradition, then their knowledge of the divine name would be the same as that of Mosheh; and if they did not know it by tradition what proof had they that this was really the name of God? They would have been required to ask another, question, viz., What proof is there that this is really His name? In truth, what is fitting for us to believe is that they were subjected to slavery by a mighty king and here Mosheh, who had fled, was returning alone merely with his staff to deliver Israel from Egypt. Therefore, Mosheh held that the matter must be considered carefully for the Israelites would ask him: By what power have you come? For by virtue of the power fittingly applicable to Him, His name must needs be determined. Consequently, he states, "and they shall say to me: What is His name? (*Ibid.*). Indeed, it was proper for them to ask a question such as this. Nevertheless, the name which indicates the existence of God was known to them by tradition founded upon reason as handed down by Avraham, Isaac and Ya'aqov and it is impossible that Mosheh spoke with ignorant people since God said to him, "Go, and gather the elders of Israel together" (*Ibid.* 16). Their question did not refer to the true nature of His existence since belief in God is prior to the belief in prophets.

Then God answered and said to Mosheh, "*'Ehyeh 'asher 'Ehyeh*" (I am that I am) (*Ibid.* 14). This verb is in the *Qal* form and is intransitive, its punctuation indicates clearly that it is a form of the *Qal* and it is in the first person singular. It is as though He explained that this name indicates only the existence of His essence. Hence, it states, "*'asher 'Ehyeh*". After having explained the true nature of this name by stating, "*'asher 'Ehyeh*", and having established His existence by the signification of this name, He states, "*I am* has sent me unto you" (*Ibid.*). In other words, the Being in whose existence you believe has sent me unto you. This Name had already been known to them: But, since their question was: What kind of power derives from the meaning of this name? therefore he explains it by differentiating between it and other names. And when He desired to offer a reply to

274

their question it states, "And God said moreover unto Mosheh, "Thus, shall you, say unto the children of Israel: The LORD (YHWH), the God of your fathers..:.". (*Ibid.* 15). 'It states further, "This is My name forever" (*Ibid.*.). From the word "moreover" (in this verse) it can be inferred that He came to indicate another meaning. And from the unpunctuated 'Tetragrammaton it can tie inferred that it does not denote what is indicated by the term *'ehyeh* which is a verb of the *Qal* form; Rather it branches out in two directions: it is *Qal* form to indicate His existence; and it is also a *Pi'ēl* form indicating that it is a transitive verb from which can be derived another meaning. When it states: '"This is My name for ever" and afterwards, "and this is My memorial unto all generations" (*Ibid.*) it indicates that it can have the following two, significations. That is, His statement, "This is My name for ever" is as though He had said: The belief in My existence is for ever, and the words, "and this is My memorial unto all generations" refer to the acts that come into being in the universe through the power of this name. Hence, it states, "for all generations", to indicate the divisions of the universe, namely, genesis and corruption. Through these conceptions wondrous things come to be. Accordingly, the intention of this name following its second meaning indicates that God has brought the universe into being and it is in His power to modify its order and to change the nature of any object. Upon the power of this name rests the belief in miracles. Now, when Mosheh was informed of God's name as a reply to this question he said: If I inform them of this power, perhaps they will not believe my words alone. Comp. "But, behold, they will not believe me, nor listen unto my voice" (*Ibid.* 4.1). He desired that this be demonstrated by some act. It is as though his request with regard to the performance of miracles was that they be wrought through this name so that the power of this name would be verified among them. For this reason God immediately answered, "What is that in your hand" (*Ibid.*). In truth, as a result of these signs and miracles they went forth from Egypt, and because of this Mosheh framed the basis of their question around this point. The Traditionalists speak of a name consisting of four letters, and a name of twelve letters. It is true that the name of four letters is a verb of the *Qal* form; it is intransitive and requires no additional letters. In the case of the transitive name, on the other hand, since its implications are many, its letters are also numerous. This does not mean that there is one name possessed [of twelve letters]; rather the words that explain the meaning of this name consist of twelve letters. The scholar R Shmariah of Negropont has explained this point stating that this name of twelve letters is: *'esem m'h(a)v(e)h k(o)l h(ō)v(e)h* (a Being who brings all into existence), and he is correct.[473] Consequently, this name is associated with the expression, "the LORD of Hosts", i.e., He brings into being the hosts. The reason that it is written but not pronounced is that there are included under this name the two meanings, that of the Qal form and that of the *Pi'ēl* form. Mark this. The fact that a *waw* replaces the *yod* indicates that it is fitting to mark the wow with a *dāgēsh*. Half of his name which is the term *yāh* indicates that it is of the *Qal* form; cf., "For the LORD (*yāh*) is God, an everlasting Rock" (Is a. 26.4). This form lacks a letter which is capable of receiving a *dagesh*, since it is not of the *Pi'ēl* form, and it indicates the eternity of His existence. When it desires to express the second meaning it states, "The LORD, an everlasting Rock". You must bear in mind what we have explained in connection with the homonymity of the term *ṣūr* (rock).[474]

CHAPTER 75[475]

In connection with the will of God we must decide between two views: the view which asserts that God wills through His essence, and that which holds that He wills by means of an instrument (cause), i.e., by means of a newly created will.[476] You must know the opinion of H. Yosef, may his soul rest in peace, respecting his explanation of the true nature of the will. He says: When we perceive that God performs acts in one particular way, not in another, this constitutes the true nature of His will. This statement is in accord with the words of Maimonides who asserts that the true essence of the will of a being is the faculty of conceiving a desire at one time and not conceiving it at another.[477] Now, that you know these things it is necessary for you to understand the decision of those who believe that He wills through an instrument (i.e., a created will) against the view of those who believe that He wills through His essence. This decision is founded upon three arguments: First, if God wills through His essence He does not require any created thing to induce this will. And since there is nothing to restrain Him it necessarily follows that the willed object is coexistent with the will. This would necessitate Eternity. Secondly, jest as it has been established that He wills so it has been established that He rejects. Hence, if we say regarding the will that He wills through His essence we must also say that He rejects through His essence. Now, it is inadmissible that an essential attribute should apply to one thing to the exclusion of another, and that which is included under the attribute of will is perforce included under the attribute of rejection. It necessarily follows that He would desire and reject the same thing, which is absurd. Thirdly, if we affirm that God wills through His essence it must be that all things are willed (desired) by Him. As we assert that He knows through His essence and is not ignorant of anything at all so we hold in regard to His will. It follows then that He desires a certain thing as well as its opposite, which is impossible.

The refutation of the first argument is as follows: When one's will is directed towards the attainment of a certain object, whether this object becomes an actuality or not there is no change in the will itself even though there be an external obstacle separate from the will itself.478 Now, if we affirm that God's wisdom and will are identical; that the true essence of wisdom is just action and that His will is subject to His wisdom, then as we do not know the essence of His wisdom so we are ignorant of the ways of His wisdom which cause His will to be realized at one time and not at another, though the will remains the same.

In reply to the second argument: We have already shown that the true essence of will is to desire at one time and not at another. For will is subject to wisdom and the essence of wisdom is the rightness of a matter; the rightness of a matter includes things and their negation, or let us say, existence and its opposite. Thus, when we say: He desires a thing's existence, it is the same as: He rejects its opposite, or its nonexistence, and vice versa. This is the true nature of will when we assert that one desires and rejects and that these are not two different elements in the will itself. For the will is subject to wisdom, wisdom is identical with right action; and the rightness of a matter is its positive or negative aspect. And hence the positive and negative are equally applicable to the will seeing that the will is relative to rightness. It is impossible that they be different things in the essence of the will so that will, let us say, will be related to the positive and rejection to the negative. Indeed, the exponent of these views himself states in the third argument that if He wills through His essence it necessarily follows that He desires both the positive and the negative of the same thing. Thus, he includes the negative in the essence of the will. In reality, when we say that he desires the positive it means that he desires the negation of its negative; and when we say that he desires the negative it signifies that he desires the negation of the positive. Thus, they are all included under will. In fine, when will is subject to rightness, then the essence of will is one thing, without change, substitution, or division. Of course, things related to will may undergo change and substitution with respect to rightness,[479] for rightness will be associated with them positively or negatively in accordance with tradition and time. Nevertheless, the will remains the same in its relationship to rightness. Furthermore, since will is related to rightness if it be associated with what is not right, how can the will be both right and not right? The same applies to rejection. This is impossible.

Our reply to the third argument, which asserts that since He wills through His essence it must be that He wills a thing and its opposite, is: Since we have stated that the Will follows His Wisdom and that Wisdom indicates rightness it follows that when a certain thing is right and the Will inclines toward it then the opposite of this thing is not right. Now, how can the Will incline toward it so that the Will would include both the thing and its opposite? Furthermore, what is intrinsically impossible does not necessitate a defect [in God's ability]. Willing a thing and its opposite is intrinsically impossible. Therefore, as the impossible does not necessitate a weakness in God why is omnipotent through His essence so the impossible cannot be willed by God who wills through His essence.

There are three objections against those who believe that God wills through a created will that does not reside in Him nor in anything other than Him; not in Him, because He is not a body that bears accidents; and not in anything other than Him, because there would have to be a place for the residence of the will and the will would be ascribed to it: **First objection**–They have already asserted that an accident cannot exist *per se*.⁴⁸⁰ Now, if they maintain that the desire of God does not reside in anything it follows that an accident does exist *per se*. **Second objection**–They have affirmed that the object in which desire resides must be a living being. How then can this desire be subject–less if that element which maintains the existence of the desire, i.e., life, is not present since it (the desire) exists without a subject? **Third objection**–What relationship and association would there be between God and this accident of desire when they assert that as desires through a created instrument, i. e., through a created will?

The reason that forced them to this conclusion is as follows: Rational speculation has proved conclusively that when an agent performs a certain act in one particular way rather than another, and although his knowledge includes both ways still he selects this one way, be must possess some attribute in addition to his knowledge. Regarding every attribute by which a living being is described it is necessary to inquire concerning the manner in which it is described. There are different types of attributes, viz., essential, instrumental, conditional and temporal attributes. The sages rejected the idea that He wills through His essence as has been explained previously. Nor is His will conditional upon the fact that He is a living Being, like the attribute of sentience. For then all living beings would be identical in having the same will, just as all living beings are alike in that they are sentient. They have also rejected the notion that His will is temporal. For then it would be in existence only at the time of sating, not at other times. There remains only that He wills through an instrument, i.e., through a desire. Now, this desire is an accident sad it is inconceivable that it should reside in Him since He is not a material substance bearing accidents. Nor can it reside in anything other than Him, for the place of its residing would needs be a living being and this would necessitate the attribution of the will to the being is which it resides, not to God. But, since it is attributed to God, it follows that it does not reside in anything other than Him. Hence, He desires through a desire that is subjective.

Now, as for you, reader, it is necessary that you understand that it is not compulsory to believe this notion of the Mutakallimūn concerning the divine will, viz., that He wills with a created will. For Maimonides, while discussing the Mutakallimūn views on the question of God's will, states:[481] For some of them (i.e., the Mutakallimūn), belonging to the old school, assume that when the Creator wills a thing, the will is not an element superadded to the essence of God it is a will without a substratum. He states further: For as they define the Will it is inconceivable, and some have, therefore, considered it to be a mere non-entity, others who admit its existence meet with insuperable difficulties. It appears to me that it is not necessary to believe this notion save according to the theory of the Ash'ariya which asserts that the acts of God follow His will alone, not His wisdom, lest, in their view, they be compelled to believe in the eternity of the universe, as will be explained.[482] But, in accordance with the view which asserts that the acts of God follows His wisdom, this notion is not necessary, i.e., that God wills with a created will. For since His will follows His wisdom then just as the creation of the universe took place after His knowledge, even though His knowledge preceded, so it took place after His will, even though the will preceded. For the latter follows His wisdom and He brought the universe into existence according as He saw with His wisdom, as has been explained.[483] Belief in the eternity of the universe does not follow necessarily from this because His knowledge preceded, as will be explained.

The Philosopher has asserted that the appetite faculty, when it concerns something pleasant, is termed "lust". This is a material conception and hence cannot be applied to God, exalted be He. When this [faculty refers] to vengeance it is termed "anger", and with reference to counsel it is termed "will" or "desire". It is known that "counsel" can be predicated only of an intellectual being. Consequently, God is described as "willing". Comp. "Even counsels of old, in faithfulness and truth" (Isa. 25.1).

CHAPTER 76⁴⁸⁴

Since the faculties of sensation proceed from the very essence of the vital principle (soul) our sages are correct in ascribing the attribute "sentient" to living beings, for the nature of life necessitates their being sentient. It cannot be objected, as some scholars contend, that the attribute "sentient" is not necessarily associated with living beings since they find animate beings not perfected with the five senses, as sea sponges and snails which possess only the sense of touch. For we can reply that there were not constructed in these animals those organs through which the attribute "living" would necessitate sentience. Similarly, the scholar H. Yosef replies—to those who object that if life necessarily implies sensation then hands should be possessed of sight and hearing—that the hand was not constructed in such a manner as to see and hear. Thus, they have affirmed sensation as a necessary corollary of life subject to the removal of any defect or hindrance. When we consider life *per se*—unaffected by corporeality, whence are derived defects and hindrances—these faculties must undoubtedly emanate from it. The opinion of the philosophers also inclines toward this view. For the perception which they ascribe to God is associated with life, since the term "living" is applied only to that which perceives and anything that perceives is termed "living". Although these two perceptions are different the term, "living" is applied to them homonymously.

Now, since it has been demonstrated in the preceding chapters,[485] after rational investigation, that God is a living Being, our sages arrived at the decision that God is sentient and perceives objects that are perceptible. However, their true belief is that this perception which is ascribed to God is attributed to Him in accordance with the nature of the perceptibles.

It is evident that the perception of sensation is different from the perception of the intellect as has been demonstrated by H. Yosef for the reason that knowledge can be had of the nonexistent as well as of the existent, whereas sensation applies only to the existent. This is in accord with the statement of the Philosopher to the effect that the intellect differs from sensation in the following two respects.[486] First, sensation beholds the particular, intellect the class; secondly, the intellect perceives the inner essence while sensation sees only externalities. Consequently, when a scholar desires to imagine through his intellect he can do so, but he cannot perceive through sensation save those perceptibles that are in existence.

Let us now return to our subject. We cannot be forced to the conclusion that a plurality of elements in Cad necessarily follows [from the fact that He is sentient]. For the attribute Omnipotent is different from the attribute Omniscient and nevertheless we have demonstrated that they constitute one essence because we consider matters in accordance with the relationship of things to Him. Hence, H. Yosef is correct in asserting that when God perceives by sensation it is through an attribute in addition to that by which He knows. He does not mean to say here that the knowledge is increased by the sensation, but that the attribute of sensation is different from the essence of the attribute of knowledge. The author of *Me'īrath 'Ēynayīm*[487] asserts that there is no added attribute from which he implies that His knowledge is not increased. These words do not indicate that the attribute of sensation is not different from the attribute of knowledge. The author himself clarifies this matter by stating that God knows all things that are know whether they exist or not, both before they are perceived by sensation and afterwards, yet His knowledge is not increased at the time of sensation, only the sensible object alone. Thus, he also teaches that the attribute of sensation is different from the essence of the attribute of knowledge, and this is the opinion of the scholar H. Yosef.

CHAPTER 77[488]

In this chapter we shall consider in order the arguments of our opponents who deny the perception of sensation in God. They argue as follows: We perceive the objects of sensation only by means of our senses and these senses are physical objects. The latter perceive the objects of their sensation through intermediaries, which are also material things. Hut God is removed from anything material. Hence, we cannot ascribe sensation to God. It can be replied as follows: Acts proceed from us and these acts are performed by means of instruments. We also see that acts proceed from trod. But speculation has led us to believe that God is removed from corporeality and necessity compels us to believe that God performs acts without the means of instruments. In like manner we must believe that although we perceive objects of the senses only by means of physical organs, God perceives objects of the senses without any organs; for speculation has led us to believe that He is removed from corporeality. Besides, no analogy can be drawn from the creature to his Creator; for just as we are ignorant of the perception of His essence so we are ignorant of the nature of His perceiving the objects of sensation. Another reply is that it is false to assume that an agent can make an instrument for a certain act without knowing the nature of this act; otherwise the construction of this instrument would not be properly adapted to the character of this act. For example, if a man wished to prepare a quill for writing and he did not know the nature of writing how could he prepare the quill so that it should be adapted to the nature of writing? Now, the preparation of these senses for the perception of sensible objects compels us to believe that the perception of sensation is not withheld from God, for it is inadmissible that the preparation of the senses was accidental. Even in the opinion of the philosophers who contend that nature acts you realize that every natural force is the result of [an intelligent Being that formed its nature as it is constituted since nature itself is not[488a]] a being possessed of intelligence and leadership.

Similar to the substance of this reply is that made by King David, may he rest in peace, to the people of his generation who denied sense perception in God and following this belief they denied the existence of Providence in the sub-lunar world, since the perception of particulars rests in the faculty of sensation. Thus, it states, "And they say: The LORD seeth not..... (Ps. 94.7). This signifies that if. He does not perceive a sensible object by means of sensation then neither does He know this object. But David argues against them saying, "Consider, you brutish among the people " (*Ibid.* 8), that is to say, is it possible that the Agent should make an instrument for a certain act without knowing the nature of this act? This is absurd, as he continues. "He that planted the ear, shall He not hear? He that formed the eye, shall He not look?" (*Ibid.* 9).[489] By this statement he necessitates the ascription of the senses of sight and hearing to God; for if God has made organs adapted to these senses, then sense perception is not withheld from God. With justice does he call them "brutish" and "fools".

From the statement of David we derive many benefits. David states: He that plants the ear, shall He not hear?" (*Ibid.* 8). He does not say: He that plants the ear, has He not an ear? This is in conformance with his belief that God is removed from corporeality. The reason of his opponents was the removal of corporeality from God and David asserted that even though corporeality be removed from Him nevertheless we cannot deny sense perception of God. Secondly, he does not say: He that formed sight, shall as not see? For the principle argument was that God does not perceive material things, since they denied sense perception of God. David's reply branches out into two answers. **First**, to affirm sense perception of God, as has been explained; and also to show that He perceives material objects since He makes them. For it is impossible for an agent to make an instrument unless he perceives it. The third benefit is as follows: We cannot determine from the passage, "And they say: The LORD seeth not" (*Ibid.* 7) whether this refers to intellectual perception, according to the homonymity of the verb "to see", or to sense perception, for whatever reason there may be. Consequently, David states, "He that forms the eye, shall He not look?" (*Ibid.* 9); this "looking" pertains to the senses, not to the intellect. If this were not so these verses would not contradict one another for their subjects would be interchangeable, as is explained in the science of rhetoric. Fourth benefit: Although they argued to deny the sense of sight alone, of. "The LORD seeth not" (*Ibid.* 8), David affirmed the sense of hearing by stating, "He that plants the ear, shall He not hear?" (*Ibid.* 9), to teach that all the five senses are identical in their relation to God.

The second argument: They contend that the senses are passive, receiving their impressions through intermediaries, as is explained in Natural Science, and everything that is passive is subject to change.[490] But God is removed from the ways of change. Our reply is that we cannot draw any analogy from ourselves to God; far since we perceive by means of organs and God perceives without organs how can one category include both these perceptions so that we should judge God by our standards? Consequently, God is not passive when He perceives sensible objects.

Third argument: They contend that intellectual perception is higher in rank than sense perception, even in ourselves there is a great distinction between the perception of our intellect and the perception of our senses. How is it possible then to ascribe something unworthy to God? We reply that this is not unworthy at all. On the contrary, it is a great distinction in God that no thing, however slight, is concealed from Him. We speak of intellectual perception in accordance with the nature of the things that are perceived, and of sense perception in accordance with the nature of the things perceived through the senses. For there are things that are perceived by the intellect, but not by the senses, and, on the other hand, there are things that are perceived through sense perception and not through intellectual perception, as has been shown in Natural Science. With respect to God, however, nothing at all is concealed since He has brought all being into existence from absolute nothingness; for it is impossible for an agent to make a thing without perceiving it. Hence, both sensible objects and intelligibles are perceived by God.

Fourth argument: They contend that through the senses particulars are perceived and the perception of particulars would imply a. plurality in His essence whereas we believe that He is unique and absolutely one. This can be answered as follows: Our faculty of sense perception is of a lowly nature. Nevertheless, it perceives many changing and contradictory things simultaneously without any change or variation in its essence, and without any plurality in its essence even though it is acted upon. It remains one essence and one faculty. How much more so does this apply to the perception of God who does not perceive through any organ, nor is there any comparison or relationship between our perception and His perception which cannot be included in the same category. How could change or plurality affect God's perception when it perceives a multitude of things or changing and contradictory things. This is impossible.

Fifth argument: Sensation perceives only what is in existence. Before a sensible object comes into existence one cannot perceive it by his senses; after it has come into existence he does perceive it. Now, does it not constitute a change in the essence that perceives when he perceives after not perceiving? But God is exalted far above the ways of change. Our reply is as follows: It has already been shown in Natural Science that when the lowly faculty of sensation contained with us perceives an existing thing it is affected by a slight impression. This impression is not a real stimulation like change. Nevertheless, this impression affects our sense perception since it is not free of primal matter, which is its substratum. The perception of God, however, which is free of primal matter is not beset by any affection or essential change. We have already explained in preceding chapters491 that, when a being is perfect in its essence and some act proceeds from it, if the cause which prevents this act from proceeding from it is something external to its essence then there is no change in the essence of the being that is acting. Consequently, a nonexistent thing when perceived by God after it has come into existence does not constitute a change in the essence of His perception for He is perfect in His essence and free from the taint of corporeality.

CHAPTER 78⁴⁹²

We must now consider the fact, as I have explained, that sense perception in the essence of God is distinct from intellectual perception. It appears from this that He is constituted of two elements, but this is not so. For since it has been shown that He is One in an absolute sense⁴⁹³ we believe that there is one force by which He perceives both sensible objects and intelligibles. This force is defined by the nature of things, i.e., with regard to sensible objects we term it "sense perception", and with regard to intelligibles we term it "intellectual perception".⁴⁹⁴

I am astonished at the statement of H. Aharon (the Elder) in his commentary on the Pentateuch on the expression "And God saw" in connection with our sages who described God as "feeling". He asserts that if they had described Him as "perceiving" it would be preferable.⁴⁹⁵ But did not H. Yeshu'ah state in his *Berē'shīth* Rabbah, concerning the expression "and God saw" that it is to be taken literally? The meaning is, He perceived it as we perceive it with our eyes. For sensation they employ the term perception. The Mutakallimūn have asserted that there are two types of knowledge: knowledge of that which is nonexistent and of that which is in actual existence. It is a known fact that sensible objects are conceived by an inner sense. In reality, it appears that a plurality of attributes in His essence implies a plurality of elements in

Him. Nevertheless, since reason dictates that many acts proceed from God and, besides, demonstration has proved to us His unity, hence necessity compels us to believe that although God is one and unique without combination or composition nevertheless He performs different acts. This is the belief in which we Monotheists believe. After this explanation we should believe that nothing whatever is concealed from God either among celestial or sub-lunar existents; all things are perceived by Him. Knowledge can be had of the nonexistent as well as of the existent whereas sensation applies only to the existent. Hence, knowledge includes more than sensation. From this speculation there results the belief that things are combined by knowledge and providence and this is the essential nature of providence. For the true essence of providence is "viewing with reflection".

Do not be misled by the author of *Mahkīmath Pethī* who states that we know what we cannot feel and we fell what we cannot know. For this phenomenon occurs only in us since our knowledge is created. But, with respect to God, since He knows through His essence, there is nothing created of which He did not know beforehand and nothing whatever is concealed from Him. Thus, His knowledge encompasses sensible objects both before and after their coming to be.

BIBLIOGRAPHY

AHARON BEN-ELIYAHU, The Tree of Life, edition of Delitzsch and Steinschneider, Leipzig, 1841.

The Tree of Life with Commentary, The Light of the Life, by Simha Lutzki, Eupatoria, 1847.

AHARON BEN-ELIYAHU, *Keter Torah*, Eupatoria, 1866.

AHARON BEN-ELIYAHU, *Gan 'Eden*, Eupatoria, 1866.

AHARON BEN-YOSEF, *Sefer HamMibhar*, Eupatoria, 1835.

ARISTOTLE, The Basic Works of Aristotle, edited by H. McKeon, New York, 1941.

BAHYA IBN PAQUDA, Duties of the Heart, English translation by M. Hyamson, New York, 1925.

BERNFELD, *Da'ath 'Elohim*, Warsaw, 1897, p. 452ff.

EFROS, ISRAEL, I, The Problem of Space in Jewish Mediæval Philosophy, New York, 1917.

EFROS, ISRAEL, I, Philosophical Terms in the *Moreh Nebukim*, New York, 1924.

EFROS, ISRAEL, I., Maimonides' Treatise on Logic, New York, 1938

FRANKL, P. F., Ein Mutazilitischer Kalām aus dem 10 Jahrhuadert, Wien, 1872.

GOLDZIHER, I., Vorlesungen fiber den Islam, Heidelberg, 1910.

FURST, J., Geschichte des Karaerthume, Leipzig, 1865, Vol. II, p 259 ff.

GUTTMANN, JULIUS, Die Philosophie des Judentums, Munich, 19x3.

HARKAVY, AVRAHAM, *Liqqutey Qadmoniyyoth* II, St. Petersburg, 1903.

HUSIK, ISAAC, "Jewish Philosophy", in Ency. Brit., 14th Ed., 1929.

HUSIK, ISAAC, *Sefer Ha'Ikkarim*, critical Hebrew text, English translation and notes, 5 vols., Philadelphia, 192930.

HUSIK, ISAAC, A History of Mediæval Jewish Philosophy, Philadelphia, 1941.

YEHUDAH HALEVI, *Al-Khazari*, Hebrew translation, ed., Warsaw, 1930.

KAUFMANN, DAVID, Geschichte der Attributenlehre in der judischen Religionsphilosophie des Mittelalters von Saadia bis Maimuni, Gotha, 1877.

KLATZKIN, YA'AQOV, Thesaurus Philosophicus Linguae Hebraicae et Veteris et Recentioris (in Hebrew), Berlin, 1928.

MAHLER, RAPHAEL, The Karaites (in Yiddish), New York, 1947.

MAIMONIDES, MOSHEH, The Guide for the Perplexed, Eng. translation by M. Friedlander, New York, 1936.

MALTER, HENRY, Saadia Gaon, Life and Works, Phila., 1921.

MALTER, HENRY, "Jewish Philosophy", in Hasings, Encyclopædia of Religion and Ethics, Vol. 9, pp. 873877.

MUNK, SOLOMON, Melanges de Philosophie Juive et Arabe, Paris, 1859.

MUNK, SOLOMON, Le Guide des Egares, 3 Volumes, Paris, 18561866.

NEUBAUER, A., Aus der Petersburger Bibliothek, Leipzig, 1866.

PINSKER, S., Liqquetey Qadmoniyyoth, Wien, 1860.

POZNANSKI, S., The Karaite Literary Opponents of Saadiah Gaon, London, 1908, p. 79f.

RULE, W. H., History of the Karaite Jews, London 1870, pp. 200232.

SAADIA GAON, Beliefs and Opinions, Hebrew translation ed., Slucki, Leipzig, 1864.

SCHREINER, MARTIN, Der Kalām in der judischen Literature, Berlin, 1895.

SCHREINER, MARTIN, Studien uber Jeschu'a ben Jehuda, Berlin, 1900.

STEINSCHNEIDER, M., Die Hebraischen Uebersetzungen des Mittelalters, Berlin, 1893.

VENTURA, M., Le Kalām et le Peripatetisme d'apres le Kuzari, Paris, 1934.

WAXMAN, MEYER, A History of Jewish Literature, N. Y., 1934, Vol. 2, p. 430ff.

WOLFSON, HARRY A., Crescas' Critique of Aristotle, Cambridge, 1929.

WOLFSON, HARRY A., The Kalām Arguments for creation in Saadia, Averrœs, Maimonides and St. Thomas, N. Y., 1943, Texts and Studies, Vol. 2, The American Academy for Jewish Research.

LIST OF ABBREVIATIONS

A.   Aristotle

C.   Chapter

E. H.   'Es Hayyim, Delitzsch ed., Leipzig, 1841.

E. K.   Eshkol ha-Kofer of Yehudah Hadassi, Eupatoria, 1836.

G. E.   Gan 'Eden of Aharon Ben-Eliyahu, Eupatoria, 1866.

G. K.   J. Furst, Geschichte des Karaertums, Vol. II, Leipzig, 1862.

J. J.   M. Schreiner, Studien uber Jeschu'a ben Jehuda, Berlin, 1900.

K. J. L.   M. Schreiner, Der Kalām in der judischen Literatur, Berlin, 1895.

K. T.   Keter Torah of Aharon Ben-Eliyahu, Eupatoria, 1866.

M.   Maimonides' Guide for the Perplexed, Eng. trans. by M. Friedlander, New York, 1936.

M. K.   P.F. Frankl, Ein Mutazilitischer Kalām aus dem 10 Jahrhundert, Wien, 1872.

O. H.   'Or HaHayyim, Commentary by Simha Lutzki on the `Es Hayyim, Eupatoria, 1847.

S.   Saadia Gaon, Beliefs and Opinions, Slucki ed., Leipzig, 1864.

S.M.   *Sefer Ha-Mibhar* of Aharon Ben-Yosef, Eupatoria, 1835.

NOTES

1. Comp., also S. Murk, Melanges de Philosophie Juive et Arabe. Paris, 1895, p. 154 f. See further M. Waxman, A History of Jewish Literature. Vol. II, p. 2 f.

2. See G. K. Vol. II, pp. 238-250.

3. Comp. J. Mann, Texts and Studies in Jewish History and Literature, Phila. 1935, Vol. II, p. 1417 n. 46.

4. See Mordechai Ben-Nissan, Dod Mordekhay, Wien' 1830, p. 14b. Although Aharon's birthplace is a matter of dispute among investigators (Comp. Proleg. of Delitzsch, p. IV, in E.H.) nevertheless most scholar incline towards Cairo as his birthplace. See further Encyc. Judaica, Berlin 1928, Vol. I, p. 38, s.v. Aharon Ben-Eliyahu Der Karaer.

5. In the G. E., Aharon quotes extensively from the opinions of the Doctors of the Talmud. See further J. H. Weiss, Dor Dor Wedorshaw, Wilna 1904, Vol. IV, p. 74; S. Posnanski, The Karaite Literary Opponents of Saadia Gaon, London 1908, p. 80.

6. E.H., Proleg. p. IV.

7. Op, cit., p. 262.

8.   If we accept the view of Yehudah Swawaskan (K. T., first section) that poem No. 7, alludes to our author it would appear that in later life Aharon suffered some grave misfortune.

9.   Comp. G. K., p. 272 f.

10.   Comp. the introduction of M. Friedlander in M., p. RLIII. See further I. Husik, A History of Mediæval Jewish Philosophy, New York 1916, p. 364.

11.   This can be inferred from the context in which Aharon cites this teacher. See E. H. p. 66.

12.   E. H. pp. 76 and 80.

12a.   *Ibid.*

13.   Perhaps this is the same H. Yosef as alluded to in poems Nos. 1 and 18 (in K. T.) if these verses be correctly ascribed to Aharon Ben-Eliyahu as adapted by I. Davidson, Thesaurus of Mediæval Hebrew Poetry, New. York 1933, Vol. 4, s. v. Aharon Ben-Eliyahu p. 360.

14.   See I. Jost, Israelitische Annalen, Frankfurt am Main 1839, No. 11.

15.   Comp. also A. Neubauer, Aus der Petersburger Bibliothek, Leipzig 1866, pp. 59, 121.

16.   G. K., p. 264 and n. 250.

17.   See above n. 3.

18. Regarding the title 'Es Hayyim in contradistinction to, the title Noser 'Emunim by which this work has also been called see Delitzsch's Proleg. off. cit., p. VI f. See further S. Bernfeld, Dalath 'Elohim, Warsaw 1899, p. 452; J, Mann, Texts and Studies in Jewish History and Literature, Cincinnati 19$1, pp. 661, 684.

19. Comp. S. Bernfeld, op. cit., p. 452.

20. This date is specifically stated in the last line of Aharon's introductory poem to K. T., p. la.

20a. According to the Rabbanites Scripture is to be interpreted in the light of an Oral Law that was given to Mosheh simultaneously with the Written Law. The Karaites reject this view and contend that the literal meaning of Scripture must always be observed. This constitutes the basic difference between the two in the opinion of Aharon Ben-Eliyahu.

21. Comp. I. M. Jost, Geschichte des Judentums and seiner Secten, Leipzig 1858, Vol. 2, p. 366; M. Waxman, Ibid. p. 440.

22. See J. Mann, op. cit., Vol. 2, p. 141?.

23. See Encyc. Judaica, Vol. 9, s.v. Karaer. See further S. Poznanski in Hasing's Encyclopedia of Religion and Ethics, Vol. 7, pp. 662-672.

24. This work is also known by the title Sefer Miswoth Gadol. Cf., Simha Lutzki's 'Orah Saddiqim published in the Dod Mordekhay, op. cit. p. 23a. See further the title page of Sawaskan's

edition of G. E. Two sections of this work have appeared under separate titles: one, dealing with the ritual slaughtering of animals is known as Diney Shebitah; the other, treating of incestuous marriage is called Sofnath Pa'aneah (Revealer of Secrets). See G. K., p. 277.

25. See the conclusion of this editor's introductory remarks on the publication of this work.

26. See I. M. Jost's exposition on the calendar, seasons and new year based on this work, Israelitische Annalen 1839, Nos. 11, 17, 18, 32.

26. Comp. Delitzsch, Proleg. to E. H. p. V. note 9. See further G. K., pp. 274-278.

27. For a comprehensive exposition of the separate treatise entitled Diney Shehitah see Delitzsch's study in Literaturblatt des Orients 1840, Nos. 16, 18, 28, 29, 30 and 31.

28. See the conclusion of Delitzsch's article in the Literaturblatt des Orients 1840, No. 40.

29. See the introduction of Yehudah Sawaskan to his edition of this work.

30. Comp. G. E., p. 2b.

31. In the introduction to G. E. Aharon cites the Sabers as the builders of the tower of Babel who identified the outermost sphere with God. See M. III, 29.

32. G. E. p. 176b, 179a, 182b.

33. See Aharon's introduction to the laws on ritual slaughtering, G. E.; p. 82a. On the Muslim origin of these principles and their influence upon Jewish scholars see K. J. L.

34. G. E., pp. 2b, 81a.

35. Comp. L. Dukes in Literaturblatt des Orients 1843, No. 45.

36. 36a. The Addereth Eliyahu of Eliyahu Bashyazi, "The Last Decisor", published in Evpatoria 1835, supplements rather than supersedes the work of our author.

37. See the prefatory remarks of Sawaskan in G. E.

38. For excerpts made known previously by de Rossi (1575) and, Kosegarten (1824) see Encyc. Judaica, Vol. I., p. 42.

39. An excellent study of these differences has been made by Delitzsch in the Literaturblatt des Orients 1840, Nos. 32, 34, 39.

40. Comp. further Jost, op, cit., p. 329, note 1, who cites similar instances from G. E.

41. E. H., Chaps. 20-63.

42. These poems are listed by Davidson, op. cit., Vol. 4, p. 360, s.v. Aharon Ben-Eliyahu. For further references see Encyc. Judaica, Vol. 1, p. 42; Delitzsch, proleg. to E. H. p. VI. note 13.

43. Poems No. 6 and 18 spell out in Hebrew: I, Aharon Ben-Eliyahu.

44. With regard to the poem which marks the conclusion of Sawaekan's prefatory remarks see the comments of J. Mann, Texts and Studies, Vol. 2, p. 255.

45. Thesaurus of Mediæval Hebrew Poetry, loc. cit.

46. On excerpts of the E. H. published prior to the Delitzsch edition see the latter's Proleg. p. Y. n. 8.

47. At the conclusion of this edition there is appended the complete text of the Derekh 'Es Hayyim by Caleb Abbe Afendopolo, the first part of which is included in the Delitzsch edition.

48. 'Orah Saddiqim by Simha Lutzki p. 23b., published with the Dod Mordekhay, Wien 1830.

49. *Ibid.* p. 25a. To my knowledge, only a fragment of this work is extant in the Bodleian Library, Oxford. See Neubsuer's Cat., No. 2387 (1).

50. Comp. K. J. L., p. 58.

51. Comp. this Kalāmistic influence upon Saadia, Bahya and Ibn Zaddik in K. J. L.

51a. See also Jewish Encyc., Vol. I., p. 10.

52. Comp. the Onomastikon, P. 311 of E. H.

53.　E. H. p. 5.

54.　E. H., Chap. 2.

55.　Aharon first proves creation by speculative reasoning them supports his results by Scripture. We are informed (Chap. 12) that even Avraham attained the conception of God's existence through objective reflection prior to his being endowed with the gift of prophecy. Similarly, after demonstrating the existence of Separate Intelligences, which he identifies with the angels of Scripture, and indicating their function as the intermediaries of God's Will in its effects upon the sublunar world, he cites the Psalms to sustain his views (Chap. 14). The same also applies to his ascription of sense perception to God (Chap. 77). But see E. H. p. 4.

56.　M. II, 25.

57.　See the Babylonian Talmud, Hagiga, folio llb.

58.　Comp. Husrk's introduction to his History of Mediæval Jewish Philosophy, p. XIXf. Subsequently, however, Gersonides and Crescas were much better acquainted with Aristotle through Averrœs.

59.　E. H., Chap. 15.

60.　*Ibid.* Chap. 16.

61.　Comp. Delitzsch's discussion of the style of E. H. in his Proleg. p. XIII, ff.

62. Comp. M. Steinachneider, Jewish Literature (English translation) London 1857, p. 95. See further M. Waxman, History of Jewish Literature, N. Y. 1933, Vol. 2, p. 207.

63. Comp. Steinschneider, op. cit., p. 119.

64. See J. J., p. 26. DH. Schreiner explains that the work of Yeshu'a Ben-Yehuda, originally written in Arabic, was translated into an extremely poor form of Hebrew and somehow the terminology was taken over and accepted by later Karaite philosophers. The same has occurred with Rabbinic philosophers, through the translations of the Tibbonides, as in the writings of Ralbag and Crescas.

65. Comp. the references of Delitzsch, op. cit., p. HIV, n. 23.

66. *Ibid.* p. XV. n. 25.

67. Quoted in the Moreh HaMmoreh by Shem Tob Palquera, Pressburg 1837, p. 107.

68. See the excursus on the relationship between Maimonides and Aharon Ben-Eliyahu in E. H. p. 329 ff.

69. In matters of physics, metaphysics, psychology, ethics and logic, Aharon employs Aristotelian terminology which, like the section on anthropomorphisms, appears to be taken bodily from Maimonides.

70. In his Onomastikon of the E. H., Steinachneider lists fourteen such instances, p. 304.

71. *Ibid.* p. 325.

72. E. H. pp. 26-27, where Aharon refutes the Aristotelian hypothesis of eternity.

73. *Ibid.* p. 4.

74. Such notions include: the eternity of the world, the inadmissibility of miracles, God's ignorance of particulars, the absence of reward and punishment, and Providence.

75. E. H. p. 7. See further *ibid.* p. 96 where the Philosopher is cited as the author of this distinction.

76. De Anima III, 8.

77. Physics Book I., Ch. 7. With regard to the form and matter of Aristotle it should be borne in mind that these terms are the concrete expressions of his abstract terms "motion" and "that which is capable of motion"; for it is the change of forms from one into another that constitutes motion and it is matter in which motion takes place.

78. De Caelo IV, 4.

79. Physics, I. 67.

80. Comp. Wolfson, Crescas' Critique of Aristotle, Cambridge 1929, p. 103f.

81. De Cae l o, I, 1.

82. Physics, IV, 11.

83. Metaphysics, I, 7.

84. E. H. p. 46.

85. See above note 74.

86. E. H. p. 48. Aristotle's Physics IV, 12.

87. E. H. p. 49. De Anima I, 1.

88. De Anima II, 7.

89. E. H. p. 66.

90. Physics IV, 1012.

91. Metaphysics XII, 78.

92. Physics IV, 12.

93. E. H. p. 78.

94. E. H. p. 91. Metaphysics.

95. E. H. p. 96. De Anima III, 8.

96. The Jralam Arguments for Creation in Saadia, Averroes, Maimonides and St. Thomas, pub-

lished in Texts and Studies of the American Academy for Jewish Research, N. Y. 1943.

97. E. H. p. 28.

98. Wolfson, op. cit., p. 227.

99. Guide, I, 74 (4).

100. Physics I, 7.

101. Wolfson, op. cit., p. 211 ff.

102. Physics I, 7 and Metaphysics XII, 1, 3.

103. Metaphysics XII, 6. See above note 72a.

104. E. H. p. 12, Chap. 4.

105. Topics I, 4.

106. Legacy of Islam, article on Philosophy and Theology by A.Guillaume, p. 239.

107. M. Horten, Die Philosophie des Islam, Munich 1924, pp. 61, 85.

108. Comp. E. H. p. 15, 108. See further, above n. 70.

109. The Kalāmists comprise two main factions: the Mu'tazila who were the first and more rationalistic theologians and the Ash'ariya who arose later and were more orthodox. For the primary sources on sects and schools of Arabic religious and philosophical thought see: Shaharastani,

German translation by T. Haarbriicker, Halle 1850-1851; Ash'ari abu alHasan 'Ali, Die dogmatischen Lehren der Anhanger des Islam; Leipzig 1929-33.

110. This included Karaites, e.g., Yosef alBasir and Yeshu'ah Ben-Yehudah as well as the Rabbanites alMukammias, Saadia, Bahya and ibn Zaddik.

111. See J. Gottman, Die Philosophie des Judentums, Munich 1933, p. 69 ff.

112. Isaac Israeli and David alMukammas although older contemporaries of Saadia did not, like the latter, establish a comprehensive system of Jewish religio-philosophical thought. Comp. Husik, History of mediæval Jewish Philosophy. pp. 122.

113. It is noteworthy that although Gersonides, the Rabbanite contemporary of Aharon Ben-Eliyahu, no longer regards the Kalāmistic point of view as a living issue after the deathblow dealt it by Maimonides nevertheless the Karaite Aharon assets himself as an avowed follower of the Mu'tazila. This influence was undoubtedly enhanced by Aharon's ties with his Karaite predecessors. See K. J. L., p. 57.

114. Aharon Ben-Eliyahu was firmly convinced that the doctrines of the Mu'tazila are of Jewish origin. See E. H., p. 4; M. I. 71; below n. 180. For a similar notion among the Arabs see A. S. Halkin, Moslem Schisms and Sects, Tel Aviv, 1935, p. 152.

115. E. H. Chap. 4.

116. *Ibid.* p. 15.

117. E. H. Chap. 10. See further Wolfson, The Arguments for Creation in Saadia, etc.

118. *Ibid.* Chap. 11.

119. *Ibid.* Chap. 15.

120. Chaps. 66-68.

121. Chaps. 75.

122. Chaps. 76-78.

123. The relationship between these two Magna Opera has been made the subject of a special excursus by Delitzsch at the conclusion of his edition of the Kalaam pp. 329-343. Consequently, it remains for me only to indicate, in addition to the salient points of comparison and contrast mentioned there, the supplementary and later material that has become available to me.

124. E. H. Chaps. 16-63.

125. Aharon follows the practice, which was quite current during the Middle Ages, of borrowing extensively from the ideas and words of his predecessors.

126. The former is mentioned eighteen times and the latter fourteen. See E. 2. pp. 304, 323.

127. This commentary by Kalonymos, a student of Maimonides, is mentioned by name (p. 147) and constituted an additional source of Aharon's information regarding the former's views. See E. H. pp. 343348.

128. S. Bernfeld, Da'ath 'Blohifi, Vol. 2, pp. 452, 463.

129. G. K., p. 270 f.

130. In the notes to the English translation I have indicated the sources in the Moreh which correspond to the subject under discussion in the 'Es Hayyim.

131. E. H. p. 5.

132. *Ibid.* p. 6.

133. Guide, I, Intro.

134. S. M., Eaod. p. 31a. See further S., p. 44.s

135. These notions are also taken from the same source in S. M.

136. E. H. Chap. 18.

137. E. H. Intro. p. LVIII. See further *Ibid.* p. 335.

138. *Ibid.* p. 52 f.

139. M. I, 2.

140. E. H. p. 40.

141. M. 11, 5.

142. Comp. I. Zinberg, History of Jewish Literature, Vol. 3. p. 410 ff.

143. M. I, 71.

144. E. H. p. 4.

145. *Ibid.* p. 17.

146. M. 1, 5560.

147. E. H. Chap. 72.

148. For the most authoritative sources in this much disputed field of learning see: the articles of S. Poznanski in Hasings Encyclopedia of Religion and Ethics, Vol. 7, pp. 662-672 and A. Harkavy in J. E. Vol. 7, pp. 438-446;M. Steinschneider, Die Hebraische Ubersetzungen des Nittelalters. Berlin 1893, p. 449 ff; I. Husik, A History of Mediæval Jewish Philosophy, Philadelphia 1941, especially Chaps. 4 and 16 (this most recent edition contains Prof. H. A. Wolfson's comprehensive bibliography).

149. Comp. Goldziher, Yorlesungen uber den Islam, Heidelberg 1910, p. loo ff.

150. Comp. E. H. p. 18 and Onomastikon p. 301. See further, note on English translation ad. loc.

151. E. K., 25b. See further Schaharastani, ed Haarbrucker I, 256 f.

152. See note 143.

153. *Ibid.* See further Wolfson, Kalam Arguments for Creation, p. 211 ff

154. Comp. M. II, 6.

155. L. Nemoy, AlQirqisani's Account of the Jewish Sects, published in H. U. C. A. 1930, p. 390 f.

156. See Steinschneider, HebH. Oebers, p. 449 f., but comp. Harkavy in J. E., VII. 439. See further Steinschneider, Die Arabische Literature der Juden, par. 43.

157. Kitab AlAnwar Wal Maraqib, Code of Karaite Law, edited by Leon Nemoy, New York 1939-43. 5 Vols.

158. Schreiner cites the opinions of Aharon and their respective sources in alBasir's works; K. J. L. p. 58. n. 3.

159. S. Poznanski in Hasings, Encyclopedia of Religion and Ethics VII., p. 666.

160. Steinschneider HebH. Uebers. p. 4.52 f. See M. K.

161. M. K., p. 51 n. 1.

162. See note 149.

163. M. I, 71. See further M. K., p. 5.

164. M. K., p. 52 n. III.

165. *Ibid.* p. 53. n. IV.

166. *Ibid.* n. VI.

167. E. H. p. 315 f; J. J.; M. Steinschneider, HebH. Uebers. p. 459 f.

168. E. K.

169. Comp. K. J. L: p. 33 f.

170. Published in Evpatoria 1836 together with a commentary entitled Tirath Kesef by Yosef Solomon Ben-Mosheh.

171. K. J. L., p. 57.

172. *Ibid.*

173. See further K. T. 7b.

174. In Midrashic and Apocalyptic literature Avraham is described as coming to know God through his own reasoning about the nature of the universe and its ruler who must necessarily exist. Comp. L. Ginzberg, Legends of the Jews, Phila. 1925, Vol. V, p. 217 f. Similarly, Josephus (Antiquities of the Jews, 1k. 1 Ch. 8) states that Avraham communicates the sciences of astronomy and arithmetic to the Egyptians. And later the Babylonian Talmud (Baba Bathra 16b and

Yoma 28b) asserts that the kings of the east and west eagerly besieged the door of Avraham's house in order to derive benefit from his wisdom.

175. Comp. S. M., Deut. 28a, top.

176. This is taken directly from M. II, 11.

177. Our author refers here to the nature of the celestial spheres from which proof can be derived for the existence of God, Chap. 10. See also M. II, 19 who employs a different method of proof based upon the nature of the spheres.

178. Comp. M. I, 71.

179. This is directed against Maimonides who maintains (M. II, 11) that the true knowledge which was originally the possession of the Jews was of an Aristotelian character.

180. The belief that Greek philosophers derived their knowledge from Jewish sources dates back to Josephus. In his work, Against Apion 1, 22., Josephus quotes from the noted letter of Clearchus that Aristotle, after a philosophical discussion with a certain Jew, affirmed that this Jew communicated to him more information than he received from him. See further, S. Horovitz, Die Stellung des Aristoteles bei den Juden des Mittelalters, Leipzig, 1911, p. 4. Comp. also the comprehensive treatment of this subject by I. Zinberg, History of Jewish Literature, Vilno, 1931, Vol. 3, p. 410 ff.

181. This statement provides the answer to the seeming paradox in Aharon's system; on the one hand he rejects philosophy and the philosophers and yet, notwithstanding this, his work is completely permeated by the, spirit of Aristotle. The answer is that it is only their results that he repudiates, their rationalistic method he not only accepts but advocates. See above, translator's intro. pp. XI-XIII.

182. These include among others David alMukammas, Saadia Gaon and Bahya ibn Paquda.

183. The foremost among these are Maimonides and Avraham ibn Daud.

184. This is directed against Maimonides who charged that the Kalāmistic views current among the Karaites were dictated by chance or preconceived notions. Comp. M. I, 71.

185. See below n. 192.

186. Regarding the homonymity of the term yeled see below C. 59. See further, M. II, 11.

187. Cf., primarily M. I, 71 and K. III, 65.

188. The O. H. ad loc. mentions a tradition in accordance with which Aharon wrote his philosophical treatise at the age of eighteen. See also J. Mann, Texts and Studies, Vol. II, p. 1417 n. 46.

189. Comp. Jer. 20. 9. See further M. II, 37.

190. Comp. S. M. of Aharon the Elder p. 8b. ff.

191. See Maimonides, haHiggayon, C. 8.

192. Comp. alBasir in M. K., p. 52 n. 3. See further, Introduction to this translation, p. XI f.

193. Comp. M. II, Intro.

194. Comp. A., De Anima, III, 8.

195. See above n. 184.

196. Comp. A., Physics I, 7.

197. The Delitzsch ed. is manifestly incorrect here. Cf., O. H. ad loc.

198. Comp. A., Physics IV, 11.

199. A., De Caelo, I, 1.

200. The investigators referred to are those who subscribe to the Kalāmistic conception of the nature of sublunar existence as constituted of substance and accidents, to be presented in detail in the following chap.

201. In his elaborate exposition of the nature and immortality of the rational soul (below C. 1069), which he demonstrates by reason and from Scripture Aharon presents the relevant views of Plato, Aristotle, Themistius, Alexander of Aphrodisias, Averroes and alFarabi.

202. Comp. M. II, Introduction, Prop. 4. See further A., Metaphysics II, 2.

203. Physics I, 67.

204. See O. H. ad loc.

205. Comp. M.I., 72.

206. The notion that the influence of the spheres led to the belief in astrology Aharon apparently derives from M. II, 12.

207. See A., Physics IV, 5; De Caelo IV, 35.

208. The evident answer to this is that the form exists in potentia while the element is in composition: See further O. H. ad loc.

209. Some philosophers contend that the Active Intellect endows all sublunar beings with form; others argue that the supralunar spheres are the real dispensers of form, as will be discussed in C. 14.

210. Comp. M. I, 73.

211. Similar to this distinction with regard to accidents is that of al Juwaini who distinguishes between essential and qualitative attributes. Comp. his al lrshad, p. 38 n. 1. See further K. V., 18; A., Topics I. 4.

212. Regarding the cosmological terminology of the earlier Mutakallimūn, see K. J. L., pp. 37 ff., and J. J. p. 27.

213. Comp. M. K., p. 20.

214. For the source of this method of analysis see J. J. p. 28 f.

215. See below, first section of C. 76.

216. This Aristotelian definition of "body" (De Caelo I, 1) is adapted to the Kalāmistic theory of atoms.

217. According to A. (*ibid.*); A magnitude if divisible one way is a line, if two ways a surface, and if three, a body.

218. On Kalāmistic terminology see above n. 212.

219. This notion is taken almost verbatim from Yosef alBasir. See O. H. ad loc.

220. Further on in this same chapter Aharon develops the subsidiary propositions which necessarily follow from these two conflicting views.

221. The Kalāmistic denial of the laws of nature and of causality as well as its atomistic theory is inherited from the Epicureans. See Wolfson, The Kalām Arguments for Creation, p. 234.

222. This Ash'arite view is one of the basic points of difference between the latter and the Mu'tazila. See further the Onomastikon, pp. 304-307.

223. The source of the Kalām theory of atoms, we are told by M. I, 73 (1) is "Epicurus and the

other atomists". The latter undoubtedly refer to Leucippus and Democritus. See further A., De Caelo III, A.

224. This appears to refer to a division among the scholars of investigation. But see O. H. ad loc.

225. Comp. M. K., p. 53, n. 4.

226. On the origins of this well known principle of the Kalām comp. J. J., p. 31, n. 2. See further alJuwaini, alIrshad, translated into French by J. D. Luciani, Paris, 1938, p. 29 ff.

227. See above the latter part of C. 3, where Aharon discusses the influence of the motion of the sphere through the media of light and darkness upon the disposition of matter.

228. The proposition that the Agent can exercise no influence upon what is already in existence is affirmed and demonstrated by Yeshu'ah Ben-Yehudah in his Bere'shith Rabbah. See J. J., p. 29. Yosef alBasir also treats of this matter in the Sefer Nefimoth and Nahkimath Pethi, cf., *ibid.* p. 32, n. 3.

229. Comp. M. I, 73, the sixth proposition, which presents a detailed exposition of this matter. For the view of Yosef alBasir in this regard see M. K., p. 19, also the preceding n.

230. Concerning this incomprehensible doctrine of the Ash'ariya, see Munk, Le Guide, Vol. I, p. 186, n. 1. See also M. K., p. 57, n. IX.

231. See below C. 86.

232. –

233. This refers to the second proof of C. 10.

234. This apparently refers to M. II, 19.

235. *Ibid.*

236. E. K., p. 23b, c.

237. This principle is stated almost verbatim in the Bere'shith Rabbah of Yeshu'ah Ben-Yehudah, see J. J., p. 29. Comp. also above, n. 226.

238. M. I, 73 (11). See further Wolfson, Kalam Arguments for Creation, p. 213.

239. Yosef alBasir, in his Nahkimath Pethi, devotes considerable effort to the refutation of the opinions of Benjamin Nahawandi. (Graetz, History of the Jews, Vol. 3, (1927) pp. 150-52). The latter's theory that God is too sublime to concern Himself directly with the material world and hence it must have been created by an angel acting as God's representative is disproved in the fourteenth C. of the said work. Cf., also J. J., p. 40 ff. This view of Nahawandi who maintains the eternity of matter despite his admission that it cannot do without accidents originating in time is refuted in great detail by Yosef alBasir in the third C. of his Sefer Nelimoth. Cf., O. H. ad loc.

240. These statements from the Bere'shith Rabbah are quoted in their context by J. J., p. 29.

241. Comp. M. II, 1, where he demonstrates the existence, unity and in, corporeality of God from the motion of the spheres.

242. *Ibid.* II, Intro. Propositions 2, 3. Comp. A, Metaphysics II, 2.

243. See M. *ibid.* Prop. 9. and II, 12. Comp. A. *ibid.* XII, 6.

244. This reference is to M. II, 4.

245. See below, end of C. 9.

246. Comp. M. II, 17.

247. The impossibility of the accidental infinite is demonstrated in the first part of C. 10. See also the concluding section of C. 4.

248. The 'before' and 'after' relative to time is treated in detail in A., Physics, IV, 11.

249. A., Physics, VIII, 1.

250. This is offered in refutation of Aristotle's definition of time as "the number of movement in respect of the before and after". Cf., A., Physics, IV, 11.

251. See M. I, 73 (3).

252. In the case of fire and water for example, the qualities of the former are hot and dry; of the latter, cold and moist. But the coldness of water is not as extreme as the coldness of earth, nor is the downward motion of water as extreme as that of earth.

253. Comp. M. II, 18. This C. is contained in Yosef del Medigo's "Hokhmah". See E. H. pp. XV, 249.

254. The identical mode of reasoning is employed by M. II, 18, in his example of the Active Intellect.

255. Comp. M. II, 17.

256. Aharon the Elder, S. M. 8b, also suggests this example as well as that of the relationship between fully developed man and the semen whence he originated. Maimonides, who discusses the latter example in detail (M. II, 17), states: It is therefore quite impossible to infer from the nature which a thing possesses after having passed through all stages of its development, what the condition of the thing has been in the moment when this process commenced; nor does the condition of a thing in this moment show what its previous condition has been. Cf., Bernfeld, Darath 'Eloham, Vol. 2, p. 455, n. 1.

257. Comp. M. II, 23.

258. See the latter part of the following chapter and the beginning of C. 14.

259. Comp. M. I, 74.

260. Comp. x. V, 18 (2) (4).

261. On this point see M. Ventura, Le Kalam et le Peripatetisme d'apres le Kuzari, Paris 1934, p. 21, n. 6.

262. Comp. M. Ventura, La Philosophic de Saadia Gaon. p. 105, n. 56.

263. See M. II, Intro. (1).

264. Comp. Wolfson, Crescas' Critique of Aristotle, Cambridge 1929, p.103f.

265. See above, the first part of C. 3.

266. Comp. M. II, 19.

267. Comp. A1Juwaini, alIrshad, C. 4, and p. 40. See further K. V., (4).

268. See O. H. ad l oc.

269. Comp. M. II, 25.

270. On the wisdom of Avraham and his reasoning concerning the nature of the universe see above n. 174.

271. Although Adam, Noah and others knew of God's existence they did not proclaim His name among the peoples. See O. H. ad loc.

272. Comp. Ventura, La Philosophie de Saadia Gaon, Paris 1934, p. 100, n. 32.

273. Comp. M. II, 29. See O. H. ad loc.

275a. Although the accepted meaning of the Hebrew term sod is "council", it is translated here "counsel" in conformity with Aharon's interpretation of this word.

275b. The literal translation of this phrase, based on Prov. 25. 11, is: When he enlarges the settings of the mosaic that are upon the golden apple. See further M. I, Intro.

274. Comp. M. II, 412.
275. See above, the Introduction, C. 12 and below C. 65 and 74.

276. On the theory of the spheres see the comprehensive exposition of D. Neumark, Geschichte der Judischen Philosophie des Mittelalters, Berlin, 1907, Vol. 1, pp. 533-604.

277. In his Metaphysics I, 7, A. explains the motion of the first heaven, i.e., the outermost sphere of the universe in which the fixed stars are set, from the fact that this sphere is the object of desire and the object of thought. On the development of this notion by Arab philosophers and Christian scholastics see Munk, Le Guide, II, p. 51, n. 4.

278. This reference from M. II, 3 demonstrates conclusively that in speaking of "the Philoso-

pher" Aharon refers to A. See further Afendopolo's n. on C. 14. in E. H. p. hVII.

279. M. 11, 15.

281a. The following words enclosed in brackets are
added by the Evpatoria ed. of the E. H.

280. This probably refers to Ptolemy. See Onomastikon p, 307.

281. Comp. Maimonides, *ibid* II, 4. See further H.
Malter, Die Abhandlung des Abu Hamid alGaz-
zali, F. a. M., 1896, p. XXI ff.

282. *Ibid.* end. But see *ibid.* I. 70.

283. "I do not deny", asserts Aharon the Elder (S. M.
Gen., 15a) "that the angels were created simultaneously with the heavens; for one who comprehends the secrets contained in the motion of
the spheres must admit this fact. This motion is
not due to any desire, as many have thought.
Furthermore, it is well known that the prophets
do not speak of a divine throne without its attendants".

284. On the identification of the angels with the
separate Intelligences see below n. 411.

285. Against this interpretation, Aharon the Elder,
in the S. M. Gen. 13a, argues that if angels were
corporeal beings they would perforce have had
to originate in time and space, but prior to the
creation of heaven and earth the concepts of
time and space were nonexistent. Aharon the
Younger, K. T., 7a, defends the former view by

comparing the creation of the angels with that of the universe which originated prior to time and space. He concludes, however, that the interpretation of H. Yeshu'ah is farfetched.

286. See below C. 63.

287. Comp. M. I, 76, II, 1.

288. This second proof is also adduced by Yeshu'ah Ben-Yehudah in his Ber'e'shith Rabbah. See J. J., p. 39.

289. Comp. the fifth proof of Yeshu'ah Ben-Yehudah in J. J., p. 40.

290. See J. J., p. 40 and the reference to Yosef alBasir in n. 1 of same p.

291. This proposition has been demonstrated in detail above, the first part of C. 11. comp. also C. 64.

292. Regarding this proof compare the treatment of Yeshu'ah Ben-Yehudahin J. J., p. 39.

293. Comp. M. I, Intro.

294. These four categories are taken almost verbatim from Aharon the Elder. See S. M. Exod. 31a. According to K. J. L., these views are derived from Yosef alBasir and Yeshu'ah Ben-Yehudah; Cf., further E. H. p. 199.

295. Comp. Below, the concluding part of the following C; the end of C. 19; the final paragraph of C. 63; the beginning of C. 72, 73.

296. Comp. M. I, 26.

297. For a parallel treatment by Saadia Gaon see S., p. O.

298. This matter is treated as part of Aharon's exposition on the homonymity of this term. See below C. 55 and 98.

299. Eshkol haKofer, Evpatoria 1836, published with introduction by Caleb Abba Afendopolo, p. 10 ff..

300. Comp. M. I, 46.

302a. The literal meaning of the Hebrew term employed here is: the privation of a positive property.

301. This is another instance (see above n. 280) to confirm the fact that "the Philosopher" referred to by Aharon Ben-Eliyahu is none other than the philosopher of Stagira. See A., Physics I, 67.

302. See A. De Anima I. 1.

303. Comp. Saadia's discussion of the physical organs of man ascribed to God, S., p. 50 f.

304. Comp. M. I, 8.

305. On the Kalasmistic conception of space see Munk's Le Guide, Vol. I, p. 185, n. 3.

306. The origin of this difference of opinion derives from A. detailed analysis of the concept of space, cf., his Physics IV, 12.

307. See below C. 62.

308. Comp. M. I, 1.,

309. "It therefore seems that all the affections of soul involve the body passion, gentleness, fear, pity, courage, joy, loving and hating; in all these there is a concurrent affection of the body" A., De Anima I, 1.

310. See below C. 109.

311. M. I, 1.

312. See further K. T., p. 32a.

313. See above n. 301.

314. See the elaborate exposition of the divine Chariot, C. 63.

315. Comp. M. 3, 3.

316. Comp. Aharon's interpretation of this passage in the K. T., Num. 17b. See further n. 411.

317. Comp. M. I, 4. 5.

318. In addition to denoting the special Providence that attends the things and events of sublunar existence, the "feet" of God are employed metaphorically to designate the knowledge of His might and transcendence that is acquired by the intellect as a result of investigating the nature of the terrestrial world. Comp. below C. 47.

319. Comp. M. I, 2.

320. This view of Adam's sin is reproduced in detail in the author's Biblical commentary, K. T. Gen. 22b. and 25b f. I have been unable to find any source for this singular interpretation.

321. See I Samuel 19.24.

322. Comp. C. 55 on the homonymity of the verbs "to speak" and "to say".

323. See above n. 296.

324. The insertion of this chapter at this particular point seems to be for the purpose of justifying the digression contained in the preceding C.

325. Comp. M. I, 41; S. p. 98.

326. See above. 201.

327. Comp. K. T., Gen. 90b for a broader discussion of this signification.

328. M. I. 41.

329. See above n. 301.

330. Both here and in C. 61; Aharon misquotes this verse, apparently combining it with Job 2, 11.

331. See above n. 324.

332. Comp. M. I, 42.

333. See above C. 23.

334. See p. 98 f.

335. The latter half of this verse is found in I Kings 17. 17, but the first part was introduced by the author erroneously.

336. Comp. M. I, 40.

337. See further K. T. p. 96.

338. Comp. above C. 14.

339. Comp. M. I, 4.

340. See further C. 58.

341. The problem of sense perception as an attribute of God is treated in comprehensive fashion by our author in C. 7678. See also C. 82.

342. Comp. M. I, 44.

343. *Ibid.* I, 45.

344. The same interpretation is employed by S. p. 50:

345. Comp. M. I, 11.

346. See M. I, 72.

347. *Ibid.* I, 11.

348. Aharon probably means to imply that the LORD reigns over the supralunar spheres and these indicate His glory. See O. H. ad loc.

349. Comp. M. I, 9.

350. See O. H. ad loc.

351. See; however, K. T. p. 47a:

352. Comp. M. I, 25.

353. *Ibid.* I, 12.

354. *Ibid.* I, 13.

355. This notion is based upon the similarity between man and the universe. Comp. M. I, 72.

356. Comp. *ibid.* I, 15.

357. When employed in connection with God, Saadia understands this verb as signifying a "created light" which he identifies with the Shekhinah (op. cit. p. 53). Comp. the beginning of C. 63 and n. 421.

358. Aharon conceives Ya'aqov's ladder symbolically as the ladder of existence since all created objects are interrelated like the rungs of a ladder. Cf., K. T. on Gen. 28. 12.

359. Comp. M. I, 24.

360. This is not an enact quotation.

361. The Biblical text reads, "And whatever goes upon its paws".

362. Comp. above C. 27.

363. Saadia (*ibid.*) also takes this verb as denoting a "created light". See also n. 358.

364. Comp. M. I, 21.

365. *Ibid.*

366. *Ibid.*

367. See *ibid.* II, 39.

368. *Ibid.* I, 21.

369. *Ibid.* I, 38.

370. Farther on in this C. Aharon expounds this passage as signifying that Mosheh, by means of divine assistance, apprehended a mighty and wondrous conception of God's acts such as no human either before or after him ever attained. Comp. also K. T., Exod. 116b.

371. See O. H. ad loc.

372. See ibn Ezra on Exod. 33. 13 ff.

373. This passage is expounded below, Chap, 92, in connection with the thirteen attributes of God.

374. See below Chap. 62.

375. On these attributes see further below C. 92:

376. Comp. M. 1, 23.

377. Comp. M. 1, 10. and K. II, 3.

378. On the origin and development of the notion of a "created light" see Munk, Le Guide, Vol. 1, p. 286 note 3.

379. Comp. M. 1, 22. 23.

380. Comp. M. 1, 20.

381. See below C. 114.

382. Comp. M. 1, 18.

383. Comp. M. 1, 28.

384. Comp. above, Chap. 35.

386. The realm of angels corresponds to man's head; the spheral world to his body; and terrestrial things to his feet.

385. M. 1, 28.

386. explains (De Anima, 11, 7); What is capable of taking on color is what in itself is colorless, as what can take on sound is what is soundless; what is colorless includes (a) what is transparent, etc.

387. See Ibn Ezra on Exod. 24.10.

388. Aharon the Elder comparing this vision with the theophany of Ezekiel interprets the "brick", as a symbolic representation of God's footstool and the "sapphire" as His throne. Thus, he draws a comparison with the "divided man" of Ezekiel. Like Ibn Ezra, Aharon Ben-Yosef believes the color of the sapphire to be red. This color he conceived as analogous to the appearance of the fire which Ezekiel perceived. (S. M., Exod., 49b.)

389. Cf., above C. 39.

390. Cf., above C. 38.

391. Comp. M. 1, 46.

392. This passage is incorrectly quoted. I believe it refers to Jer. 37. 10.

393. Comp. M. 1, 46.

394. *Ibid.*

395. *Ibid.*

396. *Ibid.*

397. See below C. 55.

398. Aharon Ben-Eliyahu employs the same interpretation in his K. T. (Exod. 10 Ba). The identical reasoning is found in the S. M. of Aharon Ben-Yosef (Exod. 63b).

399. Coap. M. 1, 46; S. p. 50.

400. Comp. M. 1, 68; K. IV, 3.

401. The view of H. Yosef that God creates words that are audible without the use of any intermediate physical instrument is considered in connection with the question of prophecy, below Chap.98.

402. See O. H. ad loc.

403. Cf., further K. T. 10x.

404. Comp. M. 1, 37.

405. As happens not infrequently with our author, this verse is quoted inexactly. Aharon may have had in mind Ps. 80. 20 or Ps. 119. 135. As quoted here, however, this Hebrew passage most closely resembles that of Ps. 31.17.

406. See above C. 41.

407. Comp. M. 1, 38.

408. For the Aristotelian conception of time apparently accepted by our author here see A., Physics., IV, C. 1012. But see above n. 250.

409. This allusion refers to the angels which are identified by Aharon with the separate Intelligences of A. (Metaphysics, XII; C.7, 8.). The meaning here is that Mosheh was privileged to comprehend the reality of the Spheral spirits or angels (Comp. the interpretation of our author on the passage, "And the similtude of the LORD doth he behold (Num. 12.8) in his K. T., Num. 17b.) but he was unable to conceive the true essence of God.

410. The first Jewish Aristotelian to adopt this identification was Avraham ibn Daud (Emunah Ramah, pub. by S. Weil, Frankfurt A.M. 1852, pp. 5769) who anticipated Maimonides in this matter (M.11, C. 36) although the latter treats the Aristotelian view in a far more masterly fashion. The basic distinction between Aristotle and the Jewish philosophers with regard to the creation or eternity of the universe applies here too, of course. According to A. (*ibid.*) the separate Intelligences are eternal and derive from the prime mover by natural necessity. The Jewish view, on the contrary, is that all these beings are created. See further the note on this passage in E. H. p. 377.

411. On the Homonymity of the term "rock" see C. 62.

412. Aharon construes this act as signifying the granting of divine assistance. Cf., C. 41.

413. Comp. M. I, 39.

414. *Ibid.* 7

415. *Ibid:* 43.

416. *Ibid.* 67

417. *Ibid.* 16, 52.

418. Comp. the homonymity of the term maqom in C. 20.

419. Comp. M. I, 19, 64. III: 17.

420. On the origin and development of the notion of a "created light see above n. 379.

421. The four 'ofannim correspond to the four sublunar elements; the 4iayyoth to the spheral realm; and the divided man to the Intelligences or angels. Comp. O. H. ad loc.

422. Aharon Ben-Yosef interprets the thirteen attributes of Exod. 34. 6 f. as alluding to the three divisions of existence. Comp. S. M., Exod. 68b.

423. The association of the disposition of the twelve tribes of Israel with the Chariot of Ezekiel is alluded to by Aharon the Elder in the S. M. Num. 2a. Comp. also K. T., Num. 3a., and Gen. 936.

424. Aharon develops this theme in detail in the K. T. Exod. 87b ff.

425. Aharon offers an elaborate exposition of this notion also; *ibid* p. 98a.

426. For a similar treatment of the homonymity of this term see K. IV, 3 end.

427. These two quotations serve to indicate that God's essence remains in the heavens while His glory abides in the Sanctuary. In the latter verse the terms "heart", and "eyes" are employed figuratively to denote His will.

428. M. 111, 7.

429. See above n. 297.

430. Comp. M. 1, 75.

431. See above C. 11.

432. Cf., S. M., Deut., 5b.

433. According to A, what is infinite is not in time, i. e., it is not contained by time, nor is its being measured by time, nor is it affected by time. Cf., his Physics, IV, C. 12.

434. See n. 293.

435. See Yosef alBasir's similar treatment of this proof in M. K., p. 27.

436. Compare the exposition of alJuwaini on this argument for unity in his alIrshad p. 58 f.

437. The words, "which lead" follow the Evpatoria ed.

438. Comp. M. 1, 35.

439. This is apparently in reply to the accusation of M, I, 75 (5), that some Mutakallimūn accept the doctrine of Unity purely as a matter of faith.

440. This Yosef, surnamed alQirqisani, is not to be confused with Yosef alBasir, Cf., E. H. p. 313. See also S. M. Deut. 5b. Comp., however, J. H. Weiss, Dor Dor WeDorshaw, Vilno, 1911, Vol. IV, p. 69. n. 6. and p. 85 n. 6; and S. Pinsker, Liqqutey Qadm'oniyyoth, Vienna 1860, p. 115, n. 2.

441. This statement refers back to the words of Yosef and points out their incorrectness; for if God's unity is a necessary corollary of His essence then knowledge of both is prior to Scripture.

442. It appears to me that there is no real point of difference between the two Aharons in this regard. Comp. S. M. Deut. 5b. See also M. K., p. 27. n. 1.

443. On the various degrees of authenticity see above, C. 2.

444. Comp. M. 1, 5.1. 52.

445. Comp alJuwaini, off. cit. p. 65 ff.

446. This refers to the thirteen attributes as expounded in C92.

447. Comp. K. IV, 18 (9).

448. Comp. M. I, 53.

449. See M. K., p. 25.

450. Comp. M. I, 57.

451. See above C. 28.

452. Comp. M. I, 69.

453. The Kalāmistic theory of Creation is demonstrated above, C. 10.

454. A1Juwaini points to a certain Mu'tazilite seat that also subscribes to this view and his refutation is basically the same as that employed by out author. See alIrshad P. 44f.

455a. The literal translation of this Hebrew phrase is, "Men kiss his lips" cf., Proverbs 24. 26

455b. The words enclosed in brackets are added by the Munich Ms. Cf., E. H. p. 260.

455. Comp. alJuwaini, op. cit. p. 50.

456. Comp. M. I, 58-60.

457. These words are found virtually verbatim in the S. M. Exod. 35b.

458. Comp. M. I, 51, 68.

459. See the latter part of Chap. 67; the beginning of Chap. 66 and the conclusion of Chap. 85.

460. See above C. 68

461. See n. 460.

462. Variations of this lengthy quotation are noted by M. K., p. 54.

463. On this sect see the Onomastikon of Steinschneider in E. H. p. 318. Cf., further Schahrastani, ed. of Haarbrucker, Halle 185-02, Vol. I, p. 89, and K. J. L., p. 58.

464. For the context of these quotations see M. K., p. 54 f.

465. This quotation is taken from Aharon Ben-Yosef's discussion of positive and negative attributes. See S. M., Exod. 35b.

466. Comp. M. I, 61.

467. This statement of Aharon Ben-Yosef is a verse from his poem on Unity for the Sabbath service. See O. H. ad loc.

468. M. I, first part cf C. 64.

469. The nature of identity is discussed by A. in his Metaphysics, X, 3. This reference also confirms the fact that A. is alluded to where Aharon speaks of "The Philosopher". See above notes 280, 303.

470a Comp. M. I, 62, 63.

470. Comp. K. IV, 3.

471. See further K. T. Exod. p. 16.

472. See the O. H. ad loc., which quotes another view, that the Hebrew equivalent of "necessary Existent" (*mehuyaw hammesiuth*) also consists of twelve letters.

473. Comp. above C. 62.

474. Comp. M I, 53.

475. On the question of a subjectless will and the accident of destruction without a substrate comp. Munk's Melanges, p. 325, n. I; see further alJuwaini, op. cit., pp. 43 and 67.

476. Comp. M. II, 18 (2).

477. Comp. above, end of C. 7.

478. —

479. This proposition constitutes one of the differences between the Mu'tazila and the Ash'ariya. The latter affirm the existence of subjectless accidents.

480. M. I, 75 (3).

481. See below C. 94.

482. Comp. the conclusion of C. 7., C. 68 and the end of C. 86.

483. Comp. M. I, 47. III, 16.

484. Above C. 66.

485. De Anima III, 8. See further n. 280, 303.

486. Nothing definite is known to us regarding this work. See Omomastikon, p. 319.

487. Comp. M. I, 47; II, 16.

488. 488a. The words enclosed in brackets are added by the Munich Ms. Cf., E. H. p. 262.

489. Cf., H. Y, 18 (7).

490. Comp. al-Juwaini op. cit., p. 78.

491. See the detailed discussion on this point above C. 7.

492. Comp. M. I, 47; III, 16.

493. See above C. 64.

494. Comp. the O. H. ad loc.

495. The burden of Aharon the Elder's contention is as follows (S. M., Gen. 15b, f.); It is difficult to comprehend how the Mutakallimūn, many of whom have hastened to remove every aspect of corporeality from God, have affirmed that He is sentient. They assert this to be so since He is Living and sentience is a necessary predicate of life. But the Mutakallimūn themselves have declared that He is Living, but not through life as an attribute. How, then, can they adduce proof from sublunar creatures that require an agent for their existence? Had they affirmed that He perceives, this would be acceptable. M. K., p. 15. n. 1, believes that this charge is directed primarily against Yosef alBasyatchi.